Rural Development Strategies

Published in conjunction with the
Policy Studies Organization

Rural Development Strategies

Editors

David W. Sears
Economic Research Service

J. Norman Reid
Rural Development Administration

Nelson-Hall Publishers
Chicago 1995

Project Editor: Rachel Schick
Typesetter: Alexander Graphics
Printer: Braun-Brumfield
Cover Painting: *Balconies* by Connie Vepstas. Photocollage.

Library of Congress Cataloging-in-Publication Data

Rural development strategies / David W. Sears, J. Norman Reid,
   editors.
       p.   cm.
   Includes bibliographical references.
   ISBN 0-8304-1339-1
   1.   Rural development—United States.   I.   Sears, David W., 1942–
   II.   Reid, J. Norman.
   HN90.C6R775   1995   94-24118
   307.1'412'0973—dc20   CIP
                                                                               Rev.

Manufactured in the United States of America

10   9   8   7   6   5   4   3   2   1

The paper used in this book meets the
minimum requirements of American
National Standard for Information
Sciences—Permanence of Paper for
Printed Library Materials, ANSI
Z39.48-1984.

Contents

Preface

I joined the Economic Research Service (ERS) in 1976, as head of a major division that carries out rural research. Over the years, I have become increasingly cognizant of the need for better and stronger linkages between the research community and the policy-making community. On the one hand, policymakers need to be aware of the basic facts of rural economic and community life that good research can provide them. Also, federal and state legislation and program implementation are likely to be more effective if they are grounded on a realistic understanding of rural America. On the other hand, researchers need to do a better job of presenting their work in a way that will be of genuine utility to harried policymakers.

The chapters of this book, taken together, discuss a wide range of approaches to rural development, including common-ly used traditional tools such as manufacturing recruitment as well as interesting newer approaches such as peer group lend-ing to stimulate micro-enterprise development. This book dis-cusses a variety of important rural development issues, and thus encourages both policymakers and researchers to think about the benefits as well as the costs of specific rural develop-ment strategies.

I am pleased to note that one of the co-editors, David Sears, is a current ERS researcher, while the other, Norman Reid, is an ERS "graduate" who has recently moved on to the Rural Development Administration.

—Ken Deavers, Acting Administrator, Economic Research Service

About the Contributors

Robert Blair is a senior research associate at the Center for Public Affairs Research at the University of Nebraska at Omaha, and an instructor in the departments of public administration and criminal justice. His research interests include local economic development planning and policy, and housing and community development. Prior to his academic career, Blair was in state and local government for fourteen years. He was a public works administrator, personnel director, assistant city manager, and economic developer. Blair is a doctoral candidate in political science at the University of Nebraska-Lincoln, and is managing editor of the *Journal of the Community Development Society*.

Terry F. Buss, Ph.D., is professor of public policy at the University of Akron. He has published numerous professional articles and books in economic development, entrepreneurship, training, and plant closings. He has developed rural economic development strategies for governors' offices in Maine, Arkansas, Iowa, and North Dakota and has worked on economic development issues for state agencies in Michigan, Pennsylvania, Montana, and Idaho. He has also worked in Australia, Wales, England, and Canada on development projects. From 1990 to 1994, he worked in Hungary on economic development technical assistance as a Fulbright Scholar; and from 1993 to 1995, he worked in Russia offering training programs to regional government officials under the auspices of the U.S. Information Agency.

Katherine A. Carlson has a Ph.D. in anthropology from the University of Hawaii and is an independent researcher in rural Washington state, doing both grant and contract work for local, regional, and state agencies and the University of Washington. Her recent research interests have focused on community and individual change, and include studies on social impacts of development, dislocated workers and their families, and education and training programs. Other studies are in the area of substance abuse prevention and intervention, and she has prepared formal reports and published scholarly articles across the range of these research areas. A monograph on her prison study is under revision for publication. She can be reached at Praxis Research, 267 Silver Lane, Port Angeles, WA 98363.

Carla Dickstein is a senior development officer for research and policy at Coastal Enterprises Inc. (CEI), a community development corporation based in Wiscasset, Maine. Her current work focuses on supporting the development of environmental industries, economic conversion of defense industries, and social/economic impact analysis of CEI's development programs. She received her doctorate in City and Regional Planning from the University of Pennsylvania.

Ginny Eager is the executive director of Forward in the Fifth. She is regularly asked to conduct presentations on community and parental involvement as a mechanism to improve local schools. Ms. Eager has also developed several workshops designed to increase human capacity through leadership development and group skills activities.

Philip Ehrensaft is a professor of sociology at the University of Quebec-Montreal. He is a founding member of the Agriculture and Rural Restructuring Group in Canada and has acted as a consultant to Agriculture Canada, Employment and Immigration Canada, and the Statistics Canada. His research interests include structural change in agriculture, the analysis of rural education conditions, and rural development policy.

David Freshwater is an associate professor in the Department of Agricultural Economics, University of Kentucky. His research and teaching interests are rural economic development, rural finance, and policy evaluation. He is currently a consultant to the OECD on rural policy, and has conducted several studies of the Community

Futures Program for the Canadian government. Prior to joining the University of Kentucky, he was a senior economist for the Joint Economic Committee of the U.S. Congress.

Schuyler Houser has worked, as administrator and researcher, with several tribal colleges and Indian institutions in the United States and Canada. He holds a Master of Public Administration from the John F. Kennedy School of Government, Harvard University. From 1988 until 1990, he directed the Institute for Economic Development at Sinte Gleska University on the Rosebud Sioux Reservation in South Dakota, where he and Eileen Lunderman established the micro-enterprise center described in his article. He is currently working with the Spokane Tribe in Washington, and with Salish-Kootenai College, to establish a new tribal college center.

Warren Kriesel is an associate professor in the Agricultural and Applied Economics Department at the University of Georgia. Following service in the U.S. Peace Corps, he earned advanced degrees from Virginia Tech and The Ohio State University. His research interests include industrial location, educational finance, impact analysis, nonmarket valuation techniques, and coastal erosion management. His articles have appeared in *American Journal of Agricultural Economics, Journal of Agricultural and Applied Economics*, and *Water Resources Research*.

Jules H. Lichtenstein has served as chief of the Applied Policy Branch of the U.S. Small Business Administration's Office of Advocacy. He manages small business research dealing with a broad range of issues including entrepreneurship, employee benefits, training, finance, tax, and international trade. Previously, he served in several positions in the Office of Management and Budget, Executive Office of the President, including senior budget examiner for federal economic development programs and senior policy analyst in the Special Studies Division, Economics and Government. He has also served as a senior program analyst at the Economic Development Administration, U.S. Department of Commerce. He received an M.A. in Urban Planning from the University of Washington, and a Ph.D. in City and Regional Planning from Cornell University.

Scott Loveridge is extension associate professor and program leader, Community and Economic Development, West Virginia University Extension. He previously served on the faculty of the Department of

Agricultural and Applied Economics, University of Minnesota. Dr. Loveridge's research interests are in the areas of community development policy and the economics of agglomeration.

George R. McDowell is professor of agricultural and applied economics at Virginia Polytechnic Institute and State University. He is currently living in Tirana, Albania, where he is working for Virginia Tech on a USAID project directed at restructuring Albanian agriculture. Dr. McDowell is an institutional economist trained at Michigan State University with scholarly interests in rural and agricultural development. He has particular interests in the performance and problems of complex organizations, particularly the American Land-Grant universities. His assignment in Albania is to help to develop the Agricultural University of Tirana, particularly its programs in agricultural economics.

Kevin T. McNamara is an associate professor of agricultural economics at Purdue University. His research interests in regional economics and economic impact analysis include: analysis of factors influencing manufacturing location and expansion, the impact of infrastructure investment on regional economic growth, and the impact of public development policy on local income and employment growth. Recent publications are in *International Regional Science Review, Regional Studies, Journal of the Community Development Society, Review of Regional Studies,* and *Land Economics.*

George W. Morse is professor and extension economist in community and economic development in the Department of Agricultural and Applied Economics, University of Minnesota. His research and teaching endeavors have been in economic impact assessment, strategic planning for local economic development, and business retention and expansion.

Mark G. Popovich is a consultant based in Washington, D.C. He is currently working with the National Academy of Public Administration on its "reinventing government" program. Prior to this, he spent several years as a senior research associate at the Council of Governors' Policy Advisors (CGPA)—an affiliate of the National Governors' Association—specializing in rural economic development issues. The research in chapter 9 is based on several large grants to CGPA from the Ford Foundation, Northwest Area Foundation, and U.S. Economic Development Administration, all managed by Popovich.

Glen C. Pulver is professor emeritus at the University of Wisconsin-Madison and Extension. His field of specialty is community economic development policy. During his career he has worked closely with governmental bodies, private businesses, economic development committees, organizations, agencies, and educators throughout the United States. He has extensive community-level experience in both rural and urban areas. In recent years, Dr. Pulver has spoken at major economic development policy conferences in over thirty states. He has also served as a visiting professor in Brazil and Indonesia and as a consultant to a number of national associations and development foundations.

Daniel V. Rainey is a graduate research fellow in the Department of Agricultural Economics at Purdue University. He earned a B.S. at the University of Arkansas and an M.S. at Purdue prior to entering the Ph.D. program with the Department of Agricultural Economics at Purdue. His primary research interests are economic development and public policy.

B.J. Reed is currently David C. Scott Professor and chair of the Department of Public Administration at the University of Nebraska at Omaha. Dr. Reed has published numerous articles in journals such as *Public Administration Review, American Review of Public Administration, The Journal of Urban Affairs,* and *Rural Development Perspectives.* His major research interests are intergovernmental management, community and economic development, and public sector budgeting and finance. His most recent books are *Managing Economic Development* and *Public Finance Administration.* He received his B.A. and M.S. from Fort Hays State University and his Ph.D. in Political Science from the University of Missouri-Columbia.

Richard Reeder is an economist in the Economic Research Service, U.S. Department of Agriculture. He has also worked for the U.S. Advisory Commission on Intergovernmental Relations and served on the Local Transportation Finance Committee of the Transportation Research Board. His research interests include rural public finance and economic development.

J. Norman Reid is director of the strategy development staff of USDA's Rural Development Administration. Previously, he served as deputy director of the Agriculture and Rural Economy Division, Economic Research Service, USDA. He has served as senior staff to several national commissions and task forces, including the President's

Council on Rural America and USDA's Rural Revitalization Task Force. He has authored a number of publications dealing with rural economic and social trends in the U.S. and OECD countries, entrepreneurship, rural development policy, public infrastructure, government aid programs, and regional governance, including *Rural Public Management* and *Rural Economic Development in the 1980's*. He was awarded a Ph.D. in political science from the University of Illinois-Urbana in 1975.

David W. Sears is head of the government and development policy section of the Economic Research Service. Earlier in his career, he taught regional planning at the University of Massachusetts at Amherst and he worked on a variety of research and evaluation projects at the U.S. Departments of Housing and Urban Development (HUD) and Health and Human Services (HHS). He has written numerous reports, articles, and monographs on rural development in the United States, including *Gearing Up for Success* and *Infrastructure Investment and Economic Development*. He holds a Ph.D. in regional planning from Cornell University.

Ron Shaffer is professor of agricultural economics and community development economist, University of Wisconsin-Madison/Extension where he currently directs the National Rural Economic Development Institute, which is part of the National Rural Development Partnership. Professor Shaffer has been a faculty member at the University of Wisconsin-Madison since January 1972, and has served as director of the University of Wisconsin-Madison/Extension Center for Community Economic Development since July 1, 1990. His extension efforts have emphasized working with Wisconsin communities to create comprehensive development strategies. Shaffer also teaches a graduate course and does research in the area of community economics. He has worked in several U.S. states and internationally on questions of local development strategies.

Stewart N. Smith is professor of sustainable agriculture policy at the University of Maine, Orono. His research provides insights to policies appropriate to support sustainable agriculture systems. He has served as Maine Commissioner of Agriculture, co-chair of the Governor's Rural Development Committee, and board member of the Finance Authority of Maine. As senior economist on the Joint Economic Committee, he has advised Congress on agriculture and rural development issues.

Thomas R. Smith is currently staff economist at the Energy Resources Center, University of Illinois at Chicago. He performs cost-benefit assessments of new energy technologies, policies, and technology transfer programs. He also chairs the City of Chicago's Clean Cities Economic Assessment Committee, working with the public and private sectors to encourage early adoption of alternative fuels to meet federal environmental mandates.

Cory Wanek is a graduate student and teaching assistant studying Industrial Organization in the department of economics at the University of Wisconsin-Milwaukee. His research on the importance of airports in rural areas was conducted during an internship at the Economic Research Service, U.S. Department of Agriculture. His research interests include the effects of government regulation on industrial organization and business.

CHAPTER 1

Reinventing Rural Policy Research

J. NORMAN REID AND DAVID W. SEARS

America appears to be on the edge of major changes in the way it makes and implements its public policy. The election of President Clinton, the challenge to prevailing ways of doing business represented by Ross Perot, and the Republican sweep of Congress in the 1994 elections herald a massive public desire to bring about radical changes by sweeping away old ways of thinking and acting. These changing times are reflected in the literature that has caught the public's attention. Two recent titles—*Reinventing Government*[1] and *Mandate for Change*[2]—capture the flavor of the changes, which are reported to be underway at all levels of government from Washington, D.C., to many state capitals and dozens of communities around the nation.

A basic theme that underlies this "new"—or perhaps more accurately, revitalized—approach to public policy is the belief that government—properly organized and managed—can have a significant and positive impact on the critical problems facing the nation.

Rural development is among these problems on the nation's policy agenda. Though hardly a new issue, it has been on America's back burner since the days of the New Deal. Now, following the lingering recession of the 1980s that highlighted deeper and more enduring changes underway in the rural economy,[3] rural development has assumed new prominence.

This combination of events—rural distress and the movement to reexamine public policy—provides an opportunity for a fresh look at rural development strategies. Nowhere is a searching reexamination more needed than in the area of rural development policy. Much of what today passes for rural development springs not from strong evidence but from myth. In a world where tight public finances have become a given, such seat-of-the-pants policy-making is no longer tolerable.

This volume is intended to explore rural development methods and to advance the field of rural development by presenting the most comprehensive and up-to-date information available about the effectiveness of a variety of rural policy approaches.

Terminology

Discussion of rural development policy suffers at least as much as other policy areas from terminological misunderstandings. While this volume does not pretend to resolve those issues, it is nonetheless useful to clarify the uses we make of certain terms.

First is the term "rural" itself. Though in popular usage it is often taken to indicate open country or agricultural areas, in policy use it has taken on a range of different definitions. Generally speaking, in the policy context rural is regarded as including small towns as well as open country areas.[4] While the precise definition of "small" varies widely among government programs, most include villages, towns, and even smaller cities.[5] We adopt this same broader convention.

Second is the term "development." Often, development is used interchangably with the term "growth." In fact, their meanings are quite different.[6] "Growth"refers to the expansion of total economic activity within an area. Usually, it is defined in terms of the number of jobs created or the amount by which income or population increases. Programs to stimulate growth normally focus on immediate job generation, with less or no concern about longer term results. Growth is often stimulated through spending and public subsidies that underwrite short-term expansion of economic activity.

"Development," in contrast, refers to fundamental and sustainable increases in the productivity of individuals and institutions, leading to higher per capita incomes for individuals. Development may be associated with growth, but the relationship is not a necessary one. It is quite possible to achieve development by substituting better jobs for poorer ones, with no growth in the number of jobs. Development programs focus on changing underlying conditions, and usually take a long-term perspective, making investments in institutions, facilities, and people, rather than handing out subsidies.[7] A critical point here is the distinction between "investments," where public expenditures are expected to raise the level of productivity of an area over the long term, and "subsidies," where expenditures are expected only to add to the level of resources available in the short term.

Finally is the term "strategy." As employed in policy discussions, strategy is sometimes used generically to refer to actions that promote growth or development. Used this way, strategy has taken on a variety of meanings. One can find the word used to refer to techniques for rural development; to specific public programs; to categories of programs; and to broad conceptual approaches to development. We ourselves must admit to having used the term at various times in all of these ways.

Properly defined, however, strategy has a very precise meaning that is conveyed by no other term. As a result, allowing it to be used loosely is to permit the destruction of what would otherwise be a valuable entry in our development lexicon.

Bryson[8] describes strategy development as occurring in five parts: (1) identifying visions or practical alternatives for resolving a strategic issue; (2) defining the barriers to achieving strategic objectives; (3) developing proposals for overcoming the barriers; (4) identifying implementing actions needed over the longer term; and (5) defining detailed work programs to carry out the strategy in the short term.

Bryson's discussion of strategy points in a helpful direction. As we see it, the key elements that distinguish a strategy from other descriptors—such as programs, actions, approaches, and techniques—are a focus on the longer term; linkage of discrete actions to broader objectives; and application of cause-and-effect thinking when selecting short-term actions.

It is the very nature of the challenges now facing rural development policy that makes this point about strategy worth making. Rural problems are very complex, and in most cases cannot be solved by simple or short-term actions. Instead, they require actions that integrate a number of different programs or actions over time, sometimes in an appropriate sequence, to produce sustainable enhancements in basic human and institutional conditions that, in turn, will lead to higher productivity, adaptiveness, and innovativeness. We would like to reserve the term "strategy" for just these complex and interrelated sets of actions.

Changing Directions, Changing Policy Needs

The current concern for the development of rural America coincides with basic shifts in beliefs about the formation and management of public policy. First, beliefs about the nature of rural development itself have changed.

Economic development is increasingly seen as a complex issue, no longer limited to traditional infrastructure construction and tax incentives but reaching deeply into the fabric of society. At the same time, it is more clear than ever that development is a long-term process, and not a task that can be achieved within a few years.

Second, these changes in perception coincide with rising doubts about the ability of government itself to perform up to a reasonable level of expectations. One of the hottest "reads" in Washington in recent years is *Reinventing Government*,[9] a book whose thesis is what its title implies: that America's public institutions need fundamental rethinking. The authors argue that government in its current form was invented for a different era, when problems could be handled in a compartmentalized way through hierarchical organizational structures. They examine recent trends, finding government to be unresponsive, driven by self-preservation rather than mission, ruled by special interests, reactive rather than proactive, and inwardly focused on inputs rather than taking a results-oriented stance.

Osborne and Gaebler argue that effective responses to public problems call for exactly the opposite approach. Government, they say, needs to be catalytic, community-owned, mission-driven, results-oriented, customer-driven, enterprising, anticipatory, decentralized, and market-oriented. Many of these same arguments appear in *A Mandate for Change*, highly touted as required reading for the Clinton Administration.

An Examination of Rural Development Approaches

We have two main objectives in presenting this volume. First, we offer a selection of thirteen chapters (see chapters 2–14) representing the best recent research assessing rural development techniques. In choosing these articles, we have focused on approaches that appear to be working. In doing so, we hope to describe techniques that practitioners will find helpful and present critical assessments of those approaches.

Second, we hope to point the rural policy studies profession in a direction that will enable it to meet the most important policy challenges that confront rural America and the nation. Thus, in our concluding chapter we provide an assessment of rural policy research and its readiness to enable policymakers to meet the public's rising demands for solid performance.

While the main contribution of this volume is the exploration of these thirteen approaches, we also believe it is important for rural development practitioners, policymakers, and researchers to understand the context in which they operate. Thus, our final two chapters address the contextual issue. In chapter 15, George McDowell discusses the institutional framework in which rural strategies must be implemented. In chapter 16, we conclude the volume by considering the possibilities of successfully matching development strategies with rural communities.

By no means does this volume fully respond to the rural development challenges posed by the authors of *Reinventing Government* and *Mandate for Change* or by our own injunctions about the needs within the discipline. Nonetheless, what we have attempted to do is to lay the foundation for a new, more responsive approach to rural development policy research. This work builds upon an earlier symposium of the *Policy Studies Journal*,[10] which we also edited. Together, the full set of analyses represents a solid base from which to begin a thorough understanding of the effects of specific rural development approaches.

NOTES

1. David Osborne and Ted Gaebler, *Reinventing Government: How the Entrepreneurial Spirit is Transforming the Public Sector*. Reading, Mass.: Addison-Wesley Publishing Co., Inc., 1992.

2. Will Marshall and Martin Schram, eds., *Mandate for Change*. New York: Berkley Books, 1993.

3. See, for instance, William A. Galston, "Rural America in the 1990s: Trends and Choices," *Policy Studies Journal*, 20 (No. 2, 1992): 202-11.

4. Ken Deavers, "What is Rural?" *Policy Studies Journal*, 20 (No. 2, 1992): 184-89.

5. U.S. Department of Housing and Urban Development. *Developmental Needs of Small Cities*. Washington, D.C.: March 1979, Appendix B, pp. 267-86.

6. On this point, see Edward J. Malecki, *Technology and Economic Development*. Harlow, England: Longman Scientific & Technical, 1991, pp. 22-25.

7. U.S. Department of Agriculture. "A Hard Look at USDA's Rural Development Programs." Report of the Rural Revitalization Task Force. June 30, 1989, p. 3.

8. John M. Bryson, *Strategic Planning for Public and Nonprofit Organizations*. San Francisco, Calif.: Jossey-Bass Publishers, 1988, pp. 59–60.

9. Osborne and Gaebler.

10. Special Symposium on Rural Development, *Policy Studies Journal*, 20 (No. 2, 1992).

Defining Development Targets

CHAPTER 2

Building Local Economic Development Strategies

RON SHAFFER AND GLEN C. PULVER[1]

Introduction

The persistent decline in the general economic well-being of the residents of many urban and rural communities in the United States has led to substantial public concern regarding community economic development policy. Citizens throughout the country are seeking mechanisms to close the growing gap in employment and income growth between the "have" and "have not" communities. As a consequence, local leaders, especially those in the lagging regions, are attempting to influence the rate of job and income growth in their communities through investments in physical and human infrastructure, searches for prospective employers, and selective tax and other incentives. The fundamental goal of most of these efforts is to stimulate the local economy to grow more rapidly than it would have without public intervention.

Although individuals in the private sector continue to be the primary actors in the American economic scheme, governmental officials and community organization members attempt to influence the location and expansion decisions of both local and nonlocal businesses. In rural areas especially, most of the people making these critical policy choices are volunteers.

9

Local governments are controlled by part-time elected or appointed officials. There are few full-time employees. Community organizations such as business associations, industrial development corporations, and civic groups are also operated by volunteers. Outside of large cities, few local governments or community groups have trained professional staff with the time to provide proper guidance to community economic development policy decision making.

Rural regions are clearly at a disadvantage when compared with urban areas. Their small populations reduce the number of people available for volunteer work. Each person has limited time and energy to give to clubs, organizations, and local government activities. Furthermore, the limited number of individuals available reduces the diversity of the knowledge base. A group of volunteers in an urban setting may include representatives from a wide spectrum of professions and businesses, whereas in rural regions the experience and occupational spectrum is often much narrower.

Distance is also an influential variable in the acquisition of information for both public and private decision making. In spite of recent advances in telecommunications, urban areas continue to have easier access to knowledge, technical assistance, and other critical inputs. Rural regions have a much weaker fiscal base to use in overcoming the friction of distance.

Rural areas with smaller local resource bases can, by themselves, seldom afford to employ the technical expertise needed to resolve their problems. Cities with larger resource bases can afford to do so. Without close cooperation with neighboring communities and/or state and federal governments, small rural regions are left with little help in making critical economic development decisions.

Local decisions, made without thorough assessment of the nature of present problems and realistic development opportunities, seldom produce the desired results. First, the heavy reliance on volunteers, no matter how enthusiastic, coupled with a limited awareness of the full range of economic possibilities, usually leads to a limited development agenda composed largely of the latest fads with minimal critical review of their appropriateness. Second, attempts to recreate prior economic conditions coupled with a failure to recognize the implications of changing national and international trends often leads to efforts that fail to capture new opportunities. Third, a failure to assess problems thoroughly often leads to responses that address symptoms, and do not build on the linkages among partial solutions. Thus, the end result of many local efforts is a strong feeling of frustration on the part of local leaders and the community at large.

Elements of Effective Community Decisions

Improvement in the quality of community economic development decision making, either through the efforts of local governments or community groups or through the policies of state and/or federal government, requires full recognition of certain fundamental elements.

1. There must be a group of local people who are committed to spending the time, energy, and other resources it will take to make positive local change a reality. The presence of aggressive, forward-thinking people in both the private and public sector may be the single most critical variable in community economic vitality.[2]
2. The quality of local decision making is strongly influenced by community residents' ability to distinguish between problems and symptoms, and to build coherent responses to real issues. The continued pursuit of solutions to symptoms rather than real problems seldom results in community satisfaction. There remains no real substitute for well-informed local leadership. Successful development requires local leaders with strong analytical skills, and with access to the information, data, tools, and techniques necessary for the full redress of root problems.[3] Inadequate access to current and accurate information is a serious stumbling block to local decision making.
3. Widespread citizen participation and support is critical to most decisions affecting a large segment of the community. Local residents control an array of resources either as individual residents, or businesses, or collectively (local governments and citizen groups) that affect community life. Individuals have time and skills to work, cash to spend or save; businesses make decisions on the type of technology to use, investments in buildings and equipment, and wage rates; and governments and community groups invest in schools, transportation systems, and other infrastructure and take other collective actions that influence change. With widespread community support many local resources may be brought to bear on local economic problems. Without this critical support, little can be accomplished by either the public or private sector.

4. The goals and values of a community's residents set the context for the choices perceived as needed and acceptable. For example, if the community believes it is important to keep the next generation of workers productive, residents are likely to insist their schools be of a high quality. If legalized gambling is proposed as a means of generating financial support for education, community values may judge that as an unacceptable mechanism for providing needed funds, requiring identification of another potential funding source. In short, local goals and values influence what is considered and what is deemed acceptable.

5. The full realization of local development opportunities requires consideration of a wide range of all local and external resources that may be brought to bear on community concerns. These resources include time, effort, and knowledge as well as all forms of physical and financial capital. Unfortunately local development is often characterized by such extremes as "all development comes from the fuller utilization of local knowledge, insight, and other resources" contrasted to "further local development is not possible without the injection of outside capital." The acceptance of just one perspective unduly restricts local options.

6. Finally, no amount of decision making is of value unless it is accompanied by action. The willingness of a broad spectrum of local citizens to take risks and commit resources is essential. Community economic development is not a one-time event. It is only achievable through continuing analyses, decisions, and actions over an extended time period. Limitations in time and money permit only a few concerns to be addressed at once. Furthermore, conditions change and prior decisions must be modified.

If local leaders are to make progress in influencing the rate of growth in employment and income in their community and to assure continuing economic vitality through effective decision making, all of these elements must be in place.

Components of a Community Economic Analysis Program

There are many public efforts at the federal, state, regional, and county level aimed at providing community economic development education and technical assistance. Most focus on leadership training for local citizens.[4] Others emphasize short-term technical assistance to local governments and development groups.[5] Few have the necessary institutional support to supply education and technical assistance to local leaders on a continuing basis. One effort that does have long-term support is the Wisconsin Community Economic Analysis (CEA) program.

The remainder of this chapter describes the institutional base of the program, the operational process, the program content, and some evidence of program impacts.

The Institutional Base

The Wisconsin Community Economic Analysis program is administered by the University of Wisconsin Cooperative Extension. Like most State Cooperative Extension Services, this program is funded jointly by the U.S. Department of Agriculture, the State of Wisconsin, and county governments. The core of the Wisconsin program is the Extension Community Resource Development (CRD) agent located in most Wisconsin counties. These are professionals with Masters Degrees in economics, business, natural resources, community development, or related fields. The CRD agents provide research-based educational programs and some technical assistance on local government, natural resources, and community and economic development in response to the problems of individuals, groups, and local governments in the county where they are employed. In 1992, there were CRD agents in over 85 percent of Wisconsin's counties.

The county CRD agents receive subject-matter content support from university campus-based specialists in a wide spectrum of fields. These specialists often teach university courses and all do some applied research in their field of expertise. In Wisconsin, specialists are provided in business management, community economic development, environmental sciences, government, landscape architecture, recreation business, regional planning, sociology, and other subjects of relevance. Specialists provide consultative and educational support to community leaders through the county Extension agents and to state and national agencies and organizations concerned with economic development problems.

County CRD agents are regularly informed of new ideas in community economic development. First, a monthly one-page newsletter, "Community Economics," provides continual information on research and policy topics. Second, in-service training is fundamental in the development and maintenance of the Wisconsin Community Economic Analysis program. Specialists regularly provide this training for county CRD agents. These sessions are used to examine comprehensive community economic development strategies, explain and interpret community economic analysis tools, discuss specific technical concerns such as encouraging entrepreneurship or using secondary financial markets, share experiences regarding local economic development efforts, and review the latest relevant research and government programs. The goal of the in-service training is to build a cadre of professionals who, when working in the community, have a sound grasp of the economic framework in which community choices are embedded and the capacity to develop effective educational programs and provide technical assistance on a continuing basis.

The Operational Process

Returning to the description of local economic development processes described in the introduction, the Community Economic Analysis program builds on the long-term relationship between the county Extension faculty member and the community. Specific dimensions addressed include developing a strategic perspective on choices the community can make, increasing awareness of current economic conditions and activities in the community, and building the community team to implement the strategies created.

The Community Economic Analysis program is initiated in the community through the county Extension CRD agent. The agent is typically approached by individuals in a community asking for assistance with community and economic development concerns. Together they identify local citizens with a willingness to invest time and energy in influencing the community's economic future. They identify a cross section of the community, i.e., representatives of business associations, industrial development organizations, bankers, farmers, educators, health care providers, local governments, civic organizations, churches, youth groups, and others interested in the community. These people carry the prime responsibility for serious analysis of local economic problems and development opportunities and for the involvement of the broader community in establishing specific development goals and action plans.

The CRD agent and state specialist then organize a series of local educational meetings for the group.[6] The purpose of the meetings is to help the community group gain a clearer grasp of their local situation, their realistic economic development opportunities, and to establish a plan for achieving their goals.

The Program Content

The CEA program blends strategic planning, knowledge transmission, and citizen involvement ideas in the following fashion. First, it is necessary to set any local choices in the context of ongoing changes in the state, national, and international economy. Second, it is important to build a comprehensive base of information about the local economy to enable people to confirm or deny their perceptions. Third, it is crucial for the community to examine comprehensively what they are currently doing regarding economic development. Fourth, within the context of newly-acquired knowledge, it is important to establish citizen priorities regarding desired changes. Fifth, the list of citizen priorities must be converted into a set of implementation activities.

Strategic community economic development planning demands awareness of the broader environment, which directly influences the prospects of even the smallest locality. Thus, the community economic analysis education meetings open with a review of overarching trends and their implications for economic development choices in the community. Examples include the relative stability of employment in goods-producing industries and the rapid growth in the services-producing sector during the last half century and how this alters the types of economic activities that communities may seek. Another is the relative growth of passive income (transfers, dividends, interest, rents) and its resistance to business cycle swings, weather conditions, or commodity price changes. Furthermore, recognition of the growing importance of passive income and who possesses that income (retirees) may alter a community's economic development strategies. The need to be sensitive to the rapid globalization of the economy and the growing importance of small businesses and entrepreneurship are other factors discussed. These trends are reviewed more to challenge people to recognize untapped possibilities than to give specific direction to local strategies.

The second phase of the educational series involves examining local economic conditions and comparing them to nearby communities and state trends to gain insight into both absolute and relative economic conditions in the community. While the Community Economic Analysis program compiles a large amount of data for the perusal of local citizens, it minimizes the amount of data shared in the oral presentations. Rather, the emphasis is on discerning trends and patterns, unexpected conditions, and identification of development opportunities suggested by the analysis. Heavy emphasis is placed on comparing local perceptions and secondary data to glean insights.[7]

This requires reliable current data. This is partially solved by using data collected for administrative reasons, i.e., unemployment insurance, income taxes. These data are seldom more than twelve months old, and given the caveats about coverage and other administrative nuances, provide current and relatively reliable information. Other data from the Censuses of Population and Business and Bureau of Economic Analysis are used for population, sales, and personal income. Custom-designed computer software is used to make the calculations and to summarize graphically the information.[8]

The community economic analysis tools used in the analysis include location quotients, population-employment ratios, trade area capture, pull factors, and shift-share.[9] None of these individually provides the depth of insight needed, but when several measures are examined, patterns emerge that provide insight into opportunities. Program participants are asked about unexpected results and are encouraged to put results from the analysis into the context of their own experience. Frequently, at this stage some commonly held beliefs are challenged. For example, the analysis of local income sources may demonstrate the growing share of local income held by retirees. This may be in sharp contrast to an existing perception that most local income comes from farming or some other sector. From an economic development strategy perspective, this suggests the need for greater attention by the local retail and construction sectors to the needs of retirees.

Next, the program addresses the tendency of local leaders to limit their economic development strategies to the goods-producing sector: largely expansion of natural resource-based industries such as farming, forestry, and mining; or attraction of manufacturing. This tendency is based on the historic belief that in order to improve the economic well-being of a region, more money must be brought in through the export of goods.[10] This belief fails to recognize that there are many other ways to increase regional income. Options include using existing resources, including human resources, more efficiently; purchasing consumer and industrial inputs locally rather than importing them; finding new uses for local resources; developing new technology and new products (both goods and services); and changing the institutional environment (examples include encouraging entrepreneurship and influencing the policies of external governments).

In the Wisconsin Community Economic Analysis program these options are shared with the participants as five general economic development strategies: (1) improve the efficiency of existing firms; (2) improve the ability to capture dollars; (3) attract new basic employers; (4) encourage business formation; and (5) increase assistance received from broader governments.[11] In most situations, local economies can be improved through actions taken on all of these strategies. The challenge for local leaders is to develop comprehensive community economic development programs that fit their unique needs and resources.

The next phase of the educational effort engages the community group in a systematic review of current local economic development efforts. This is accomplished using the Community Preparedness Index—a survey of development actions that might be taken by local leaders.[12] Participants are advised that the presence of an activity on the survey does not imply that it should be done; rather the purpose of the index is to compile an inventory of what is being done. This instrument serves as a teaching outline to stimulate discussion of why various activities may or may not be appropriate in that community. Furthermore, it opens participant discussion about current actions and whether they are sufficient. For example, the discussion may discover that a community promotional brochure has been developed but languishes in a storage cabinet, causing the group to discuss a brochure distribution plan.

The next aspect of the series of meetings is the process of identifying the full range of problems local leaders feel need to be considered. These problems are prioritized by the group. They then proceed to develop very specific action plans for each of the highest priorities. Planning includes a discussion of specific goals and objectives, a review of the forces that may assist or hinder the achievement of each goal, what will be done, who will do it, and when it will be done. There is a clear consideration of prospective cooperating agencies and organizations, both local and nonlocal, whose participation in further planning and action is absolutely essential. The success of the entire program hinges on the capacity of the local CRD agent and the community leaders to engage other federal, state, and local agencies and institutions in the search for solutions. Supplemental external knowledge and financial resources are almost always needed. Cooperation is a must that is emphasized.

The educational product of the series of meetings is a cadre of local people with strong insight and knowledge about economic development trends and realistic economic development opportunities for their community. In addition, they have the outline of an action plan that they can use to take advantage of those opportunities that they judge appropriate. The plans are theirs and not those of an external consultant/expert.

The county Extension Community Resource Development agent, who has conducted much of the educational program, continues working with the community group, serving as a catalyst and provider of additional information that local leaders might need. The community's continuing access to this professional is a powerful part of the Wisconsin Community Economic Analysis program. Often priority issues such as tax incentives, small business incubators, mainstreet revitalization, solid waste disposal, and housing development require additional educational programs. Original action plans may prove inadequate and require revision. Knowledge of new government programs may be important. The global economic environment shifts rapidly and the entire educational meeting series will need to be revisited regularly.

Evidence of Impact

The Wisconsin Community Economic Analysis program has been subjected to four formal internal evaluations.[13] First, participants from the initial eight communities involved with the program were surveyed to determine the extent to which their primary community goals had been achieved one year after the end of the meeting series. Participants were also asked to comment on the value of the program, including CRD agent assistance. Second, twenty-six additional communities were included in a similar survey two years later. Third, a survey of CRD agents was used to produce information for a summary of economic development successes attributed to the Community Economic Analysis program. Fourth, using secondary data sources, annual rates of change in total employment and per capita income of participating communities before and after the program were compared with similar nonparticipating communities. These two measures were used because changes in local jobs and incomes were the most frequent stimulus to participate in the program.

None of these evaluations singularly provides a completely unbiased measure of the worth of the program, but collectively they demonstrate that the program has had a positive impact. The strongest single indicator may be the high regard in which it is held by the participants. Furthermore, the detail that follows clearly indicates that the participants attributed specific changes to the Community Economic Analysis program. Numerous small incremental events characterize local economic development. Large changes are the exception. Thus, these evaluations necessarily contain many examples.

Survey 1

In 1984, seventy-two of the participants in the first eight communities involved in a community economic analysis were interviewed by the Program Development and Evaluation Staff of the University of Wisconsin/Extension (UWEX) for their reactions to the Community Economic Analysis program and what had happened since.[14] The respondents were asked to describe the amount of progress made on the top goals identified at the end of the program. Of the goals identified, 37 percent related to business and industrial development; 28 percent related to community public relations; 5 percent each related to transportation, local government, and long-range planning; and 3 percent to education.

For all six of these general goals, over half of the respondents (and for four of the goals, at least two-thirds of the respondents) felt either the goal had been achieved or visible progress had been made. Respondents perceived relatively more progress on issues not directly related to a narrow definition of economic development, indicating the capacity of the CEA program to crystallize local initiative on locally perceived issues.

Specific forms of progress on business and industrial development goals occurred as follows: assisted two local businesses expand; worked with a nursing home expansion; worked with three new business start-ups; acquired first occupant of an industrial park; helped two communities acquire grants to install infrastructure; reactivated a local development group; produced community profiles; and increased awareness of the multijurisdictional nature of economic development.

The participants identified water and sewer improvements; renewed efforts to repair sidewalks and streets; created more parking; increased interest in historic preservation; increased use of special tax assessments to fund downtown projects; and attracted two physicians as evidence of progress in community facilities.

The goal of community public relations represented two ideas: (1) building awareness among nonresidents about the qualities of the community, and (2) the increased awareness among local residents about local economic development efforts. Regarding the first, one community started a new ethnic festival to build on its Dutch heritage. Also, some participants pointed to increased promotional efforts to bring tourists to the community. Progress on internal public relations was indicated by statements of improved relations between businesses and community, and increased community spirit and involvement.

In one northern Wisconsin community, a transportation task force evolved from the program participants and worked with the Wisconsin Department of Transportation to accelerate highway improvements for tourism, local manufacturers, and farm commodities.

A sense of increased appreciation of business concerns and approachability of governmental officials characterized statements of progress toward community government goals. Acquisition of grants needed for economic development projects were other forms of progress.

The effect of the Community Economic Analysis program on long-range planning appeared in several responses, indicating that the Community Economic Analysis program was instrumental in a strategic planning effort by 200 people over a six-month period in one community.

Survey 2

In 1986, a second survey very similar to the first was sent to participants in the Community Economic Analysis program in twenty-six communities.[15] In all cases at least one year had elapsed since the original educational series had ended. The initial eight communities were not included. The survey instruments were customized to list the community-specific priorities participants had identified at their earlier meetings. Usable responses were received from 154 participants.

As in the first survey, participants were asked to assess how much progress had been made toward accomplishing their previously identified community priorities. Progress was reported on all of their top five priorities, with 59 percent reporting progress on the number one priority, including 25 percent reporting much or great progress. Progress on the other priorities was as follows: second, 53 percent; third, 53 percent; fourth, 68 percent; and fifth, 36 percent. Reports of little or no progress ranged from 13 percent on the highest priority to 39 percent on the fifth. The lack of accomplishment regarding the fifth priority may be an indication that leaders in small localities can give only so much time and energy at one time to community actions.

When asked if the program had contributed to the economic well-being of the community, two-thirds of the participants indicated that it had. When asked if the Community Economic Analysis program was worth doing, over 80 percent said that it was and 6 percent said that it was not. Nearly 85 percent of the participants indicated that they would recommend the program be done in other communities and less than 5 percent reported they would not.

Three out of five of the program participants felt the follow-up provided by the county Extension Community Resource Development agent was valuable. Many commented that they would have liked even more follow-up than they had received.

The participants were also asked to state where they worked and the agencies and organizations they represented at the meeting. The categories were not mutually exclusive: 34 percent reported they were either elected or appointed local officials; 47 percent indicated that they worked for businesses, banks, or were farmers; and 57 percent said they were representatives of Chambers of Commerce, industrial development corporations, or other civic groups.

Survey 3

A 1988-1989 survey of CRD agents identifies specific events that the agents attributed to the Community Economic Analysis program.[16] The responses represent CRD agents' interpretations of community activities evolving from the Community Economic Analysis program. These outcomes are categorized according to the five elements of a comprehensive community economic development strategy. A brief synopsis of selected outcomes gives a sense of the types of outcomes.[17]

Increasing the Efficiency of Existing Businesses. The community of Rosholt (1989 population of 554) approached the Wisconsin Development Fund to help a major local employer expand into several vacant buildings in the village. The firm stayed in the community, expanded employment to sixty people, and anticipates adding another forty people.

Tigerton (1989 population of 885) became more sensitive to local businesses as a result of its Community Economic Analysis program and worked with a local tool and die shop so it could expand locally and add jobs for local residents. The firm worked with local workers to provide skills training.

Capturing Existing Markets. Mauston (1989 population of 3,486) felt that its downtown appearance was repulsing shoppers. They hired a landscape architect to help them redesign downtown parking, traffic flows, and signage standards. Downtown merchants also worked with the Small Business Development Center on merchandising and management. The most obvious outcome was that the Chamber of Commerce purchased and reconditioned forty dumpsters to remove clutter at back entrances to stores.

Seymour (1989 population of 2,868) decided that one way they could attract people to their downtown was to build on the historic fact that the first hamburger was created there in 1885. An annual hamburger cook-off was created to attract people to the community. The water tower was painted to look like a hamburger.

Gilman (1989 population of 871) created a multi-community Taylor County Log Cabin Arts and Crafts Festival that attracts over 1,000 people to the community. Other festivals include Sauk Prairie's (1989 population of 5,225), Eagle Day in January (the city is a winter home for bald eagles); or Burlington's (1989 population of 8,780) building on the reputation of Nestle's to create a "Chocolate City" festival.

Attracting New Basic Employers. The City of Jefferson (1989 population of 5,783) identified the need for an economic development committee to manage its efforts. This led to hiring a consultant to evaluate their industrial attraction program. Eventually a computerized site inventory was built and current socioeconomic information was made available to prospects.

Florence County (1989 population of 4,237), with no incorporated municipalities, attracted four manufacturing firms to its industrial park that was built after the Community Economic Analysis program. The county was also involved in helping one firm locate housing for the relocation of some of its headquarters management team to Wisconsin from out of state.

Acquiring Funds from Broader Levels of Government. Fort Atkinson (1989 population of 10,161) identified improvements in the local airport as crucial to local manufacturing retention and expansion. A transportation committee was formed by the city council to address the issue and to work with the State and FAA on improvements. Tentative approval of a $720,000 grant for runway expansion, taxiways, land acquisition, and beacons will enable the airport to accommodate twin-engine aircraft year-round.

Oconto Falls (1989 population of 2,752) conducted a Community Economic Analysis in the spring of 1983. Industrial development was identified as a high priority. During the summer of 1983, the Federal Emergency Jobs Bill became available to communities that had experienced substantial economic decline and had conducted public forums to build strategies addressing those concerns. The

Community Economic Analysis program allowed the community to meet the preconditions for the support. They were awarded a $590,000 grant to assist their industrial development efforts. They were able to assist a local company to expand from sixty to ninety workers.

Superior (1989 population of 26,914) in the extreme northwest corner of Wisconsin has experienced long-term economic decline and perceived disinterest by Wisconsin state government in their plight. The most obvious manifestation was delays in the completion of four lanes on Highway 53, which affected tourism and logging. Through a series of community "lobbying" events at the state capitol, they were able to get the Department of Transportation to commit $35 million to upgrade the highway. The City also hosted Wisconsin State Government when it officially moved to Superior for one week in mid-summer 1989.

Tomahawk's (1989 population of 3,562) Community Economic Analysis program identified housing concerns. They used that interest plus Community Development Block Grant funds for housing rehabilitation and weatherization, and to purchase and convert a gravel pit into a city park.

Annual Rates of Change Computed from Secondary Data

In comparing annual rates of change in community wage and salary employment and per capita adjusted gross income over time it is possible to identify whether a shift occurred and conclude that the Community Economic Analysis program was *one* of the reasons that shift occurred. Each community's annual rate of change are compared before and after the year of the program. To correct for local trends, annual rates of change for comparable communities are calculated to indicate if any shift occurred in those communities also.[18]

In table 2.1, the average annual rate of change for communities conducting a Community Economic Analysis is compared both before and after the program and against communities used for comparison in the actual CEA program. The analysis uses the year of the Community Economic Analysis as a common ending point for the "pre-CEA" and common beginning point for the "post-CEA" calculations. The time of the analysis varies with the community. The first communities conducted programs in late 1982 and the last ones included in this analysis occurred in 1988.[19] Thus, pre-CEA represents annual percent change in per capita adjusted gross income (from 1977) or wage and salary employment (from 1979) through the

Table 2.1: Average Annual Rates of Change (in percents)

	Pre-CEA	Post-CEA
Per Capita Adjusted Gross Income		
CEA Communities (n = 48)	5.78%	6.55%
Comparison Communities (n = 93)	6.30	6.55
Total Wage and Salary Employment		
CEA Communities (n = 55)	−.40[a]	7.26[a]
Comparison Communities (n = 111)	.42[a]	4.15[a]

a. 10 percent or better significant difference between pre- and post-CEA annual rates of change.

year of the CEA. For the post-CEA, the change represents what happened from the year of the CEA to 1989.

The CEA communities display a more dramatic shift in employment trends than in income. There is a significant change between the pre-CEA and post-CEA rates of change in employment, but not income. There is no significant difference between the CEA and comparison communities. While the Community Economic Analysis program is not the sole cause of the change in economic trends for these communities, it plays some part in the shift. The description of specific types of community activities (described earlier in this section) gives some insight into how these communities caused the shift in trends.

Implications

The beginning of this chapter offered a brief description of local economic development efforts in rural communities. The Wisconsin Community Economic Analysis program addresses each of those dimensions. The program with its local delivery mechanism (county Extension faculty) represents a way to overcome the barriers of distance in acquiring knowledge[20] and adds analytical insight in order to expand the range of economic development options the community considers. The presence of a county Extension faculty member, with major program interests in community and economic development issues, increases the likelihood that a wide spectrum of community interests will be included as well as provides continued support to part-time local officials and volunteers through the implementation phase.

The county Extension Community Resource Development agent, who has conducted much of the educational program, continues working with the community group, serving as a catalyst and provider of additional information that local leaders might need. The community's continuing access to this professional is a powerful part of the Wisconsin Community Economic Analysis program. Often priority issues such as tax incentives, small business incubators, mainstreet revitalization, solid waste disposal, and housing development require additional educational programs. Original action plans may prove inadequate and require revision. Knowledge of new government programs may be important. The global economic environment shifts rapidly and the entire educational meeting series will need to be repeated regularly.

Although the Wisconsin Community Economic Analysis program provides most of the fundamental elements necessary for successful community economic development decision making, it is clearly not the only way that federal, state, and local policymakers can address local economic problems. It is an outgrowth of nearly thirty years of commitment by the University of Wisconsin-Extension to the delivery of public policy education focused on natural resources, economic, and community development to people throughout the state of Wisconsin. This thirty-year commitment has built the Community Resource Development agent and campus-based specialist system that is the professional staffing base for this specific educational program.

Each state and region in the United States possesses unique resources and conditions. The institutional base necessary to provide continuing educational and technical assistance may differ from place to place. Other institutions such as community colleges, regional planning organizations, and/or state agencies might also serve in this role. In some states, funds are appropriated for communities to hire private consultants as well as for public entities to provide the basic educational and technical assistance needed for community economic development. Whatever the institutional approach, the assistance must be tailored to local needs, provided by a reliable source, readily available, flexible in approach, accessible over time, and broadly financed.

One of the important lessons learned from the Wisconsin experience that is far too easy to overlook is that community economic development issues do not resolve themselves quickly or through casual and intermittent contact. This requires an institutional commitment to the continued placement and support of staff with responsibility in issues of economic and community development, local government education, and natural resource management so that they are able to build the long-term working relationships needed with the communities and neighborhoods to solve their problems.

There is no single program approach that is preferred over all others. There are many models that might be followed in organizing community groups, holding educational meetings, and providing ongoing technical and educational assistance. Workbooks outlining alternative models have been produced by the North Central Regional Center for Rural Development, the Western Regional Center for Rural Development, the Rocky Mountain Institute, the Edison Electric Institute, Pioneer Hi-Bred International, Inc., and others. All place primary emphasis on the education of a relatively small but important group of local leaders. These programs are sometimes criticized for reaching so few people directly. Most of the program models, however, emphasize the importance of reaching out for broader citizen involvement. Although conceptually well designed, the common weakness of most is that they are short-term efforts with little provision for education and technical assistance over time. In the long run, community leaders are left to fend for themselves. This does little to provide the catalytic help that makes volunteers most effective. Consequently, smaller rural communities receiving short-term assistance may experience a spurt of activity, but quickly fall back into a dormant state.

There is considerable variety in the content of the various program models. Some place a great deal of emphasis on leadership development and less on helping communities develop specific action plans. Conceptually, they are based on the belief that well-trained leadership can identify community problems and will acquire the necessary support, both internal and external, to resolve them. The Wisconsin Community Economic Analysis program may be properly criticized for its limited emphasis on leadership development itself. Most of the programs devote a great deal of time to environmental scans including an examination of global and local economic conditions. All call for the maximum use possible of mechanisms for acquiring the perspectives of the wider community (surveys, town hall meetings, special interest panels). Few spend as much time in detailed economic analysis as does the Wisconsin program. All the programs universally insist that the definition of community goals and objectives and the determination of appropriate action strategies are the responsibility of the people of the community. Local decisions and actions are primary in determining the future of local residents.

The ultimate institutional support base, program design, and content are not critical as long as they meet the fundamental requisites for sound individual and community decision making. What is critical for the future of rural America (and many inner-city neighborhoods as well) is that education and technical assistance in community economic development be made available on a widespread and continuing basis. Without it, many regions of the United States will continue to fall farther behind.

NOTES

1. Professor and Professor Emeritus of Agricultural Economics, University of Wisconsin-Madison/Extension.

2. DeWitt, John, Sandra S. Batie, and Kim Norris, *A Brighter Future for Rural America? Strategies for Communities and States,* Washington, DC: Center For Policy Research, National Governors Association, 1988; and Glen C. Pulver, "The Changing Economic Scene in Rural America," *The Journal of State Government,* Vol. 61, No. 1 (January/February 1988): 3–8.

3. If this is not in the community, then they must search for this technical assistance elsewhere. The technical assistance must be tailored to local needs; provided by a reliable source; readily available; flexible in approach; and accessible over time.

4. Some examples include programs designed by the Rocky Mountain Institute, the Heartland Center for Leadership Development, Pioneer Hi-Bred International, Inc., Regional Rural Development Centers, and many university extension programs. A detailed review of those programs is beyond this chapter.

5. These tend to be associated with regional planning agencies, utility companies, state development agencies, and private consulting firms.

6. These represent the initial and formal portion of the education effort. They typically require ten or more hours of contact time over three or four weeks. The crucial informal and repetitive educational effort is provided by the county Extension CRD Agent. This makes the regular in-service training especially important in order to maintain the quality of this integral portion of the CEA program.

7. An example of insight gained is one community (4,000 people) that was convinced they needed a CEA to improve the effectiveness of their industrial development program and solve their economic development problems. A simple and quick analysis of their employment structure uncovered that the local employment share in manufacturing was more than three times the national average. This stimulated discussion of what other local development strategies might need to be considered.

8. Paul, Alan, Tom Lesiewicz, Ron Shaffer, and Glen Pulver, "Design Documentation for CEAS: Community Economic Analysis Software," *NCCI Software Journal,* Vol. 2, No. 1 (November, 1986).

9. Hustedde, Ron, Ron Shaffer, and Glen Pulver, *Community Economic Analysis: A How To Manual,* North Central Regional Center for Rural Development, Ames, IA, 1984.

10. This includes selling higher valued products and services and developing niche markets as well as increased volume of existing exports activities.

11. Pulver, Glen C., *Community Economic Development Strategies*, G3366, University of Wisconsin-Extension, June 1989.

12. A copy is available from the authors.

13. None of the evaluations asked about changes in community activities pre- versus post-CEA. Rather, their purpose was to determine the amount of perceived progress on identified community goals.

14. Forest, Laverne, and Connie Wilsrock, "Community Economic Analysis Program Evaluation," Program Development and Evaluation Unit, University of Wisconsin-Extension, April 1985.

15. Danz-Hale, Dawn, "CEA Follow-up Survey," unpublished manuscript, Dept. of Agricultural Economics, University of Wisconsin-Madison/Extension, February, 1987.

16. Smith, Rachael, "Community Economic Analysis: 1982-1989 County Samples," Community, Natural Resources, and Economic Development Program Office, University of Wisconsin-Extension, August 1989.

17. In some cases these outcomes are goals identified in the program, others are spin-offs from emerging community development efforts. The data do not permit a consistent delineation of categories to which the response belongs since respondents were not asked to link the observed community actions with Community Economic Analysis program goals.

18. Comparison communities are selected as part of each Community Economic Analysis program. The general criteria for selecting a comparison community includes similar population size, similar economic function (county seat, area trade center, tourist destination), and same general area of the state. The comparison communities differ from the CEA communities by the absence of a Community Economic Analysis program.

19. Because of data availability and insufficient time for any change to occur, no community conducting a Community Economic Analysis program after 1989 is included in the analysis.

20. It must be remembered that knowledge is different from information.

CHAPTER 3

Applying Strategic Planning to Rural Economic Development

ROBERT BLAIR AND B.J. REED[1]

Local economic development can be defined as an organized effort by communities to stimulate private investment in order to increase opportunities for employment, expand the tax base, broaden the area economy, and generally improve the quality of life of citizens. Communities can undertake a variety of activities to reach their economic development goals. Because resources are needed for economic development, however, it is important that program activities and strategies are appropriate, achievable, and effective. Communities that fail to focus their economic development strategies are likely to waste valuable resources.

There are several reasons why rural communities especially need to carefully select economic development strategies. First, most rural communities depend on local volunteers more than do their urban counterparts (John, Batie, and Norris 1988). Consequently, selecting strategies that are compatible with the use of voluntary resources is important. Second, many small community economies developed around natural resource-based industries (e.g., agriculture, mining, and forestry) have decreasing capacity to generate income and employment (National Commission on Agriculture and Rural Development Policy 1990). Hence, rural localities have fewer

viable development approaches since most local strategies are derived from the existing economic base. Finally, in addition to declining economies, many rural communities also face population decline
and an aging population base (Brown and Deavers 1987). These
trends affect the level of development resources, the characteristics
and availability of labor, and the nature of options. Overall, rural
communities have fewer resources and fewer choices for economic
development.

One approach to identifying development activities used by a
growing number of communities is strategic planning (Eisinger
1988). Strategic planning has been described as the "most appropriate approach" for communities engaging in local economic development (Blakely 1989). This approach has also been portrayed as the
process that best integrates the factors that ultimately determine
success or failure in state and local economic development including
the "identification of local needs and resources; adaptation to external constraints; local leadership that stimulates collaboration among
public, private, and nonprofit organizations; and sustained effort
over many years, sometimes decades" (Luke et al. 1988).

This chapter explains why strategic planning is a viable approach to selecting achievable economic development actions appropriate to rural communities. The components of the strategic planning process will be outlined, its importance as a planning approach
to rural development illustrated, and a community-based approach
used in Nebraska described. Finally, evidence from a case study of
Nebraska communities is examined to determine the effectiveness of
strategic planning as a method of selecting rural development strategies.

Strategic Planning and Economic Development

Strategic planning is one of the most discussed techniques in economic development today. After twenty years in the private sector,
this process was adapted by many public organizations in the early
1980s. Various authors have listed five, six, eight, or more steps in a
typical process (Bryson 1989; Koteen 1989; Sorkin, Ferris, and Hudak
1984). However, all agree that there are at least four major components of the process:

- Mission or Goal Identification.
- Review of External and Internal Environments.
- Setting of Priority Strategies and Action Steps.
- Implementation and Evaluation.

Several elements make strategic planning distinct from long-range planning. First, it places heavy emphasis on the community's environment, both external and internal. In this way the process attempts to look at factors that influence the community. Understanding where the community has been and where it is now can contribute to the ability to capitalize on opportunities, mitigate threats, improve on existing strengths, and reduce weaknesses. Long-range planning, on the other hand, focuses on a trend line from the present. "It answers the question of how to get the job done" rather than how to change the job to fit emerging trends (Mercer 1991).

Second, strategic planning is action- and implementation-oriented (Bryson 1989). Long-range planning has been criticized for its lack of pertinence to the real situations faced by organizations or communities (Bryson 1989). Strategic planning builds this pertinence into the process by carrying out a reality-based analysis of the environment and by emphasizing actions steps, implementation, and evaluation.

Finally, strategic planning differs from a traditional long-range planning approach in its attempt to link implementation techniques and approaches to action planning (Koteen 1989). Strategic planning advocates argue that the process emphasizes the importance of operationalizing action plans. Action plans are a key component of the process, assigning responsibilities and time frames to projects and activities to better ensure their implementation (Sorkin, Ferris, and Hudak 1984). Long-range planning often lacks this critical component.

But strategic planning is not without detractors. Concerns fall into three major categories: (1) the rationality embedded in the process often results in proposals that ignore political reality; (2) many public organizations lack the capacity to participate in strategic planning; and (3) strategic planning often places too much emphasis on process rather than on results (Reed, Reed, and Luke 1987).

None of these criticisms, however, point to a fatal flaw in strategic planning. For instance, criticisms focusing on the limitations of rational decision-making approaches often fail to recognize the adjustments that can occur in the strategic planning process to adapt to a particular political and cultural context. In addition, weak organizations can, over time, develop a capacity to productively engage in strategic planning. Strategic planning may be better suited to participatory decision making in the public sector rather than "top down" approaches often employed in the private sector. Finally, strategic planning does not, by its nature, have to focus on process rather than results. In sum, there is little evidence that these three concerns are endemic to strategic planning (Swanstrom 1987).

Strategic Planning and Rural Development

In spite of criticism, strategic planning for economic development is increasingly used by many rural communities. One reason is the desire of local leaders to respond to the growing distress of many rural places. Also, strategic planning techniques appear to help communities acquire many of the elements that research and experience indicate are needed for successful local development.

The signs of rural distress include declining population, business out-migration, and serious erosion of rural economic base industries (Brown and Deavers 1987; John, Batie, and Norris 1988; National Commission on Agriculture and Rural Development Policy 1990). A number of community economic development programs that use strategic planning approaches or techniques have been developed in recent years to help communities respond to rural distress. Notable examples include programs sponsored by the National Association of Towns and Townships (National Center for Small Communities 1985) and the North Central Regional Center for Rural Development (Ayres et al. 1990). Other efforts are underway in Iowa, Kansas, and many other states.

In addition to addressing specific and immediate distress-related problems, strategic planning helps communities undertake many of the activities and obtain many of the components needed for a broad-based successful local economic development effort. An important component is the development of a range of diverse local strategies (Malizia 1986). Because of intra-community diversity, each local strategy should be comprehensive in nature (Brown and Deavers 1987; Luke et al. 1988). Strategies might recruit business, targeting both service and manufacturing firms (John, Batie, and Norris 1988); attract investment; increase local spending; and/or expand the local share of community spending (Shaffer and Pulver 1987; Kane and Sand 1988).

Economic development strategies should reflect local strengths and resources (Luke et al. 1988; Redwood 1988). Frequently encouraged are local strategies that take an entrepreneurial approach (Eisinger 1988; John, Batie, and Norris 1988); those that focus on self-development (Green et al. 1990); those that emphasize the expansion and retention of existing industries (John, Batie, and Norris 1988; Morse 1990; Olsen and Blair 1990); those that help new or small firms grow (Malecki 1988; Teitz 1987); and those that maximize linkages among local firms (Smith 1985). Strategic planning, because it focuses on goal identfication by the community participants, tends to emphasize local strengths and resources.

Local implementation is often a critical ingredient of economic development. Strategies that reflect area strengths are best implemented locally (Council of State Governments 1989). Local implementation occurs when a participatory approach is included (Ryan 1987; Wallis and Schler 1988; Cawley 1989; Strange et al. 1990). Because of the devolution of the federal system, many communities are forced to take more responsibility for their economic development (Vogel 1990; Schweke and Toft 1991). The action plan, a product of participatory strategic planning, contains provisions for the local implementation of strategies.

While local implementation is essential, outside assistance is usually needed (John, Batie, and Norris 1988). Naturally, a primary source of economic development assistance is state government (National Governors' Association 1988; Reed and Paulsen 1990). The ability of communities to make external connections to state, regional, and national economic development resources is deemed critical (Humphrey, Ericson, and McClusky 1989). A strategic action plan provides for linkages to external resources to support local projects.

A planned approach has also been identified as a crucial component in local economic development. Because public resources are increasingly employed, a plan is needed to ensure their efficient use (Eisinger 1988). A plan will facilitate a long-term economic development process (Blakely 1989; Northeast Midwest Institute 1989); systematically set goals (Vogel and Swanson 1988); and anticipate the changing nature of economic activity and the public role in stimulating economic growth (Luke et al. 1988). Strategic planning is based on a structured approach.

Organizational and leadership capacity have been identified as important elements in local economic development (Rubin 1986). The capacity of a community to undertake economic development is influenced by leadership levels (Paulsen and Reed 1987; Walzer and Kapper 1989; Reed and Paulsen 1990); the existence of local champions, or "sparkplugs" (John, Batie, and Norris 1988); and the "readiness" of a community to undertake an effort (Reed, Reed, and Luke 1987). Organizations need to have sustained efforts, emphasizing finance (Green et al. 1990), industrial sites, and infrastructure needs (John, Batie, and Norris 1988). Since most strategic planning projects involve a cross-section of the community, local leadership and organizational capacity are likely to be improved.

Finally, there are a number of economic and demographic factors that influence local economic development. Important factors include population size and per capita income (Paulsen and Reed 1987); economic environmental turbulence (Rubin 1990); and local government institutional and managerial arrangements (Stevens and McGowan 1987; Feiock and Clingermayer 1986; Sharp 1991). At the same time, because of demographic and economic factors, there are limits to local economic development (Power 1989). These factors are examined in strategic planning by a systematic review of the external and internal environments.

In sum, there are a variety of reasons to believe that a local strategic planning effort can make a strong contribution to rural economic development.

Strategic Planning in Nebraska

Efforts to build an effective vehicle for rural economic development strategic planning began in Nebraska during the mid-1980s. Public Administration faculty at the University of Nebraska at Omaha (UNO) and Community Development Division staff of the Nebraska Department of Economic Development (NDED) formed a joint venture to test the feasibility of economic development strategic planning on a community-wide basis (Reed, Reed, and Luke 1987). The approach was adapted from the model in the Public Technology, Incorporated strategic planning guide (Sorkin, Ferris, and Hudak 1984). That preliminary project provided the groundwork for a planning grant from the U.S. Department of Housing and Urban Development to NDED in 1986 to assist "rural communities recently experiencing economic dislocation." In cooperation with NDED, UNO provided assistance on the strategic planning project. Modifications to the original planning model were made and tested in the field at six pilot locations. In 1988, four additional communities participated in strategic planning projects.

The result of these efforts was Strategic Training and Resource Targeting (START), which began in 1989. It is now the primary mechanism for delivering community-wide strategic planning services for local economic development in Nebraska. The program is operated through the Center for Public Affairs Research (CPAR), a public policy research and community outreach department of UNO. Staff who oversee the program include trained facilitators, economists, and economic development specialists. The program provides on-site technical assistance, and participant materials that include computer software for community analysis and self-help training and planning manuals. START has provided strategic planning assistance to more than forty communities in Nebraska.

START is a self-help, community-based approach to economic development that assists local leaders in developing a strategic plan to improve the area economy. START relies on a local team of twenty-five to thirty volunteers to complete the initial strategic planning process in five to six months. This process leads to action plan implementation, evaluation, and revision. The local volunteer team has three components. A *local leader* manages the overall program within the community and serves as the spokesperson for the project. A second component includes a *resource team* of six to eight people who complete specific logistical and support tasks, such as recording activities, preparing for planning meetings, conducting community surveys, compiling data, providing information to the public, and working with the committees. The last component is the local *steering committee*, consisting of all the volunteers who participate in the strategic planning sessions—analyzing data, identifying issues, developing strategies, and initiating the actions needed for plan implementation.

The heart of the START program is the structured strategic planning process that the steering committee follows to identify the strategies that will comprise the local action plan for economic development. The program contains a seven-step process.

1. *Local Organization*. In this first step, communities interested in participating in the process send their requests to the START staff. A member of this staff will visit with the community leaders to describe the process and carry out an initial evaluation of community readiness. Communities are also expected to have identified resources ($1,000 fee, payable to START, meeting facilities, staff or volunteer support, and so forth) necessary to carry out the effort. When all these items are in place, the community is scheduled to participate in the process.

    A START organization is formed or integrated into the activities of an existing body. Local leaders are identified through the initial community contacts. These individuals come from a wide variety of leadership positions including chambers of commerce, development corporations, city and county government, and so forth. The selection of local leaders is critical since they will shepherd the process and ultimately will be responsible for its overall success. Local leaders along with other START initiators usually become the resource team. The resource team makes the determination of who will serve on the committee that will actually take part in the planning process. START staff make recommendations about the mix of local participants necessary for a successful process; however, the local leader and resource team, through a consensus-building process, make the final decision.

2. *Analysis of External and Internal Factors.* Two structured planning sessions are held to focus on the scan of environmental issues. Typically, each session is four hours long. Steering committee members are broken into small groups, each with assigned discussion leaders to facilitate dialogue. In the first session, the external environment is discussed. During this session the committee focuses on threats and opportunities facing the community. The process highlights actions outside the community that create threats that might be mitigated or opportunities that can be capitalized upon. The steering committee analyzes income, population, and employment data; and state and national economic trends.

   The second planning session focuses on the internal environment to gain an understanding of community strengths and weaknesses. Efforts are made to identify issues over which community residents have some control. Strengths represent objects for the community to maintain and build upon. Weaknesses can be strategic targets for reduction or elimination. Steering committee members focus on attitude survey results and community organizational and infrastructure inventories in attempting to identify internal issues for further discussion.

3. *Identification of Key Issues.* During the second planning session the participants identify key community issues. These issues are gleaned from the external and internal scan analysis. Key community issues may include topics as diverse as downtown deterioration, lack of job opportunities, need for additional recreational programs, or poor community image. Often as many as twenty key issues are initially identified by the steering committee. It is necessary then to reduce them to a more manageable number. A series of secret votes are conducted so that only the most important concerns or issues, as seen by the steering committee, are considered for further action.

4. *Development of Strategies.* A critical part of strategic planning is the development of action strategies to address the key issues selected. First, it is necessary to take the top issues (usually around ten) and then place them in priority order. This is

accomplished during the second planning session by a matrix exercise where each steering committee member ranks each of the top issues in terms of their importance and how well the community is addressing them. The individual rankings are then grouped and a visual image of the consensus surrounding each issue is presented. This process permits the steering committee to focus on those issues that are both important and not being addressed effectively. Where there is not group consensus, further discussion helps clarify the differences, and it is then decided whether the issue should continue to be considered.

Next, task forces are formed to begin the development of action strategies for the highest priority issues, usually around four or five. The task forces include both steering committee members and occasionally individuals from the community who have a special interest or expertise in the priority development issue.

5. *Formation of Action Plan.* These local task forces then prepare drafts of action strategies. These strategies are reviewed by economic development specialists from the START staff and elsewhere who then help the task forces refine and clarify elements of each strategy. Where development specialists and task force members disagree on particular elements of the strategy, the specialists defer to the task force members recommendations. This is done to ensure that ownership in the action plan remains within the community.

   At a third general planning session the various strategies are submitted and discussed by the steering committee. Duplications are eliminated and differences resolved. The final strategic plan is then operationalized into a community action plan. The plan is then presented at a town hall meeting.

6. *Implementation of Action Plan.* As mentioned earlier, steps 1 through 5 take approximately five to six months. The action plan, however, contains specific timetables for the completion of activities and the names of parties responsible for various action steps. Some of the activities in the plan may be short term, others may be long term. The community assumes responsibility for implementing the plan.

7. *Monitoring of Plan.* No plan is perfect or complete; monitoring, adjustment, and refinement are needed. Evaluation is essential to strategic planning, and local leadership plays a critical role in this step. The success of the overall plan depends heavily on the local leaders, as well as resource team and steering commit-

tee members. To this end, plans are reviewed six to twelve months after action plan implementation begins. This provides an opportunity for community participants to reflect on how well implementation of the action steps is proceeding. START staff help facilitate this evaluation. Based upon this evaluation, action plans are modified, activities eliminated or new ones added to reflect changing conditions and changing capacities. This monitoring allows START to become a dynamic rather than static process.

While a self-help and community-based approach is generally considered essential to the success of a local economic development effort, it was pointed out earlier that outside support and assistance is also paramount (Paulsen and Reed 1987; John, Batie, and Norris 1988; Humphrey, Ericson, and McCluskey 1989). START staff provides technical assistance in the development of plans, trains resource team members on their responsibilities, facilitates activities included in the strategic planning sessions, and arranges action plan monitoring meetings. And finally, START helps mobilize the economic development resources from state and federal agencies needed for implementation of the local plan.

It is apparent that the completion of a START program requires community volunteers to commit many hours to the effort. While it is very difficult to calculate the average number of person-hours devoted to the strategic planning program, it is possible to estimate a range of time for the various steps in the process. Because the number of hours depends on the number of people involved in a particular community, the number of people surveyed, the number of action steps and development objectives in the plan, and the overall scope of the project (e.g., single community versus regional), it is only possible to estimate a range of hours. Also, because of the structured nature of steps 2 through 5 in the START program, estimates for these steps will be more reliable than estimated for steps 1, 6, and 7.

Step 1 includes not only the organizational phase but also the recruitment of volunteers, training resource team members, and generation of community interest; it is estimated that 150 to 200 person-hours are needed, depending on the nature of the community. Steps 2 through 5 are the structured phase of the strategic planning program, including the data collection, formal planning sessions, and action plan formulation. The total number of person-hours needed are estimated to be between 1,200 and 1,500, with the variation explained by the size of the steering committee and the number of persons surveyed. The number of person-hours needed to accomplish steps 6 and 7, the implementation and monitoring stages, are dependent on the amount of work that the steering committee has created for itself in the development of the action plan. Estimates for these stages would be 500 to 600 person-hours.

Research Methodology and Data Analysis

Because START has been in operation since 1989, the experience of several communities can be analyzed. It is possible to assess the ability of the program to help rural communities identify and select achievable economic development strategies by examining the outcomes of local planning efforts. Accordingly, a basic case study design was deemed appropriate as a research approach to analyzing START.

A single case study design where the START program is evaluated was chosen. The design, however, includes multiple units of analysis. Communities that participated in START are examined as individual units of analysis. Findings from the individual projects are then aggregated, giving us an assessment of the START approach.

In order to ensure that community activities, or outputs, might conceivably be attributed to START, it was necessary to limit the study to those communities that completed the START program. Only outputs that occurred after or during START were included. In addition, since the focus of this chapter is on rural development, communities located in metropolitan counties or with populations that exceeded 20,000 were excluded from the case study.

Seventeen START projects were included in the case study, consisting of twelve community projects, one multi-community project, and four county-level projects. Geographically, the projects were dispersed around the state. The seventeen action plans, completed between August 1989 and July 1990, were comprehensive in nature. They contained sixty-six different development strategies.

The communities in the study met general rural population and economic criteria. Populations in 1990 ranged from 650 to 13,130, with a median population of 1,916. Thirteen locations lost population from 1980, and the average loss per location was 8.3 percent. Eight of the START projects were in agricultural dependent counties, where farm earnings accounted for 20 percent or more of total labor and proprietor income (Bender et al. 1985). Eight more were in counties with less agricultural dependency and more economic diversity, but with no population centers of 10,000 or more. One project was located in a regional trade county, where there is a community of 10,000 or more in population (Johnson and Young 1988).

Data from the attitude surveys, action plans, and program evaluations were analyzed. The business and community attitude surveys provided ratings of residents on community services and facilities, city leadership, job opportunities, and citizen opinions on the allocation of resources for local economic and business development. This information provides a sense of community attitudes about local economic conditions and organizational capacity to improve the economy. Looking at action plans gives a sense of how the strategic plan responded to these perceptions. Local action plan documents listed priority development goals of the community and the action steps needed to satisfy priorities. Participant evaluations of the START program rated the usefulness of various planning activities, the capability of local participants, and the expected outcomes of the strategic planning process. This provides an indicator of how the participants themselves felt about the utility of the process. The local leaders were also interviewed regarding implementation. Progress toward meeting action plan goals is an indicator of successful implementation. Specific program outputs were also examined.

By compiling the data from the individual local projects an aggregated data base was created. The evaluation has three components: the overall evaluations of participant programs, local action plan strategies, and the outputs of the implementation efforts. Analysis will focus on the following evaluation criteria: the ability of START to help rural communities select achievable and effective economic development strategies.

Findings

Participant Evaluation of START

In order to evaluate the success of the START process, the Center for Public Affairs Research at UNO surveyed the steering committee participants who had participated in the process. The surveys were taken approximately two months after completion of the process but before the six month review of progress in action plan implementation. Table 3.1 shows selected responses from the survey for communities included in the case study, and the results are summarized below.

START was seen by the respondents as an effective process for organizing the community and for building a broad-based coalition

Table 3.1: START Evaluation Survey—Mean Participants' Ratings (n percents)

	Excellent	Good	Satisfactory	Fair	Poor
Steering Committee					
Broad representation across community sectors	35%	40%	16%	6%	4%
Ability to follow through on future projects in the action plan	16	36	30	13	5
Local Leader					
Ability to organize tasks and people	34	41	16	4	4
Small Group Discussion					
Relevance and importance of questions	24	53	16	7	0
Importance of issues	33	41	15	6	5
Task Forces					
Enthusiasm for task force plan	25	44	18	8	5
Action Plan					
Realistic and doable objectives	28	45	18	6	4
Relevance to improvement of local economy	27	38	19	10	6
Ability to serve as an ongoing plan for the future	28	40	20	7	5
Overall rating of START Economic Development	21	53	16	6	4

to carry out strategic planning. The survey asked participants how they viewed the representation of the committee in terms of covering a broad spectrum of interests and concerns. Roughly three-quarters of those responding felt the representation as either excellent or good. Only 4 percent felt it was poor.

Organizing strategic planning efforts is especially challenging in rural development efforts because START involved individuals from throughout the community rather than from a single organization or sector where values and mission may be more clearly defined and homogeneous. Interests of participants are likely to be more diverse, value conflicts may be more pronounced, and commitment to development may vary considerably. START was seen by respondents as an effective way to deal with these organizational and diversity issues.

Local leaders also play an important role in this organizational process because they help make decisions about the composition of the steering committee and help set the agenda for the strategic planning efforts. Again, three-quarters of the respondents saw the local leaders' ability to organize tasks and people as either excellent or good.

Concerning the internal and external environmental analysis, START used small group discussions as a way to break down myriad issues to a manageable size and help facilitate the exchange of ideas and issue identification. Discussion questions were developed by START to help facilitate small group discussions. Most respondents found the discussion questions relevant and important to the identification of key issues. When asked to evaluate the importance of the issues identified in the process, three-quarters of the steering committee members found them to be excellent or good. However, 11 percent believed they were not very important to the rural development aims of the community.

The final stages included the development of strategies and the formation of an action plan. The steering committee members were asked several questions to gauge attitudes about the action plan strategies. Respondents were fairly positive about the realistic nature of the action plan objectives; three-quarters saw them as excellent or good. Four percent ranked them as poor. The overall plan developed by steering committee task forces received similar support. Nearly two-thirds believed the action plan would be relevant to improving the local economy, while one-sixth were more skeptical. Two-thirds of the steering committee respondents believed the action plan was good or excellent in serving as an ongoing plan for the future.

Finally, the strategic planning process success rests on its ability to foster implementation of the action plan itself. Most steering committee members remain optimistic about the possibilities of action plan implementation. This optimism is tempered, however, by some concern about the ability to translate the plan into action. When asked about the steering committee's ability to follow through on projects in the action plan, over half believed it was excellent or good but almost one-fifth believed it was only fair or poor. The overall participant evaluation of the START process, however, was quite positive, with almost three-quarters believing it was excellent or good. These results demonstrate that while the START process is considered to be valuable by most of those who participated, there is concern about follow-through and implementation. This may be reflective of planning processes in general or it may represent apprehension about personnel, political, or financial resources necessary to carry out activities. Some of the apprehension may have come from the realization of the size of the community development task at hand.

Action Plan Strategies

An important outcome of START is the actual development of a community action plan. The plan is a set of action strategies that guide the community in reaching development goals. Since START participants identify the community goals and develop the strategies to meet these goals, an examination of the strategies contained in the plans of the case study communities will help indicate whether the planning process followed is an effective one for selecting appropriate strategies. Strategies were first sorted into categories so they could be analyzed. They were then examined to see how they relate to community attitudes and evaluations once the progress of their implementation was evaluated. Strategies were also compared to empirical research regarding rural needs.

One way to reduce and categorize the many and diverse strategies included in the plans is to conduct a content analysis of the plans. The content analysis used here consisted of a two-step process. Step 1 was the sorting of 249 development activities of each of the seventeen plans into like categories. Key words were identified in each of the development activities. The key words relate to a specific set of actions or activities that have an identifiable result. Examples of actions are forming a local economic development corporation or developing a community center. Activities might also include the organization or mobilization of local resources to accomplish a task in the future, like identifying a symbol for the community or improving the retail environment downtown. Similar key words were combined, forming sixty-six specific action steps.

Step 2 was grouping action steps into broader development strategies. Strategies refer to the collection of similar action steps that have a common end result, like attracting business, improving community image, or developing downtown. Nineteen different development strategies were identified, and the sixty-six action steps placed into the appropriate strategy.[2] Table 3.2 is a listing of broad development objectives contained in local action plan strategies, and the number of communities selecting at least one of the action steps included in that objective.

An examination of table 3.2 shows that "traditional" economic development strategies, like existing business assistance, community promotion, and business attraction, are not among the top five strategies included in local action plans. Undertaking activities to improve the community image, the attitudes of the residents, or the physical appearance of the town was a strategy selected by nearly all of the communities in the case study. These sets of action steps are

Table 3.2: Priority Action Plan Strategies

Local Action Strategy	Number of Communities Selecting Strategy (n = 17)
1. Community Image/Attitude/Appearance	15
2. Retail/Main Street Development	14
3. Improve Community and Public Service	13
4. Recreation Development	12
5. Local Development Organization	12
6. Existing Business Assistance	11
7. Community Promotion (Marketing)	9
8. Development Finances and Resources	9
9. Business Attraction	8
10. Tourism	8
11. Housing	7
12. New Business Development	6
13. Infrastructure Development	6
14. Area Cooperation	5
15. Education Improvement	5
16. Leadership Development	4
17. Transportation Improvement	4
18. Health Care	3
19. Work Force Development	3

related because they pertain to how the community is perceived by those outside, as well as inside, the community. This top strategy is indirectly related to economic development since it strives to present a favorable impression of the community; employment, income, and investment—traditional measures of economic development—would occur later. The community of Oxford, for example, saw external image as a key concern and developed action plan elements incorporating the production of a village directory, the organization of a village cleanup day, and the creation of a community welcoming committee. Other communities developed actions such as improving the attractiveness of open space, enhancing the physical image of their downtowns, and removing various eyesores throughout the area.

The next most prevalent strategy, retail and main street development, links directly to economic development. David City focused on several retail issues including the recruitment of a fast food franchise, improved marketing, and acquiring additional clothing and shoe retail outlets. Other communities focused on removing vacant storefronts, renovation of buildings, development of business retention programs, and so forth. Improvement of community and public services, and recreation development, the next two strategies listed in table 3.2, seem to pertain to improvements within the community and have little direct relationship to economic development. Superior listed recreation development actions such as constructing a running track, building new tennis facilities, improving the swimming pool, and improving a specific park. Two communities began investigating the possibility of developing a regional landfill as a strategy for improving public services; Clay Center researched the need and eventually funded a professional development position.

Number 5 in table 3.2 is the improvement of the local development organization. While this strategy pertains to economic development, it is generally concerned with activities undertaken prior to engaging in economic development efforts. Developing organization capacity led to many types of action steps. Albion proposed the creation of a county-wide foundation as part of an effort to expand fund-raising capacity. Valley County developed a regional organization and brochure. Stuart established a local development corporation.

While table 3.2 is an informative description of the various strategies selected by the communities, it does not yet tell us if these local strategies, selected by strategic planning processes, are effective approaches to rural development. One way to understand the impact of a number of specific development strategies is to place them into broader development categories that are more easily analyzed. Since many of the action plan strategies have an obvious relationship to each other, it is possible to place them into groups according to their objectives. Table 3.3 shows the local action strategies grouped into six development objectives that can be described as follows:

- *Infrastructure.* The improvement of physical facilities.
- *Quality of Life.* The improvement of intangible community assets.
- *Organizational.* The upgrading of the community's internal capacity.
- *Local Support.* The supporting of specific local economic development efforts.
- *Industrial/Community Promotion.* The attracting of outside jobs and investment, customers, and visitors.
- *Business Development.* The facilitating of local business growth by increasing community support and assistance.

Table 3.3: Local Action Strategies and Rural Development Goals (in percentage of total strategies)

Local Action Strategies	Development Objective	Broad Goal
Transportation improvement Infrastructure development Improve community and public services Develop housing	Infrastructure (18%)	Community Development (34%)
Improve health care services Recreation development Education improvement	Quality of Life (16%)	
Leadership development Local development organization Facilitate area cooperation	Organizational (15%)	Pre-Economic Development (34%)
Development finances and resources Enhance community image/attitude/ appearance Work force development	Local Support (19%)	
Business attraction Develop tourism Promote community	Community Promotion (14%)	Economic Development (32%)
Assist existing business and industry Assist retail and downtown business New business formation	Business Development (18%)	

These six development objectives, as shown in table 3.3, can then be grouped into comprehensive goals important to the overall development of the community:

- *Community Development.* Objectives that do not directly relate to economic development, but focus instead on broader community improvement goals.
- *Pre-Economic Development.* Objectives that prepare the community for local development activities.
- *Economic Development.* Objectives that engage in specific activities and undertake substantive projects.

By computing from all the strategies selected by the communities the percentage for each development objective and goal, it is possible to learn more about the nature and scope of the rural development priorities of the communities in the case study. Once these priorities are determined the effectiveness of strategic planning can be measured by examining community attitudes, empirical research, and outputs of the process. Table 3.3 shows the percentage of strategies for each development objective and broad goal. It is interesting to note that the communities in the case study have distributed the number of strategies equally among the three broad goals. While communities choose substantive economic development activities, they do not neglect those activities that pertain to basic community needs or those necessary to prepare for economic development efforts. In other words, community leaders who participated in the START strategic planning program did not ignore broader local development goals when selecting economic development-related strategies.

One assumption of START is that there is a connection between the environmental scan, the stakeholder perceptions of issues, and the strategies the steering committee selects. The stakeholders for strategic planning are the members of the community. Advocates of strategic planning argue that action steps are more likely to succeed if they flow from a clear understanding of the factors that impact on development, and the values and issues that stakeholders view as important (Bryson 1989). One way to measure issues and stakeholder concerns is through an analysis of citizen and business employer attitudes. Specifically, do the action plans address the concerns raised by these stakeholders? If they do, it is an indicator that action plans are derived, at least in part, from the concerns articulated by these stakeholders. Table 3.4 presents case study averages for selected citizen attitude survey responses. Table 3.5 presents selected responses from the business attitude survey.

In general, both surveys show that the strategic planning committees responded to general stakeholder input when they focused on a number of economic development strategies as outlined in table 3.3. The citizen's survey had very low ratings on the availability and quality of local job opportunities. More than half gave fair or poor responses to these two questions. Both the business and citizen surveys supported local development strategies that strive to attract new business and industry. However, the citizen's survey did not support the expanding existing business strategy as highly as the local business respondents (55 to 90 percent). Community businesses directly benefit from this economic development strategy. The survey provides support for the action plan goals identified in table 3.3.

Nearly a third of citizen and business respondents gave a rating of fair or poor to the responsiveness of city government and leadership. These attitudes help explain why the actions plans were de-

Table 3.4: Rural Citizen Attitude Survey—Communities' Average[a] (in percents)

	Excellent	Good	Satisfactory	Fair	Poor
Rating of the responsiveness of the city government and leadership to the needs of the citizens	5%	26%	36%	23%	10%
Ratings of city services					
Fire	46%	34%	9%	7%	4%
Police	18	35	26	15	6
Street Maintenance	12	34	29	18	8
Library	28	39	18	9	4
Ambulance	41	37	12	6	3
Planning	7	28	37	16	8
Sewage	16	41	29	9	3
Rating of the overall availability of job opportunities	3%	10%	26%	33%	25%
Rating of the overall quality of job opportunities	5%	9%	24%	33%	27%

	Yes	No
Support for local development strategies		
Attracting new industry	87%	12%
Attracting new retail business	81	16
Attracting new service business	74	23
Expanding existing business	55	42

a. Totals may not equal 100 percent because four communities in the case study included non-response rates.

veloped with almost a third of the strategies relating to the pre-economic development goal, where issues pertaining to organization and community preparation are addressed. Also, the high priority placed on enhancing community image by the START communities (number 3 overall) is consistent with the emphasis placed on that factor by the business survey respondents.

Finally, even though both the citizen and business surveys generally rated city services favorably, concern existed about planning and condition of streets. Perhaps participating in START is one way to address the issue of planning. Table 3.3 identified a third of the total development strategies concerned with community development objectives. Street maintenance and other public works and service needs are addressed in this objective.

Another way to evaluate strategic planning strategies is to examine the progress of their implementation over time. Local leaders from the communities in the case study were asked a series of questions regarding the status of their action plans. Since the communities in the case study completed their action plans between August 1989 and July 1990 and the interviews were not conducted until October 1992, at least two years elapsed in most cases between plan completion and questions regarding the status of implementation. There was sufficient time for activity to occur in the communities.

Local leaders were asked to rate on a scale of 1 to 5 the progress of the individual priority action strategies in their plan. The responses for the separate strategies were placed into broader categories of development objectives, as described in table 3.3, and then

Table 3.5: Rural Business Attitude Survey—Communities' Average[a] (in percents)

	Yes	No
Factors that would improve business operations		
Better transportation routes	27%	71%
Improved community image	60	38
Better cooperation among area merchants	50	48
More support from chamber of commerce	36	62

	Excellent	Good	Satisfactory	Fair	Poor
Rating of responsiveness of local government and leadership to the needs of the business community	4%	29%	37%	23%	8%
Rating of city services					
Fire	48%	42%	7%	2%	0%
Police	18	43	23	12	3
Street maintenance	13	39	28	13	6
Planning	6	36	37	16	5
Sewage	20	51	23	4	1

	Not important	Important
Importance of local development strategies		
Attracting new industry	16%	83%
Attracting new retail business	27	72
Attracting new service business	33	65
Attracting tourism	46	53
Expanding existing business and industry	9	90

a. Totals may not equal 100 percent because four communities in the case study included non-response rates.

averaged. Following are the average ratings, on a scale of 1 to 5, for communities in the case study, by development objective:

Local Support	3.79
Infrastructure	3.50
Organizational	3.50
Community Promotion	3.43
Quality of Life	3.25
Business Development	3.10

Another way to examine strategic planning is to see how actions in the case study relate to research on effective local economic development. While there has been little empirical work, there is a small body of applied and anecdotal research on the topic of economic development strategies. START's efforts mirror the experiences in other states. Work through the North Carolina Institute of Government has found that a strategic planning approach has been successful in producing measurable progress among communities in community and economic development activities (Jenne et al. 1988). Savannah, Georgia, completed a "Target 2000" program that led to the creation of task forces and work programs to implement action plans in a wide variety of areas including economic development (Mercer 1991). The National Association of Towns and Townships has noted several successful small-town strategic planning efforts including retail development (Landers 1991). Other authors have highlighted the use and effectiveness of the process in areas outside economic development. Nutt and Backoff note case studies of a local library, a state social service agency, and a large non-profit agency to demonstrate the usefulness and diversity of approaches to the strategic planning process (1992).

One economic development researcher divided local strategies into two groups: growth-based strategies that focus on expanding the existing export base of the community; and development-based strategies that strive to diversify the local economy by developing a mix of new goods and services for the community (Malizia 1986). Malizia's recommendations for both types of strategies focused on the expansion of existing industrial and service firms. Other researchers similarly encourage rural development practitioners to consider activities that "maximize local economic linkages" among companies in the community (Smith 1985), or "improve the efficiency of existing firms," (Shaffer and Pulver 1987). An examination of table 3.2 shows that START communities have placed high priority on development strategies that emphasize the growth of local firms. This emphasis by

START communities on local business is consistent with a recent study of 103 "self-development" projects showing that "business retention and expansion/downtown revitalization" efforts were present in 31 percent of the communities surveyed (Green et al. 1990). It appears that START communities have selected development strategies that are consistent with the experts even though they were identified with little outside advice.

In addition to identifying local economic development strategies, research has identified other factors that contribute to the growth of rural communities. Research sponsored by the National Governors' Association discovered that growing rural communities are characterized by their sustained efforts, pro-growth local attitude, active leadership, and ability to access outside resources (John, Batie, and Norris 1988). Table 3.2 shows that START communities have emphasized similar strategies; namely, those that enhance the community image and improve local attitudes, facilitate area cooperation, and strengthen the local development organization.

Outputs of Implementation Efforts

The final way to assess the effectiveness of strategic planning is to examine the community-based activities, or outputs, that were generated by the planning process. In other words, what are the results of the implementation efforts? Data for this portion of the study were collected from newspaper and journalistic reports, state development agency reports, discussions with development specialists in the field, interviews with START participants in the community, and a telephone survey of START local leaders in the seventeen case study communities.

A qualitative approach to gathering output information was considered the best method because of the nature of the data. It is important, of course, to ensure that the outputs were to a large degree the product of the strategic planning process. First, there is the temporal factor, the outputs needed to occur after the completion of the planning process or initiated during it. Second, the output needed to be the result of some aspect of the local action plan, either as a specific action step, strategy, or development objective. And finally, the output needed to have some definite activity taken on the part of the community, not just discussion. A specific action needed to occur.

Table 3.6 is a description of selected outputs of communities in the case study according to development objective. The table shows a wide range and variety of local development efforts. Some efforts

appear very fundamental in nature, like forming a development
group, while others are quite sophisticated, like purchasing and
reselling property to an industrial prospect. In general, table 3.6
illustrates that the outputs of the communities that undertook a

Table 3.6: Selected Outputs of Strategic Action Plans

Development Objective	Completed Activity
Infrastructure	Formed a housing corporation.
	Developed plans for taking advantage of highway relocation.
	Purchased utility company for city.
	Formed housing development group.
Quality of Life	Secured federal financing for a community center.
	Recruited a new physician.
	Received grant to build downtown park.
	Renovated building to hold community meeting.
	Relocated a hog operation that was in the middle of town.
	Built a minipark.
Organizational	Hired a part-time economic developer.
	Formed a leadership development group.
	Raised local funds for development efforts.
	Bankers formed an organization to help finance development projects.
	Developed a community reinvestment CD to raise funds.
Local Support	Started an economic development corporation.
	Development group meeting regularly.
	Secured a CDBG grant to construct a day care center.
	Formed a regional development group.
Industrial Development	Purchased building, resold to manufacturer.
	New livestock operation began in area.
	Encouraged agricultural supply and wholesaler to locate in town.
	Assisted a food processor in the purchase of a local firm.
Community Promotion	Developed brochure promoting tourism in multi-county area.
	Organized a new community festival.
	Developed community logo and theme.
	Made a new entrance to city museum and historic park.
	Developed promotional program around heritage.
Business Development	Received CDBG grant to open restaurant.
	Got new retail business in town.
	Secured federal grant for local firm to expand employment.
	Developed plan for downtown improvement.
	Formed group of retired business executives to help new business.

strategic planning program are not focused on one set of development objectives or goals (as shown in table 3.3), but are engaged in a variety of both simple and complex development tasks and activities.

It appears from table 3.6 that START has helped generate a significant amount of local effort in the implementation of development strategies. Arguably, this increased activity is the result of the capacity-building characteristics of strategic planning.

Another way to examine the outputs from strategic planning is to assess the progress after a period of time. As previously described, about two years after completion of an action plan, local leaders from the case study communities were asked about specific activities resulting from the START efforts. Local leaders were also asked about some general community development outputs. In terms of the quality of the local efforts in implementing the START plans, on a scale of 1 to 5, local leaders rated the efforts at 3.5, indicating a better than moderate effort. START, it appears, has some local capacity-building ability. Also, when asked about the impact of START on the community's overall development efforts, local leaders gave a rating of 3.7. A significant effort was rated at 4.0. It is interesting to note that this was at least two years after the plan was completed. Overall, the development output occurring in case study communities, when viewed by local effort and program impact and rated by local leaders, appears to be positively influenced by START.

Brief Illustration

An abbreviated description of the implementation efforts for a specific community-based activity will be helpful in assessing the effectiveness of the strategic planning process. Two communities are described.

The community of Wayne, with a population of 5,000, a relatively large manufacturing base, and a state college, was experiencing severe shortages of day care providers. This issue was of such magnitude that it was affecting the ability of the community to attract employees and adult students. The START committee identified day care for children as one of the five priority development objectives in their action plan. A day care task force was formed and an extensive data collection process undertaken. As a result of these efforts the community received a $165,000 Community Development Block Grant from the state for the construction of a child care center.

The city of Superior, a community of 2,500, in 1985 lost their major employer that had been the backbone of the area economy. Superior appeared to have lost its vitality and identity. For several years the community leadership was unsure how to respond to these problems. The START program was the spark that ignited the town to take action. At the town hall meeting when the action plan was presented, nearly 10 percent of the population attended. The five task forces formed through START recruited half of the attendees to help with activities. Enthusiasm for the community was generated, and large projects like downtown renovation and historic preservation were initiated. While the accomplishments of these tangible efforts are just beginning, the intangible benefits of pre-economic development objectives, like organizational improvement and building local support, are evident. Superior was honored by an organization of state and local economic development volunteers for using strategic planning as an effective way to address community needs.

Conclusion

The purpose of this chapter was to demonstrate that strategic planning can be an effective approach for selecting achievable strategies that are appropriate to rural development. A case study of seventeen communities participating in a strategic planning program (START) in Nebraska was the method of analysis. Three different sources of data for each of the communities in the case study were analyzed: community attitude surveys, participant evaluation of START, and the community action plans.

Obviously, as shown by this chapter, with any planning process, problems will arise. While the START approach had been thoroughly tested and many difficulties eliminated through the pilot efforts, not every community effort has proved uniformly successful. Several obstacles in the process have been identified.

First, the mix of steering committee members is critical to the overall success of the effort. In some cases individuals were excluded from participation for various reasons. This often reduced expertise on the committee or removed someone who may later be critical to the successful implementation of a particular strategy.

Second, data used for the environmental scan was not always complete or current. This may limit discussion of issues or occasionally lead to invalid assumptions being drawn for the data presented. Also, there is a constant struggle in how to present information. If presented in too much detail, committee members may find themselves unable to decipher the key issues that come from that information. On the other hand, if the data is summarized in too general a fashion, key issues may be lost.

Finally, the process itself depends upon quality facilitation. When hidden agendas or latent hostilities surface as part of the process, without high quality facilitation, serious difficulties can arise. This happened on occasion. Where possible these issues need to be raised early in the process so they can be resolved before they affect the ability to build consensus on specific strategies.

Despite these problems, the data showed that participants felt positive about the strategic planning process. About three-fourths of the respondents to the evaluation survey gave high ratings to the composition of the steering committee, the abilities of the local leader, and the importance of the identified issues. There were equally positive feelings about the realistic nature of the local action plan. The respondents were, however, concerned about the ability to follow through with projects included in the plan, and this is evident from the interviews with local leaders. More follow-up was identified as a way to improve START.

When the various local strategies contained in the plans are placed into like categories, economic development is the highest community priority. While the emphasis on economic development is consistent with community preferences, other concerns expressed in the attitude surveys are also addressed in action plans. For example, several action plans have strategies directed at image improvement and organization development. Several action plans have strategies directed at improvement and organization development. Finally, when the specific components of the plans are evaluated, there is evidence that significant progress has been made toward addressing many of the issues identified in the planning process.

Overall, the case study indicates that the strategic planning process is evaluated highly by the participants, the strategies are comprehensive in nature, and the plans address issues and concerns identified by the participants. In summary, it can be said that START, a strategic planning program, has a positive impact in identifying and implementing appropriate rural development strategies.

NOTES

1. Jamison Lucchino assisted in data collection for this chapter.
2. The authors are indebted to Dr. Russell Smith for his assistance in the development of the content analysis approach.

REFERENCES

Ayres, Janet, Robert Cole, Clair Hein, Stuart Huntington, Wayne Kobberdahl, Wanda Leonard, and Dale Zetocha. 1990. *Take Charge: Economic Development in Small Communities*. Ames, Iowa: North Central Regional Center for Rural Development.

Bender, Lloyd D., Bernal Green, Thomas Hady, John Kuehn, Marlys Nelson, Leon Penrinson, and Peggy Ross. 1985. *The Diverse Social and Economic Structure of Non-Metropolitan America*. Rural Development Research Report No. 49. Washington, D.C.: Economic Research Service, U.S. Department of Agriculture.

Blair, Robert, and B.J. Reed. 1993. Economic Development in Rural Communities: Can Strategic Planning Make a Difference? *Public Administration Review* 53: 88–92.

Blakely, Edward J. 1989. *Planning Local Economic Development: Theory and Practice*. Newbury Park: Sage.

Brown, David L., and Kenneth L. Deavers. 1987. Rural Change and the Rural Economic Policy Agenda for the 1980s. *Rural Economic Development in the 1980s: Preparing for the Future*. Washington, D.C.: Economic Research Service, U.S. Department of Agriculture.

Bryson, John M. 1989. *Strategic Planning for Public and Non-Profit Organizations*. San Francisco: Jossey-Bass Publishers.

Cawley, Richard. 1989. From the Participants' Viewpoint: A Basic Model of the Community Development Process. *Journal of the Community Development Society* 20: 101–11.

Council of State Governments. 1989. *The Changing Arena: State Strategic Economic Development*. Washington, D.C.: Council of State Governments.

Eisinger, Peter K. 1988. *The Rise of the Entrepreneurial State: State and Local Economic Development Policy in the United States*. Madison: University of Wisconsin Press.

Feiock, Richard C., and James Clingermayer. 1986. Municipal Representation, Executive Power and Economic Development Policy Activity. *Policy Studies Journal* 15: 211–29.

Green, Gary P., Jan L. Flora, Cornelia Flora, and Frederick E. Schmidt. 1990. Local Self-Development Strategies: National Survey Results. *Journal of the Community Development Society* 21: 55–73.

Humphrey, Craig R., Rodney Ericson, and Richard McCluskey. 1989. Industrial Development Groups, External Connections, and Job Generation in Local Communities. *Economic Development Quarterly* 3: 32–45.

Jenne, Kurt J., Thomas Lundy, Ed Kitchen, and John M. Link. 1988. Strategic Planning: Three North Carolina Communities. *Popular Government* 53: 21–26.

John, DeWitt, Sandra S. Batie, and Kim Norris. 1988. *A Brighter Future for Rural America? Strategies for Communities and States*. Washington, D.C.: National Governors' Association.

Johnson, Bruce B., and Joel Young. 1988. Trends in Sales of Retail Goods Across Nebraska's Counties and Communities. Agricultural Research Division Report No. 160. Lincoln: University of Nebraska.

Kane, Matthew, and Peggy Sand. 1988. *Economic Development: What Works at the Local Level.* Washington, D.C.: National League of Cities.

Koteen, Jack. 1989. *Strategic Management in Public and Nonprofit Organizations.* New York: Praeger Publishers.

Landers, Susan. 1991. Use of Local Strategic Planning Can Help Small Towns Move Toward Successful Futures. *Townscape* August: 5–8.

Luke, Jeffrey, Curt Ventriss, B.J. Reed, and Christine M. Reed. 1988. *Managing Economic Development: A Guide to State and Local Development Strategies.* San Francisco: Jossey-Bass.

Malecki, Edward J. 1988. New Firm Startups: Key to Rural Growth. *Rural Development Perspectives* February: 18–23.

Malizia, Emil E. 1986. Economic Development in Smaller Cities and Rural Areas. *The Journal of the American Planning Association* 52: 489–99.

Mercer, James L. 1991. *Strategic Planning for Public Managers.* New York: Quorum Press.

Morse, George. 1990. *The Retention and Expansion of Existing Businesses: Theory and Practice in Business Visitation Programs.* Ames: Iowa State University Press.

National Center for Small Communities. 1985. *Harvesting Hometown Jobs: A Small-Town Guide to Local Economic Development.* Washington, D.C.: National Association of Towns and Townships.

National Commission on Agriculture and Rural Development Policy. 1990. *Future Directions in Rural Development Policy.* Washington, D.C.: Economic Research Service, U.S. Department of Agriculture.

National Governors' Association. 1988. *New Alliances for Rural America.* Washington, D.C.: Task Force on Rural Development.

Northeast Midwest Institute. 1989. *Revitalizing Small Town America: State and Federal Initiatives for Economic Development.* Washington, D.C.

Nutt, Paul C., and Robert Backoff. 1992. *Strategic Management of Public and Third Sector Organizations: A Handbook for Leaders.* San Francisco: Jossey-Bass.

Olsen, Duane A., and Robert F. Blair. 1990. Adapting Business Retention and Expansion Models to Rural Communities: A Nebraska Case Study. Paper presented at the annual Conference of the International Community Development Society. Little Rock, Arkansas.

Paulsen, David F., and B.J. Reed. 1987. Nebraska's Small Towns and Their Capacity for Economic Development. In Russell Smith, ed., *Nebraska Policy Choices: 1987.* Omaha: University of Nebraska at Omaha.

Power, Thomas Michael. 1989. Broader Vision, Narrower Focus in Local Economic Development. *Forum for Applied Research and Public Policy* Fall: 40–49.

Redwood, Anthony. 1988. Job Creation in Nonmetropolitan Communities. *The Journal of State Government* 61: 9–15.

Reed, B.J., and David Paulsen. 1990. Small Towns Lack Capacity for Successful Development Efforts. *Rural Development Perspectives* 6(3): 26–30.

Reed, Christine, B.J. Reed, and Jeffrey S. Luke. 1987. Assessing Readiness for Economic Development Strategic Planning: A Community Case Study. *The Journal of the American Planning Association* 53: 521–30.

Rubin, Herbert J. 1986. Local Economic Development Organizations and the Activities of Small Towns in Encouraging Economic Growth. *Policy Studies Journal* 14: 363–88.

Rubin, Herbert J. 1990. Working in a Turbulent Environment: Perspectives of Economic Development Practitioners. *Economic Development Quarterly* 4: 113–27.

Ryan, Vernon. 1987. The Significance of Community Development to Rural Development Initiatives. *Rural Development in the 1980s: Preparing for the Future*. Washington, D.C.: U.S. Department of Agriculture.

Schweke, William, and Graham S. Toft. 1991. The New Localism: "You Can't Wring Your Hands and Roll Up Your Sleeves at the Same Time." *The Entrepreneurial Economy* 9(2): 3–9.

Shaffer, Ron, and Glen Pulver. 1987. Community Economic Development: Forces, Theories, and Policy Options. *Economic Development for Rural Revitalization*. Ames: North Central Regional Center for Rural Development.

Sharp, Elaine B. 1991. Institutional Manifestations of Accessibility and Urban Economic Development Policy. *Western Political Quarterly* 44: 129–47.

Smith, Russell L. 1985. Economic Development Strategies for Nonmetropolitan Areas. Occasional Papers Series, No. 85-1. Vermillion: Governmental Research Bureau, University of South Dakota.

Sorkin, Donna L., Nancy B. Ferris, and James Hudak. 1984. *Strategies for Cities and Counties: A Strategic Planning Guide*. Washington, D.C.: Public Technology, Inc.

Stevens, John M., and Robert P. McGowan. 1987. Patterns and Predictors of Economic Development Power in Local Governments: A Policy Perspective on Issues in One State. *Policy Studies Review* 6: 554–68.

Strange, Marty, Gerald Hansen, Patricia E. Funk, Jennifer Tulley, and Donald Macke. 1990. *Half a Glass of Water: State Economic Development Policies and The Small Agricultural Communities of the Middle Border*. Walthill, Nebraska: Center for Rural Affairs.

Swanstrom, Todd. 1987. The Limits of Strategic Planning for Cities. *Journal of Urban Affairs* 9: 139–57.

Teitz, Michael. 1987. Planning for Local Economic Development. *Town Planning Review* 58: 5–17.

Vogel, Ronald K. 1990. The Local Regime and Economic Development. *Economic Development Quarterly* 4: 101–12.

Vogel, Ronald K., and Bert E. Swanson. 1988. Setting Agendas for Community Change: The Community Goal-Setting Process. *Journal of Urban Affairs* 10: 41–61.

Wallis, Allan D., and Daniel Schler. 1988. Rational and Reflective Models of Community Action. *Journal of Community Psychology* 6: 403–17.

Walzer, Norman, and Shawnelle Kapper. 1989. *Issues and Concerns of Small City Officials in Illinois*. Macomb, Illinois: Illinois Institute for Rural Affairs, Western Illinois University.

PART II

Mobilizing Institutions
for Development

CHAPTER 4

Catalyzing Bottom-Up Development with National Policies: Canada's Community Futures Program

DAVID FRESHWATER AND PHILIP EHRENSAFT

Bottom-up, community-directed local development initiatives are increasingly seen as a central element of rural development policy. Virtually all successful examples of rural development are found in communities where the local populace is the key force in the development effort (Economic Council of Canada 1990; John, Batie, and Norris 1988). Yet, there are relatively few cases where communities have successfully implemented locally-based initiatives. Lack of organizational capacity has been seen as a limiting factor in many rural areas (Bowles 1981; Shaffer 1989). Even where rural regions have the potential to organize themselves for local development, difficulties in assembling and focusing the human and material resources necessary to foster bottom-up development thwart progress.

This suggests that assistance by senior levels of government in the form of supplemental resources can help communities to build a consensus for locally-based development, define a development strategy, link and coordinate the efforts of adjacent communities, and foster local enterprise. The assistance provided can be thought of as seed capital that provides the means for a community to reach a stage where development becomes self-sustaining. Canada's Community Futures Program (CFP) provides an important example of this type of assistance to other countries that are interested in national initiatives to catalyze locally-directed rural development.

In this chapter we provide the results of our research on how the Community Futures Program has been implemented in four different types of rural community. The observations and conclusions we reach are based upon extensive interviews with individuals in those communities and with program officers charged with managing the program. While the sample of four communities is not large, we believe that it provides a reasonable indication of the capacities and limitations of the program as a stimulus to locally-based economic development.

The main strategy of CFP is to catalyze bottom-up community development by creating a new local organization that is focused on economic development and has a large enough budget to be a significant player within the community. An inherent tension exists in the mandate of CFP. The program is consistent with one strand of neo-conservative thinking in that it is decentralized and supports local entrepreneurship. On the other hand, there is a degree of public planning that is inimical to some neo-conservatives (Prince and Rice 1989). Four main features distinguish the program:

1. A definition of "community" in terms of labor market areas rather than administrative boundaries, which encourages clustering and cooperation by adjacent rural municipalities. Generally these labor market areas have populations in the 30,000 to 35,000 range.

2. A Community Futures Committee (CFC), which includes representatives from key economic and social groups in the community. The CFC is the lead element of the strategy and receives a $400,000 budget over five years to hire permanent staff and consultants to help the community formulate and execute a local development approach.

3. The CFC oversees a Business Development Centre (BDC), which receives a $1.5 million capital grant plus an operational budget to hire a professional manager. It supports small and medium enterprises through management counseling and supplementary loans.

4. The CFC oversees several additional program options including the Community Initiative Fund (CIF) for joint federal-community financing of major projects; an independent employment program that supports the start-up of small businesses by unemployed persons; funding for the purchase of specialized local training; and funding for relocation.

The Community Futures Program was initiated in 1986 by Employment and Immigration Canada (EIC). By the spring of 1991, there were 214 Community Futures Committees in operation covering the majority of Canada's nonmetropolitan areas. Funding for the 1991–1992 fiscal year was just under $200 million. Each community in the program can receive in excess of $2 million dollars in assistance over the five-year period of operation. If the same kind of program were to exist as part of U.S. rural development legislation, this would imply annual expenditures of $2 billion (in U.S. currency) directed towards catalyzing bottom-up development. In late 1991 the Canadian government announced that the program would be extended for a second five-year period, and that eligibility would be extended to qualifying urban neighborhoods in major centers as well as nonmetropolitan places.

To become eligible for the program the area must meet EIC criteria in terms of level of unemployment, size, and degree of economic disruption. In addition, EIC considers the potential for success, the degree of need, the likely degree of local cooperation, and regional balance in the allocation of funds. Communities do not apply directly to EIC; they are selected. A "sunset clause" limits the support of a Futures Committee and Development Centre to six and five years respectively. Renewal of the program has resulted in a commitment of another five years of funding to virtually all existing CFCs.

Major issues that arise in examining the effect of the community Futures Program include:

1. To what extent can a national government successfully implement a local self-help program? Can a national bureaucracy really let go of enough central control mechanisms for local self-help to take place, and will localities really self-organize in new ways rather than going through the motions just to receive the newest source of funding?
2. How do you keep national and provincial politicians at enough distance from local decision makers to allow genuine community self-organization, while leaving some room for politicians to have a voice in program decisions? How do you manage the program so that local leaders have a significant degree of autonomy while giving senior government politicians enough input into the process that they view it as a resource rather than a threat?

3. To what extent is it possible to define and use local labor markets that map into a viable cluster of communities as the basis for defining a common development strategy?
4. Can a committee based on local elites, representing key economic and social groups, be a source of innovation when one barrier to local development may be the desire of this elite to preserve its dominant position in the community? Conversely, is it a viable option for a nationally-initiated program to seek out representatives from outside the existing power structure when the likely result will be a rallying of these leaders against the program?
5. How does one design a national program that is flexible enough to take account of the wide diversity of nonmetropolitan economic structures, income levels, and potential for development, while at the same time maintaining enough structure to allow monitoring of the effectiveness of individual programs?
6. Is the current level and form of federal funding and technical assistance "optimal" in the sense of providing sufficient resources to catalyze sustainable development, but not so great that the hunt for federal support becomes the predominant objective of the community?

In the balance of this chapter we describe the basis for EIC support and additional features of the program. We then turn to four case studies that are the basis for our assessment of the program. The case studies are Community Futures projects in two regions: the Eastern Townships of Quebec and the Interlake area of Manitoba (figure 4.1). The Eastern Townships region is a microcosm of the diversity of Canada's nonmetropolitan economic activities: it contains rural manufacturing centers as well as mainstream agricultural, forestry, and mining production. The Interlake area is a predominantly rural, marginal economic region that is north of, and beyond the daily commuting range to, Manitoba's political and economic capital, Winnipeg. The chapter concludes with a discussion of the strengths and weaknesses of the CFP approach to rural development.

The EIC Role in Nonmetropolitan Labor Markets and Public Policy

As in the United States, the recession of the early 1980s had a more severe impact on rural areas and small, single-industry communities than on Canada's metropolitan regions. The front-line federal agency dealing with these pressures in nonmetropolitan areas is Employ-

FIGURE 4.1. Community Futures Case Study Areas

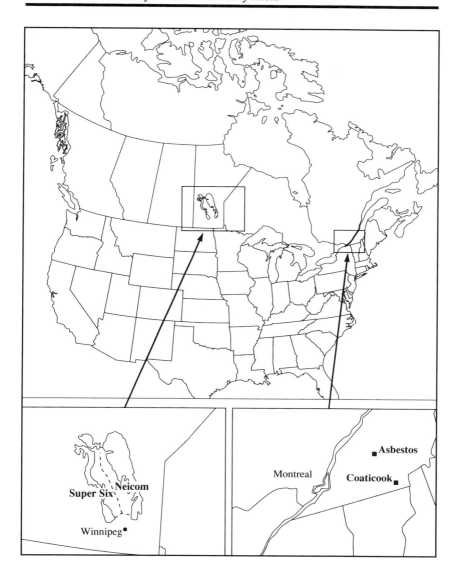

ment and Immigration Canada. EIC has a key role for three reasons: its broad labor market development mandate, its ability to deal directly with the rural populace, and the general federal government equalization responsibility. The origins of CFP trace directly back to earlier programs operated by EIC that provided project assistance to high unemployment areas (Price Waterhouse 1990).

The involvement of EIC in development programs aimed at nonmetropolitan labor markets is a logical extension of its basic role. EIC has responsibility for the administration of unemployment insurance in Canada and also operates job placement centers and worker training programs. The degree of responsibility and level of support for each of these programs is considerably more generous than in the United States, making EIC a more potent force in labor markets than the U.S. Department of Labor. In particular, a policy providing extended unemployment insurance benefits in areas with high rates of unemployment has resulted in EIC providing major transfer payments to much of rural Canada.

EIC is the only federal department with constitutional authority to deliver services directly to the Canadian public. The Canadian Constitution generally reserves the direct provision of services to the provinces and they have closely guarded it. However, through the Unemployment Insurance Act of 1940, the provinces formally ceded responsibility for unemployment insurance and policy to the federal government. Over time, the federal role enlarged to include policies aimed towards prevention of unemployment. EIC's present mandate is to "facilitate adjustments required at the national, regional and local levels for the effective functioning of the Canadian labor market" (Price Waterhouse 1990: 8). As a result, EIC has had a relatively long history of developing and delivering programs that focus on improving labor markets.

The third factor underlying the Community Futures initiative is that Canada, unlike the United States, has a formal constitutional commitment to equalization payments and programs that ensure access to a basic set of social programs across the country (Savoie 1990). Community Futures has to be assessed in terms of this formal agreement to equalization, which inherently includes considerable pressure to maintain communities.

Decentralizing the Community Futures Program

The thrust of the Community Futures program is place-specific in two senses. First, the Futures Committee and the Community Initiatives components of the CFP target the social processes of building community consensus and action for local economic development. This contrasts with the Business Development Centre component, which focuses on individual entrepreneurs. Second, the CFP generally emphasizes creating long-term employment opportunities in target communities, rather than options that encourage mobility by individuals to labor markets with better current job opportunities.

The Community Futures Committee

The Community Futures Committee (CFC) component is the most innovative and ambitious component of the CFP, although not the most ambitiously funded. The Committee is the "window" between the community and EIC and potentially other forms of federal assistance. It is composed of ten to twelve local residents with an interest in economic development, and is charged with developing and implementing a development strategy for the community by catalyzing the community. The role of the CFC is not so much to deliver development through its direct actions; rather it is to stimulate and link the actions of others.

Federal financial support is used to hire a full-time local coordinator, pay the rent and the secretary, pay consultants, and take care of other routine operational expenses. In areas where competing development institutions exist, the limited budget can have the advantage of making the existing local leadership feel more comfortable with the Committee's objectives of catalyzing new ways of conceiving and organizing the community's future, since the CFC is not directly involved in delivering employment or funds. The downside is less perceived clout for the Committee compared to more conventional local economic development institutions.

Conversely, in areas where there is limited existing development leadership capacity, the CFC budget provides a major infusion of resources. In these areas the CFC staff person may be the only full-time person engaged in development activity. In many of these areas, higher funding levels would induce a problem of reaching limits on the capacity of the community to take up the funding and put it to good use.

The Business Development Centre

The Business Development Centre (BDC), with its permanent $1.5 million capital grant, is one of the main carrots that first attracts communities to the CFP. The grant is used to establish a revolving loan fund that can be augmented and retained by the BDC through favorable loan decisions. It can also be lost through poor decisions. A primary function of the BDC is to provide management consulting resources to small and medium enterprises that would normally have little access to such service. The BDC fills a useful niche for local economic development since existing economic development organizations typically focus on industrial recruitment. Its lending services are intended, in most cases, to supplement loans advanced by local banks and credit institutions.

Small-scale enterprises generated a large portion of the new jobs that were created in Canada during the 1980s, and the BDC is a valuable resource for local job creation. But, the BDC has the potential to subvert the larger process of catalyzing new forms of community organization. The BDC's evident and well-funded role can lead to an implicit disregard for the work of the Futures Committee. There is a certain degree of risk that a community will establish and run a Futures Committee in a pro forma manner, for the primary objective of getting a Business Development Centre. While this adds a valuable resource to the community, little will be accomplished with respect to instilling new ways of conceiving and organizing local development. The most important counter to this risk is the degree to which the Employment and Immigration staff person responsible for overseeing the local Futures Committee takes the community innovation objective to heart and intervenes in support of the program's intended catalytic role.

Other Program Options

The CFC can engage in other program options, including sponsoring a specific Community Initiative project that will provide a key element of infrastructure or create a new thrust in employment. These projects are the other major inducement to participate in the program. EIC and other federal agencies will provide additional financial assistance to these projects. The CFC can also recommend that EIC provide additional job training or relocation assistance as part of the CFC development program. The key point in this context is that the CFC has to take the initiative in implementing these options.

On the Ground

Understanding the implementation and effectiveness of a nationally initiated nonmetropolitan development program requires a targeted approach to local case studies. Four initial sites for case studies to suggest performance indices for the Community Futures Program were selected. They were chosen to be representative of conditions the program encounters and to provide a pairing of nearby regions, where one had a Community Futures Committee that was off to a strong start and the other was experiencing difficulties.

Two of the regions have mainstream economies that have come under stress during the last two decades: the counties of Coaticook and Or Blanc, both located in southeastern Quebec. This region was initially settled by Loyalist settlers and their descendants during the early nineteenth century. Since 1945, francophones have constituted an increasing majority of the regional population. Coaticook is a prime dairy county of 16,000 people on the Canada/U.S. border. It also includes a small industrial city of 6,000, with an economy centered around textiles and wood products. Policy intervention previous to the CFP was mainly sectoral in Coaticook.

Or Blanc, which translates as "white gold," is centered around one of the world's largest asbestos mines located in a small city appropriately named Asbestos. Until the collapse of the asbestos market from 1980 onwards, it was one of the more prosperous mining counties in Canada. Population declined from 30,000 in 1976 to 20,000 in 1986. Since 1980, Or Blanc has an intense history of federal and provincial intervention to build an alternative economic base for the community.

The economically marginal Interlake region, located in the western province of Manitoba, was chosen as the site for the third and fourth case studies. Towns in the Interlake area are small, service-oriented communities providing no higher order functions; there is no dominant community in the area. There is a long history of policy intervention attempting to demarginalize the Interlake region. In 1967, the area was designated by the federal government as one of the target areas of the Fund for Rural Economic Development (FRED). Over the next ten years FRED funds were used to develop public infrastructure, primarily roads, and provide training for local residents (Decter and Kowall 1990).

Three Community Futures Committee areas have been designated in the Interlake Region. The first is in the southern portion of the region, and is in many respects a bedroom community area for Winnipeg. We focused on the two CFC areas in the northern, nonadjacent part of the Interlake region: the North East Interlake Community Futures Committee (NEICOM) and the Super Six Community Futures area in the northwestern section.

In both cases the CFC projects are aggregations of multiple local government units, most being the equivalent of counties in the United States in terms of function and powers. The NEICOM area has a population of 15,000, while the population of Super Six is under 7,000. The southern part of the NEICOM area has some of the better agricultural land in the Interlake and the area has the best developed recreational facilities. Not only is the NEICOM area endowed with better resources, it has a longer history of collective action. NEICOM existed as a planning and financing entity under the EIC LEAD program that preceded the CFP. The Super Six name is taken from Highway 6, which runs through virtually all the communities in this sparsely populated area. Unlike NEICOM these communities had no formal linkage prior to Community Futures.

Targeting and Clustering Program Regions

A major objective of the Community Futures program is the clustering of adjacent rural communities in order to increase the effectiveness of local development strategies (MacDonald 1992). This objective has less to do with involvement in new trends in thinking about rural development than with the program experience of EIC civil servants, which indicated that local institutions such as the BDCs need some minimal population and market threshold in order to function effectively.

In principle, boundaries of the new clusters were to be defined on the basis of labor markets rather than on existing administrative boundaries. The latter, more often than not, correspond poorly to either labor, commodity, or consumer markets. In practice, most of the CFC local areas ended up corresponding neither with adminis- trative boundaries nor with labor market areas. This is especially true in the Prairie provinces, which contain three-quarters of Canada's agricultural land and is reflected in the Interlake area.

Nonmetropolitan administrative and market areas do overlap, however, in the province of Quebec. Each of the two Quebec areas being studied, Coaticook and Or Blanc, involves roughly a 90 percent overlap between county boundaries and local labor and shopping markets. While county governments have interesting potential as a vehicle for local development, they are weak in terms of spending, taxing, and decision-making powers. As in other Canadian prov- inces, the provincial government has kept power centralized in its hands.

The Mainstream Regions. At the time that the CFP was estab- lished in 1986, both Coaticook and Or Blanc had relatively high average incomes relative to other nonmetropolitan counties. How- ever, Coaticook had an unemployment rate that was above the provincial average, although lower than that of many other nonmetropolitan regions. And, if not for out-migration or early retirement by workers who were laid off in Asbestos, the county would have had one of the higher rates of unemployment in Canada.

Where the Community Futures Committee has functioned well, as it has in Coaticook, the experience can have an important impact on transforming consolidated county government from a weak institution into a functioning cluster. In this case, the role of the CFC has been to help bridge a gap between the two sectors—manufacturing and agriculture—that characterize the county. Industrialization began in the mid-nineteenth century and until the early 1970s, the town of Coaticook had a stable industrial economy and blue-collar work force. Plant closings, a combined effect of industrial restructuring and the recession of the early 1980s, put an end to this stability. At the same time, the Canadian dairy marketing board system transformed local agriculture; while the number of dairy farmers has declined in regions like Coaticook, the remaining farm enterprises are prosperous and stable in a manner that was not imagined thirty years ago.

The Community Futures Committee has served as a bridge that brought mutually suspicious urban-industrial and farm interests around the same table and helped build a consensus for common actions for local development. As the committee process unfolded, city dwellers perceived that the remaining farm operators now ranked among the wealthier and most entrepreneurial members of the community. Manufacturing and commercial interests also began to see the stabilizing role that Coaticook's dairy sector played in buffering the local economy from the business cycle fluctuations.

The CFC has provided an institution that buffered inter-municipal political conflicts by bringing new faces and voices to the discussion. A consensus was created that the Committee's first major project should be an Agricultural Initiatives Centre. What is most important from the perspective of local development is the implicit understanding that next time around it will be the turn of another interest to receive community support.

The contribution of the Futures Committee process toward strengthening the effectiveness of clustering in Or Blanc county cannot be examined apart from the larger question of the local difficulties in establishing the CFC. Or Blanc was one of the first consolidated counties to be established in Quebec. Its boundaries correspond well to labor and shopping markets. The collapsing asbestos market forced both local actors and higher levels of government to look beyond the one large mining company that had been the center of gravity for both economic and cultural activities.

A new examination of the relatively neglected farm and forest sectors was part of the search for new opportunities. In turn, this meant linking the town of Asbestos and rural municipalities into effective alliances. When the CFC was established, the county already had six years of intensive clustering and strategy-building under its belt. Local leadership was reluctant to go through the CFC process with its emphasis on strategic planning, which was viewed as redundant. The question here is whether the CFC process was, in fact, redundant in this particular context, or whether the CFC process had the potential to increase the effectiveness of clustering and rethinking local development. The earlier strategic plan, while technically sound, had not been endorsed by the local community. Although a second effort at strategic planning may not have resulted in different alternatives, it could have created a process for building community solidarity and support.

The Marginal Regions. Historically, the Interlake has been considered a well-defined region in Manitoba. Both the federal and provincial governments have treated the area as a single administrative unit, despite the presence of significant intraregional differences. Within the area there is a reasonably strong sense of identity with other communities as part of a region. However there has been little to translate this feeling of regional identity into collective action. The limited internal dynamics of the area and the weak economic base have reduced the incentive and capacity to form linkages. With no higher order centers in the Interlake there is limited internal trade. In this environment EIC initiatives, with their requirement that communities act collectively, provided an impetus for organization. Without this external pressure and in the absence of a dominant community there was little incentive for local governments to risk their autonomy.

The particular grouping of the communities into two committees reflects both the history and the features of the region. Historically, Lake Winnipeg and Lake Manitoba provided the primary transportation link among communities, so people tended to associate on a north-south rather than east-west basis. Highway improvement reinforced this behavior, since the major roads run north-south. As a result, the initial formation of the NEICOM group under an earlier EIC program followed the natural pattern of communication. The NEICOM area also contains the largest towns in the Interlake and was the beneficiary of the bulk of the investment made under an earlier major federal development program (Decter and Kowall 1990). This not only provided a better base upon which to build, but it also gave local leaders experience in dealing with federal programs.

Super Six was in a sense created as a residual area because NEICOM had already carved out its territory. Closure of a military base in the mid-1980s triggered efforts by the local Member of Parliament to establish Community Futures as part of the adjustment package. In order to include enough people to qualify for the CFP, the boundaries of Super Six were pushed well beyond any meaningful notion of a local labor market area. Despite this, there is a form of clustering developing in the area. This reflects the role of Highway Six as the only major road and the impossibility of any single community in the region achieving the mass "to go it alone."

In both cases there are few internal reasons to organize, but there are increasingly strong external reasons. In both cases a structure is required in order to reach the critical mass necessary to attract visitors, afford marketing, and facilitate local efforts to stimulate economic growth.

Creating the Committee and the Community Futures Plan

The creation of a bottom-up local development initiative by the Ministry of Employment evolved piecemeal from the learning experiences of EIC staff as they tried to help nonmetropolitan communities cope with job losses during the 1980s. Experience with earlier rounds of programs that preceded Community Futures led to the perception that focusing on individual entrepreneurs was not sufficient to generate job growth. It was necessary to place this lending within the context of an overall strategy for job creation. In turn, the first experiences with developing local strategies led to the perception that representation and participation of leaders from all economic and social interests in the community was necessary if the strategies were to be taken seriously.

Creating the Community Futures Committee. The CFC is the key element in the strategy of stimulating local development. The objective of the Futures Committee component of the CFP is to catalyze the community into working together in new ways in order to rethink its economic future in a more integrated and long-term fashion. "More integrated" means that specific projects are linked through a strategic plan that will prepare the area for sustainable locally-based development. "Long-term," in the beginning (i.e., 1986), was conceived of as a five-year period during which EIC would provide new resources to get the process off the ground; the expectation was that at the end of the five years, the community would assume full responsibility. By 1991, it was recognized that phase 2 funding was necessary, as more than five years is required to achieve program goals.

Achieving "more integrated" development is inseparable from the process of selecting the Futures Committee. Ownership of the local development strategy was to be transferred from EIC to the community through the CFC board. The paradox was that bottom-up development was to be catalyzed from above. Despite firm commitment of EIC staff to creating a new approach to nonmetropolitan job creation, the bottom line is that the CFP was created by civil servants from the federal government, the areas designated for program eligibility were designated by the federal government, and the Community Futures Committee members were selected by EIC staff in the regions.

The caliber of the EIC staff is an important factor in the success of the transfer. These people have a diversity of backgrounds. Many came from EIC's Industrial Adjustment Service (IAS), where they were involved in industrial restructuring and had strong business skills. Another source of talent was people who had worked in earlier community development programs operated by EIC and had a strong background in human relations. While it is possible for the program to work without a strong EIC staff person, chances of this happening are slim. This places a great responsibility on the staff person.

The representative nature of the CFC board can be short-circuited in several ways. First, if municipal politicians dominate the committee, the CFC will simply provide another monthly forum for existing local political conflicts. Second, if municipal politicians do not have what they perceive as sufficient representation on the committee, it is going to be hard to get their action on any strategic development plan. Third, the local Member of Parliament has the formal right to veto the list of proposed committee members. If the committee membership is viewed as being stacked by the MP, the community consensus-building process will be knocked off track. Fourth, if committee membership does not include representatives of social and cultural groups as well as enterprises and politicians, a crucial element in community mobilization will be missing. Finally, any fledgling organization can be thrown off track by "bad chemistry" among key participants from both the senior government and community sides. Avoiding these pitfalls depends on the skills of the local EIC staff representative, complemented by a dose of good luck.

Much of the effectiveness of the CFC is linked to the time and energy that the chair puts into the Committee. Candidates for this position are typically busy people with other community responsibilities. The chair must spend long hours making the committee process work and must also have strong conviction that consensus-building for strategic planning is an important step forward. There is an incentive for the chair to do a serious job since he or she will have to live a long time in a small community that does not easily forget. In addition, a check may be provided by a strong EIC representative who persistently prods the Committee to part with old habits.

Selection of a strong local coordinator is also crucial to the success of the process. The day-to-day work of coordinators involves three main activities: organizing or attending meetings; holding office hours to meet with people seeking advice on where to hunt for resources supporting individual or group job creation projects; and contacting government and private agencies to seek support for development initiatives proposed by the CFC. In order to work well, the coordinator's role involves striking a balance between getting along well with all the players and having the independence to prod people off beaten paths.

The Community Plan. The innovative objectives for the Community Futures Program were to get an atypical geographical and sectoral diversity of local interests around the same table in order to get them to create and enact a new vision of their community's economic future. One vehicle for accomplishing this was to be an in-depth study of the community's pluses and minuses with respect to economic development, to be performed by a competent consulting firm in cooperation with the local community. Committees were permitted to spend roughly $30,000 to $40,000 on hiring a consulting firm. EIC's objective in providing these resources was to avoid both make-work projects for local residents and quickie jobs by outside consulting firms.

Many of the commissioned plans, whether well or poorly performed, have gathered dust. The pluses and minuses of the Community Futures Plan as a document are secondary, however, to the manner in which communities are involved in and act upon the strategy-building exercise. When it works well, new energy and thinking can be unleashed, by debating different trajectories for the community's future. Successful applications of community futures are characterized by debate followed by consensus. Where the community develops a vision as a result of the planning process it is not important if the formal plan is relegated to a file drawer. Conversely, a strong plan that lacks community support is unlikely to be implemented, as the process of catalyzing local support for development did not take place.

In each of the case studies events have now overtaken the original plan, limiting its usefulness. Making the Futures Plan a living document, one that would be continually reexamined and reevaluated in the light of the Committee's experiences, could make an important contribution towards local development. It would help communities to think about their development in a more integrated and long-term manner and also help them to establish priorities. The idea of the Community Futures Plan is solid, but it frequently loses its catalyzing impact within a year or two after completion.

What Does the Community Futures Program Really Do, What Could It Do, and How Long Does It Need to Do It?

As with all programs, actual implementation differs from the concept envisioned at the time of formation. The informal operation of the Community Futures Committees diverges from the CFP's formal program design but ends up by meeting, in good measure, the program's objectives (Freshwater and Ehrensaft 1993). One risk for the program is that the second phase will involve more administrative controls that will move the Committees toward working in a more orderly but less effective manner.

Generally, the first priority of a Committee is to establish a Business Development Centre. In principle, the BDC should operate within the parameters of the Committee's plan. In practice, the BDC operates at arm's length from the Committee as a quite effective small business counseling service with supplementary lending activities. Because the BDC produces direct and tangible results in the form of new enterprises and jobs, it is viewed quite positively by community leaders.

When the larger budget of the BDC is added into the equation, the implication is that this formal option of the Community Futures Program can be interpreted as its pillar. This is true both for communities and elite managers in EIC, who can readily measure the results of the BDC's work and relate them to the ministry's mandate. In terms of the entrepreneurs who are supported by the BDC, this is more likely to proceed in terms of individuals approaching the Centre with promising ideas rather than in relation to the Futures Plan or the Committee's orientations.

In each community the BDC has developed a significant role in financing small business. Because the BDC has the opportunity to lend money on flexible terms or even take an equity position, it can provide funding where banks or other commercial lenders cannot. In this regard BDCs are similar to community development corporations in the United States. BDCs have been able to improve access to commercial credit in two ways. First, they are prepared to take subordinate positions to banks; and second, banks respect the extensive investment analysis that BDCs require before becoming involved with a client. In addition, they provide clients with ongoing accounting and management help.

The second thing that a Community Futures Committee does is to put together plans for major projects under the Community Initiatives Fund (CIF) option. There are two basic criteria for EIC support of the community projects: (1) they are "innovative," and (2) the community must raise a major part of the funding itself in order to receive EIC's dollars. While the first criterion is open to a wide range of interpretation, it is basically a requirement that some significant extension of the economic base be undertaken. The second criterion is intended to break old habits of dependency and ensure that the community place considerable stock in their proposal. The CIF projects are important not only for the new economic capacity that they bring but also for the alliances and expectations that are created in putting the projects together.

In the three communities that had undertaken projects, the potential to utilize the CIF was the main attraction for involvement by local citizens in Community Futures. While other features of the program were attractive, it was the ability to implement a long-standing concept that pulled people in. In each case the EIC funds were a relatively small part of the total package, but because other money was conditional on the community being able to carry out certain actions, the CIF money was essential. As a result, the CFC received credit that was disproportionate to its actual outlay because its funds were the last to be committed.

In Coaticook, the Agricultural Initiatives Center serves as a combined dairy farming training center for third world students, a demonstration farm (run by a multinational firm) for developing marketable organic farming technologies, and a farm tourism center. In the two Interlake CFC areas, the projects involve recreation and tourism centers that can help realize the region's tourism potential. In the NEICOM area, funding was secured to assemble a package of land to construct a hotel/conference center/retail center in Gimli on the lake beside a major marina. The community recognized the need for this type of facility well before the CF program was implemented, but lacked the resources to carry it out. In Super Six, an existing beach development at Steep Rock was obtained from the province and is being upgraded by adding a marina, campgrounds and permanent cottage sites. The idea for this development also existed well before the creation of Super Six, but once again resources to implement it were lacking.

In both Coaticook and the Interlake, there are clear expectations that, next time around, it will be another sector's or another town's turn to get the major project. It is this kind of cooperative alliance that hopefully will provide future projects after the formal Community Futures Program fades into the sunset. However, the question is, how many legitimate future projects exist? Particularly in the marginal areas, there may not be many more projects that have the potential to generate a return on the investment. Although communities may be willing to use outside funds for additional projects, will they be willing to use their own?

The downside of the major project emphasis is that the successful funding of projects may be related more to a region's political connections and skill in packaging its proposal than to the intrinsic value of the proposal. While there is nothing illegitimate about seeking such support, the search can move towards pork barrel politics that reinforce old habits of dependency. There are inevitable grumblings by some regions that other regions got their projects because they are located in a riding represented by a particularly powerful MP, but there is more than a grain of truth in the grumblings.

Given the limited personnel and financial resources of a Committee, energies get focused on the major project. This can lead to a downplaying of the coordination and planning role that is the intended core of the Committee's responsibility.

The independent employment option can make a valuable contribution to local job creation, but it parallels the BDC as being an activity that runs on its own steam and involves decisions that are weakly linked to the Committee's plans and priorities. Under phase 2, this option has been transferred to the local Canada Employment Centre; the technical requirements for running the option resulted in the perception that it did not fit well within the CFCs capacities.

The labor mobility option may make sense for some communities, but there has been little inclination by Committees to explicitly pursue outmigration as a viable option for significant numbers of local residents. It is typical for local residents to be painfully aware of people moving out but not to incorporate the fact that new people are frequently moving in, especially the managers and professionals manning key local institutions. Attitudes of the local population on migration issues lean strongly towards maintaining the local population rather than seeking the best opportunities for individuals, which could require that people leave the community.

Conclusion: Reconciling Goals and Implementation

In conclusion, we return to the six major issues raised at the beginning of the chapter that concern the conflicts between program goals and implementation.

1. To what extent can a national government successfully implement a local self-help program? Can a national bureaucracy charged with program oversight really let go of enough central control mechanisms for local self-help to take place, and will localities really self-organize in new ways rather than simply go through the motions just to satisfy bureaucrats and receive the newest source of funding?

When the CFP was launched, neither EIC nor the Futures Committees had a precise definition of program goals and implementation procedures. These emerged from practice and learning, which ultimately was a contributing factor to the success of the program. The central bureaucracy loosened its hold partly because this is what the creators of the program intended and partly because they were uncertain as to what they should hold on to. In principle, federal programs should have clear goals and implementation methods. However, when the federal government does not have a clear idea of how to define or accomplish goals but does recognize that action needs to be undertaken, this type of program may be the best that ·can be expected.

The degree of local control varies with the capacity of the community and the management approach of the regional EIC office. In general, where communities have built the capacity they have received control. Committees in successful areas like Coaticook and NEICOM have developed enough credibility in the community that they now can influence development. It is less clear whether the communities truly believe in the Community Futures process. As long as federal funds for the partnership are available, the communities appear to be willing to make good faith efforts to live up to their part of the agreement. When the federal funds disappear some communities are certain to let the concept lapse. However, some will keep the ideas alive. What proportion of failures is enough to judge the program a failure remains to be seen.

By the end of the first phase the federal program managers were facing growing pressure by EIC's internal evaluation unit and external auditors to show what Community Futures had accomplished. Pressure increased to tighten oversight and management control to ensure accountability for the use of federal funds. In 1994 the entire future of the program was thrown into doubt as the federal government reassessed the role of EIC as a result of a worsening budget deficit and a change in political philosophy.

2. How do you keep national and provincial politicians at enough distance from local decision makers to allow genuine community self-organization, while leaving some room for politicians to have a voice in program decisions? How do you manage the program so that local leaders have a significant degree of autonomy while giving senior government politicians enough input into the process that they view it as a resource rather than a threat?

Once again the results are mixed. In some CFCs, politicians from all levels of government are actively involved in the program. Federal, provincial, and local officials view it as an important vehicle that provides them with local media and public exposure, but associated with their pure political interest is a significant degree of support for the actions of the CFC. In other cases there has been little direct interest by politicians at the provincial and national level. Somewhat surprisingly, in some cases Community Futures has provided a way to go around local political institutions and leaders and create a new forum for the discussion of local issues. Not surprisingly this has not endeared the program to the local political establishment.

As Community Futures becomes more successful, the threat of co-option by politicians at all levels increases. Once there is something to take credit for, the political process shows more interest. However, in a time of budget cuts the endorsement of politicians may be necessary to protect the program. As long as the committees are prepared to do the work and allow the politicians to share in the credit the present structure should remain viable.

3. To what extent is it possible to define and use local labor markets that map into a viable cluster of communities as the basis for defining a common development strategy?

In principle this made some sense, particularly from the perspective of EIC. However, in the majority of cases Community Futures areas are not organized around local labor markets. Various factors, including the fluid nature of labor markets, make this an unrealistic goal. Prior clustering and political pressures are at least as important in defining CFC boundaries. Nevertheless, in many areas clustering of communities appears to be taking place. The CFP process provides a significant reason to bring the various interests together to work for their mutual benefit.

4. Can a committee based on local elites, representing key economic and social groups, be a source of innovation when one barrier to local development may be the desire of this elite to preserve its dominant position in the community? Conversely, is it a viable option for a nationally-initiated program to seek out representatives from outside the existing power structure when the likely result will be a rallying of these leaders against the program?

In rural communities, failure to bring local elites on board can doom a development effort to failure. For the most part, the level of financial and technical support provided by EIC is enough to stimulate these groups' interest. There are enough new resources available that local leaders feel compelled to participate to protect their position. Since Community Futures requires these elites to come together on neutral ground and limits the influence of any single group, it is also easier to establish good faith bargaining. In cases where a small number of groups have seized control of the Committee, as in Asbestos, results have been less encouraging.

5. How does one design a national program that is flexible enough to take account of the wide diversity of nonmetropolitan economic structures, income levels, and potential for development, while at the same time maintaining enough structure to allow monitoring of the effectiveness of individual programs?

The answer to this issue lies in the comments on the first point. It is impossible to clearly and precisely define a program to address the diversity of needs and capacities of rural communities. In this sense the vagueness of the original CF goals and implementation procedure was its salvation. This allowed individuals who knew each community to tailor the program to local needs. In this sense the program did what it was supposed to do. It provided financial and technical resources to community-based economic development strategies.

From an administrative perspective, Community Futures has had the advantage of being embedded in the Canadian Jobs Strategy (CJS). Since it is only a minor part of CJS and the entire CJS program has been devolved to a regional level there has been considerable opportunity for flexibility in implementation. No region in the country operates Community Futures in the same way. As noted earlier, there is growing concern in Ottawa that they may have lost control, and with the termination of the Canadian Jobs Strategy there is no longer a broader context in which to embed Community Futures.

6. Is the current level and form of federal funding and technical assistance "optimal" in the sense of providing sufficient resources to catalyze sustainable development, but not so great that the hunt for federal support becomes the predominant objective of the community?

Clearly not. Funding for CF has increased each year, providing money for new areas and supplemental funds for older projects. Yet progress to a sustainable structure of community development in most communities has been slower than anticipated. One feature of CF is that all areas get the same level of funding. Thus, Super Six is eligible for the same support as Coaticook, despite major differences in population, resources and capacity. Arguably, smaller, more remote areas need greater support than those with more internal resources, but it is not clear that the current funding system provides appropriate amounts on an area-by-area basis.

The amounts of money provided by the program are relatively modest, even in terms of the budget of the local communities. However, since virtually all the existing funds in the budget of the community are already committed, the fact that new funds are made available in sufficient quantity to do something is critical to attracting local interest. The money brings them to the program; whether they buy into the underlying principles remains to be seen.

No community ever believes it has enough time or money to reach its goals, and no organization thinks that their grant should not be renewed. Standing back from this cliche, our observation is that most Committees were unlikely to have become self-sustaining if the Community Futures Program had not been renewed for a second, five-year phase. By self-sustaining, we mean that communities have been changed by, and become committed to, the Futures Committee process, as demonstrated by a willingness to put up all or part of the Committee's budget when EIC funding runs out. In part, the slow rate of progress reflects the incremental way in which the program was implemented, but it mainly reflects the continuing economic pressure on these communities.

Program evaluations conducted in 1990 confirmed EIC's hands-on conclusions that there was much work to be done in training and supporting both Community Futures volunteers and EIC's own staff if community strategic planning and new local partnerships were to become a lasting feature of the targeted communities'organizational capacity (Price Waterhouse 1990; Ehrensaft, Freshwater, and Thurston 1991). Such efforts were begun soon after. Whether they will continue in the current environment, where the program has lost its philosophical support and context, is yet to be seen. While the terms of the contract between the CFCs and the federal government will be honored, there is a clear loss of enthusiasm at the federal level. The big question mark is whether many or most of the selected Community Futures regions really have the will and capacity to generate their own strategies and development alliances when phase 2 of the CFP comes to an end in 1996.

REFERENCES

Bowles, R.T. 1981. *Social Impact Assessment In Small Communities*. Toronto, Ontario: Butterworths.

Decter, Michael, and Jeffrey Kowall. 1990. *Manitoba's Interlake Region: The Fund For Rural Economic Development Agreement*. Local Development Paper 18. Ottawa: Economic Council of Canada.

Economic Council of Canada. 1990. *From The Bottom Up: The Community Economic Development Approach*. Ottawa: Supply and Services Canada.

Ehrensaft, Philip, David Freshwater, and Lynn Thurston. 1991. *Goals and Measures: The Community Futures Program*. Unpublished report prepared for Employment and Immigration Canada.

Freshwater, David, and Philip Ehrensaft. 1993. *Initial Results from the Implementation of Canada's Community Futures Program*. Research Report 57, Department of Agricultural Economics, University of Kentucky, Lexington, KY.

John, Dewitt, Sandra Batie, and Kim Norris. 1988. *A Brighter Future For Rural America?* Washington, DC: National Governors Association.

MacDonald, Dennis. 1992. "Canada's Community Futures Program Stimulates Multicommunity Collaboration." In P. Korsching, T. Borich and J. Stewart (eds.) *Multicommunity Collaboration: An Evolving Rural Revitalization Strategy* RRD 161 North Control Regional Center for Rural Development, Ames, IA.

Price Waterhouse. 1990. *Final Report: Role Review and Community Impact Analysis of the Community Futures Program*. Unpublished report prepared for Employment and Immigration Canada.

Prince, M. J., and J. J. Rice. 1989. "The Canadian Jobs Strategy: Supply Side Economics." In K. Graham, ed., *How Ottawa Spends, 1989–90*. Ottawa: Carlton University Press.

Savoie, Donald. 1990. *The Politics of Public Spending In Canada*. Toronto: University of Toronto Press.

Shaffer, Ron. 1989. *Community Economics*. Ames, IA: Iowa State University Press.

CHAPTER 5

Stimulation of Economic Development Through Worker Cooperatives

CARLA DICKSTEIN

Since the mid-1970s, interest in worker cooperatives and other forms of employee ownership as part of a local economic development strategy has grown in North America and Europe. Cooperatives have special characteristics that are particularly well suited to the rural context and deserve consideration for rural enterprise development.

This chapter first defines a worker cooperative and successful cooperative performance. It then discusses theoretical reasons for supporting cooperative development in rural areas, the conditions likely to lead to success or failure, and the empirical evidence of the economic development impact from case research of worker cooperatives in Canada, the United States, and Europe. It also draws on examples from the kibbutzim in Israel. Although the kibbutzim are total cooperative communities, their enterprises have a high degree of worker participation and self-management (Tannenbaum 1974). Economic development impacts are then discussed in terms of (1) creation or retention of local jobs; (2) equity benefits for disadvantaged groups; (3) institutional change; and (4) long-term growth and innovation.

A Definition of Successful Worker Cooperatives

Worker cooperatives are firms that are controlled by their members who are workers. Despite some divergences, the following basic cooperative principles have applied to worker cooperatives.[1] First, membership is open and voluntary. Second, there is democratic control at all levels of the enterprise based on one member, one vote. Third, interest paid on share capital is limited. Fourth, workers share in any profits, usually in proportion to their work contribution. Fifth, some part of the cooperative's profits is devoted to worker education. And sixth, cooperatives cooperate among themselves. If a worker cooperative is consistent with these principles, then its success depends on operating an economically viable and democratically-managed business in which workers have the knowledge and capacity to participate in the decision-making process and ultimate control of the cooperative.[2]

It is apparent from this definition that cooperatives differ fundamentally from private firms. Control of the firm is based on personal rights derived from a worker's labor contribution rather than on property rights derived from a capital contribution (Ellerman 1984a). Cooperatives also differ from employee-owned firms, such as firms with an employee stock ownership plan (ESOP). The membership right in an ESOP is based on share ownership and not on the functional labor role in the company (Ellerman 1984a: 262). ESOPs have been established primarily for tax advantages, without creating widespread employee ownership (Blasi 1988: 240). Many ESOPs systematically have excluded lower- and middle-paid workers and have allocated stock in favor of more highly-paid employees (p. 119). Only a handful of "democratic ESOPs" give workers full control of the firm and comply with the above definition of a worker cooperative.[3]

Advantages of Worker Cooperatives

Worker cooperatives are an alternative institutional approach to economic development that increases local control of economic activity and changes the incentive structure of enterprises. A cooperative structure can benefit the community and workers and improve business competitiveness.

Because cooperatives are worker-controlled rather than corporate or absentee-owner controlled, it is more likely the business will stay where the workers live. Cooperatives have been used successfully as a defensive strategy to buy out closing businesses and retain jobs in the community. Companies that have been mismanaged or unable to pay the high returns required by corporate interests may be sufficiently profitable for the workers to maintain them and secure their jobs. According to Bradley and Gelb (1983), this example of "asset restructuring" should be considered a form of local industrial policy that moderates the velocity of economic change and industrial restructuring.

Cooperatives also provide greater flexibility for job retention during recessionary periods. Labor is considered a fixed rather than a variable cost over the short run in cooperatives although labor costs can be manipulated over the long run (Ellerman 1984b). Members can decide to reduce hours or wages and spread the work among themselves to provide job security.

When cooperatives are structured properly and have sufficient inputs of production, they have been known to increase productivity and provide better job quality.[4] Greater worker participation in decision making is generally thought to improve business performance by increasing worker motivation, job satisfaction, and personal dignity and eliminating conflict between labor and management. Cooperatives improve job quality mainly by increasing the job responsibility of their members and developing self-management skills. Overall pay and benefit levels, which also contribute to job quality, depend on the industrial sector and market conditions. However, because workers share in profits, they can earn more than in comparable private firms, assuming the cooperative is profitable.

Conditions for Success and Failure

Formation of cooperatives is rare in societies dominated by private enterprise and materialistic values. Our social, cultural, and legal institutions reinforce the existing system and its values. Like other small businesses, cooperatives can succeed if they have sufficient inputs of production. However, few incentives exist in our present society for cooperatives to mobilize those resources.

The greatest difficulty cooperatives face is attracting and retaining talented entrepreneurs and managers. Shared control and limited rewards make cooperatives less desirable than private firms to most entrepreneurs unless they are committed ideologically to cooperatives.

A second problem is raising sufficient capital. Although small businesses often suffer from undercapitalization, the cooperative structure creates even greater difficulties. A cooperative must raise equity capital almost entirely from its members, assuming that it permits equity capital at all.[5] Nonmembers have little incentive to invest if they have no voting rights with their share purchase. Conventional financial institutions are commonly unwilling to lend to cooperatives either because of outright bias or because unfamiliarity with cooperative structures makes it difficult for them to under-write loans.[6] The employee stock ownership plan (ESOP) is usually chosen over a cooperative structure in buyouts of closing firms or conversions of family-owned firms. It offers tax advantages for raising equity capital from company contributions and leveraging debt capital from conventional lenders without requiring workers to invest their own capital in stock ownership. However, it only benefits firms that can afford high initial transaction costs of setting up ESOPs and that pay taxes. Thus, it is not suitable for most start-up firms.

A common criticism of cooperatives is that they are perceived as unable to innovate, reinvest, and sustain growth. In fact, their long-term performance has been highly variable depending upon the enabling conditions for their formation—i.e., their economic, politi-cal, and social environment, and their internal ideological and orga-nizational characteristics.[7] Historically, cooperatives have tended to develop countercyclically during oppressive economic, political, and social conditions. Economic crisis, rather than ideology, has been the key catalyst for their formation. Cooperatives have developed more extensively in areas with some history of operating cooperative structures and/or a cooperative or socialist ideology. Government support—in the form of grants, favorable terms for borrowing capi-tal, favorable taxation policies, preferential treatment in awarding government contracts, and establishment of barriers to outside in-vestment and trade—has been important in sheltering the develop-ment of cooperatives in an otherwise hostile environment.

Experience has also shown that worker cooperatives do not survive well as isolated enterprises because of discrimination against cooperatives and because their small size[8] limits their internal ability to undertake specialized functions.[9] They must create systems of cooperative enterprise for mutual support (Jordan 1983). Coopera-tives have achieved economies of scale through joint purchasing and marketing of goods and services and have gained access to financial, technical, and managerial resources by forming federations and support organizations (Jackall and Levin 1984; Dickstein 1988; Corn-forth et al. 1988; Quarter 1989).

Frequently, cooperatives are simply way stations until the economy turns around and there are more attractive job or financial opportunities. Cooperative "degeneration" has occurred in several forms: members have sold out to nonmember shareholders for financial gain; they have barred entry to new members and hired non-member labor in order to hoard profits;[10] or they have relin-quished control to managerial elites who possess specialized technical knowledge, expertise, and leadership skills (Dickstein 1991).[11] Some of the degeneration problems can be minimized through legal structures that prohibit nonmember control and hired labor or require worker education and training for workers to gain self-confidence and business skills (Dickstein 1991). However, legal structures can be manipulated. Ultimately, if cooperatives are to remain cooperative and grow over the long term, members must also have some ideological commitment to cooperative principles.

In capitalist economies, worker cooperatives have thrived better economically in rural areas than in urban areas for several reasons. Cultural and community bonds, as well as lifestyle preferences, tie people to rural areas and create strong preferences for local work. The relative isolation of rural areas means that cooperative members have fewer lures to the wider labor market and to more materialistic lifestyles. Rural cooperatives have a better track record than urban cooperatives in retaining entrepreneurial and managerial talent, although this is still a problem. However, these cultural, social, and geographic characteristics are not sufficient conditions for cooperatives to take hold in rural areas. The work force must have education and training. Most importantly, cooperatives must be seen as central to a community development strategy; this centrality has been frequently found in communities experiencing repression of ethnic and cultural minorities, plant closings in single industry towns, or years of exploitation in resource-based economies.

The Record of Worker Cooperatives in Rural Areas

Worker cooperatives have been formed in rural areas through new starts; buyouts of existing firms that have closed or are about to close; and, less frequently, conversions of successful private businesses (either because of benevolence of the owner or as a succession strategy for family-owned firms). They have developed in a variety of sectors: primary and secondary production in forestry, agribusiness, manufacturing, services, and tourism as discussed below for selected cases.

Forestry Cooperatives

Quebec forestry cooperatives were first formed in 1938 as labor pools that worked on a contract basis for large companies or the government. They provided supplemental wages for subsistence farmers, and in some regions, they were the only employers (Talbot-Dagenais 1986: 24). By the end of 1988, forty-seven Quebec forest cooperatives had spread throughout the province, with 3,500 members and a total of 4,300 people employed (Gavin 1991). Some cooperatives were over thirty years old, with multimillion dollar sales.

The cooperatives have become highly mechanized over the last ten years and are recognized as industry leaders, particularly in silvicultural work.[12] Diversification of work has been a key issue in order to extend the work season and increase members' income. Growth has been largely in forest management. Cooperatives have also diversified into seedlings and tomato production in their greenhouses, equipment supply, and secondary production. Some have developed saw mills and have a minority participation in a privately controlled pulp and paper enterprise and a wafer board plant (Clement and Martel 1990). More skilled labor, such as forest engineers, technicians, and biologists, is now required.

Since 1980, the Quebec government has sheltered the cooperatives' growth by allowing them to negotiate direct contracts for forest management and reforestation of public lands with the Ministry of Energy and Resources. Otherwise, they would have had difficulty gaining the expertise and technology in the field. By 1985, the cooperatives formed a federation responsible for lobbying, marketing, product development, and technical assistance to distressed cooperatives. The record of cooperation among cooperatives, however, is still spotty. One cooperative shared its technology for reforestation with other cooperatives, allowing all of them to grow in the field. On the other hand, territorial restrictions among cooperatives have tended to favor competitors rather than the cooperative sector. Each cooperative has its prime territory of operations, and some cooperatives refuse to let others fill contracts they cannot handle (Clement and Martel 1989).

The positive economic climate in the 1980s in Quebec left the forestry cooperatives with shortages of manual labor, which hinders long-term growth. Workers have started other, more lucrative ventures, with easier work conditions and better pay. The cooperatives have also lost managers to other enterprises because of lack of adequate financial remuneration (Clement and Martel 1989). With recession and cyclical decline in sales of processed forest products, the cooperatives may have less difficulty retaining workers and managerial talent.

The plywood cooperatives in the Pacific Northwest are the longest surviving cluster of U.S. worker cooperatives. From the first cooperative formed in 1921 with 125 workers, the plywoods grew to twenty-seven cooperatives in the early 1950s. By 1982 only eleven cooperatives remained with a total membership of 2,000. The decline was partly due to financial success (seven cooperatives were sold to conglomerates or to private investors with worker-owners making substantial profits in some cases). Cooperative performance was also affected by pressures facing the entire industry: environmental demands requiring large capital expenditures, locally depleted timber, and up to 400 percent increases in the price of raw materials (Berman 1982: 175). According to Gunn (1984: 102), the 33 percent failure rate was still favorable by national standards. Some of the cooperatives formed from buyouts of closing plants eventually failed but still provided local employment up to fifteen to twenty-five years (Gunry 1984: 103).

Berman (1982) documents a number of other favorable economic impacts of the plywoods. The hourly return to members of the cooperatives has been above the union average in most cooperatives, and in some, it has been consistently at 50 percent or more above union averages. Continuous operation has meant higher annual income for members. The plywood cooperatives have also demonstrated superior productivity of member-workers according to measures of physical volume of output per man-hour of work, quality of product, and economy of material use. Value added per labor hour in some cooperatives is more than twice that of conventional plants.

The cooperatives have done better than the plywood industry as a whole in surviving economic downturns. In the recession period of 1982, their market share rose to 20 percent because they were able to retain their niche in high quality sanded plywood, one of the most stable portions of the market. Members have also been willing to reduce their incomes or, if necessary, lay off nonmember workers who make up 10 to 50 percent of their labor force (Gunn 1984). However, Gunn points out a number of financial pressures the cooperatives face over the long run, including substantial new capital investment to meet environmental requirements and dramatic rises in the price of timber. If their prices rise, substitute products that can be made more cheaply in other countries become more competitive.

The plywoods' record on democratic self-management is mixed. Although they hire large numbers of nonmember workers, they provide members with substantial ownership and control of the enterprise.[13]

Agri-industrial Cooperatives

Agri-industries are another common sector for rural worker cooperative models. The Acadian town of Evangeline, Prince Edward Island, developed Old Barrel Chips, a potato chip factory to process locally grown potatoes as part of the town's overall cooperative strategy to provide local economic opportunities and preserve French culture and community. With a total of fifteen consumer, credit, and worker cooperatives and only 2,500 people, Evangeline claims to be cooperative capital of the world (Arsenault 1988). The potato chip factory started in 1987, with twelve people employed in the plant and five in sales, and has grown to nineteen people in the plant and sixteen people in sales. Sales are now over $2 million, exceeding projections by at least a year. The quality of jobs is better than other jobs available locally. Pay is close to industry rates, and benefits are somewhat better.[14] So far, profits have not been distributed. The cooperative has had no problem recruiting members in an area where unemployment is 14 percent in the winter and 6 percent in the summer.

A more comprehensive model in the agricultural sector is the regional cooperatives formed by the kibbutzim and moshavim cooperative communities in Israel over the last forty years in order to extend services and improve economic conditions of the member communities (Daniel 1982). These cooperatives increase the integration of the agricultural sector by developing equipment plants and processing services. Nonagricultural sources of employment were needed for workers displaced by mechanization in agriculture and for second generation farmers and other immigrants to the regions. One example is Mifale Haemak, a regional cooperative founded in 1957 in the lower Galilee and owned by thirty-two kibbutzim and twelve Moshavim. In 1982 the cooperative owned the voting stock of a poultry slaughterhouse, chicken reprocessing plant, hatching egg cleaning plant, cotton gin, fruit processing plant, avocado packing plant, flower packing plant, cold storage facility, data processing office, pool of agriculture machinery, and feed mill. Total turnover was $150 million.

Regional cooperation and integration have added value to production. Daniel (1982: 5) also notes that farmers control the process of integration rather than depending on outside suppliers and distributors. The settlements also benefited from the training and experience of their members involved in managerial positions in joint enterprises.

Industrial Cooperatives

The best-known industrial cooperatives are the Mondragon cooperatives in the Basque country of Spain, which began in the mid-1950s. As of 1985, Mondragon's eighty-six industrial cooperatives had created 15,183 jobs and generated $1,001.10 million in sales, of which $277.32 million (28 percent) was from exports (Morrison 1991: 256). The cooperative complex as a whole at the beginning of 1988 had 166 cooperatives and had created 21,000 jobs spread throughout the four Basque provinces (Morrison 1991: 8).

The secondary support organizations formed by the base cooperatives have also had important economic development impacts both for the cooperatives as well as for nonmember private sector firms in the region. Mondragon's applied research and development cooperative, Ikerlan, develops advanced technologies and production processes for both cooperatives and for private firms, which pay a higher fee. Most noteworthy is Mondragon's cooperative bank, the Caja Laboral Popular. By the early 1980s it ranked twenty-sixth among banking institutions in Spain. Financing from the Caja has been instrumental in fulfilling the cooperatives' main goal of creating local jobs. In recent years its lending capacity has outstripped the investment opportunities within the cooperative system, and it now has the authority to lend to private enterprise in the Basque region (Wiener and Oakshott 1987: 25).

Productivity of cooperative firms has been high. Thomas and Logan (1982) compared the Mondragon industrial cooperatives to the 500 largest Spanish industries on the basis of (1) value added per factor of production, (2) value added per person, and (3) value added per fixed assets from 1971 to 1977. In the years comparisons could be made, the cooperatives performed better on all measures, but were losing their lead in labor productivity due to the priority placed on employment creation.

The cooperative system also demonstrated it could weather the recessionary period of the late 1970s and early 1980s far better than the private sector. Through wage flexibility and work sharing, as well as retraining and placement of workers in other growing cooperatives, the Mondragon cooperatives had far lower unemployment rates than other Basque firms (Whyte and Whyte 1988).

The other impressive group of rural industrial cooperatives is in the kibbutzim. In 1986 there were 269 kibbutzim in Israel with 126,700 members. Secondary industry employs 23 percent of the kibbutz labor force and contributed about $1.6 billion (Canadian) of sales in 1986. Twenty-seven percent of sales is from exports (Profile of the Kibbutz Movement 1989). According to Blasi (1986: 65), the kibbutz developed many of the most important sectors of Israeli industry, such as plastics and electrical equipment, and operate some of the largest and most mechanized plants. Studies have also shown that the kibbutzim outperformed conventional Israeli enterprise on various productivity and profit measures.[15]

Despite their dramatic impact on developing their regional economies, both Mondragon and the kibbutzim are more vulnerable to exogenous economic forces as they open up their economies to international competition. In order to compete in the new European Economic Community, Mondragon must substitute technology for industrial jobs. Future employment expansion is projected in some high-paid, but many more low-paid, service jobs (Morrison 1991: 214). The kibbutzim must also compete in the context of a triple digit inflation rate in Israel. As of 1989, one-third of the kibbutzim were having financial difficulties (Profile of the Kibbutz Movement 1989: 13).

The cooperative systems in Mondragon and the kibbutzim are unique in terms of their scale, the numbers of industrial cooperatives, their impact on the local economy, and their commitment to cooperative enterprise. Both environmental conditions and social values were conducive for successful industrial cooperative startups. Severe economic depression and political repression during Franco's regime eliminated other career options for young educated Basques (Whyte and Whyte 1988: 33). Political persecution of Jews in Europe shaped the commitments of early kibbutz settlers to socialism and communalism (Blasi, Mehrling, and Whyte 1984: 301). The founders were also exposed to cooperative principles and models. Mondragon's entrepreneurs were students of Father Jose Arizmendi, who emphasized Catholic principles of social doctrine and cooperation and exposed his students to nineteenth century cooperative communities and mutual aid organizations (Blasi, Mehrling, and Whyte). For the second generation in both cooperative systems, strong cultural traditions, family and friendship networks, and isolation from other labor markets and life-styles were important factors in reinforcing the cooperative option (Bradley and Gelb 1983; Katz and Golomb 1974).

These systems also had governmental support and favorable economic conditions. After the first kibbutz members proved their ability to settle and defend their communities, the kibbutzim then received financing, land, and services from the Jewish National Fund and the Histadrut, Israel's labor union (Blasi, Mehrling and White 1984: 301). Later, the Israeli government provided subsidies both for settlement and for economic development, particularly in export sectors. Mondragon benefited primarily from sheltered domestic markets during Spain's isolation from international markets under the Franco regime (Thomas and Logan 1982).

Industrial cooperatives formed in Mondragon and the kibbutzim not because capitalist enterprises failed, but because capitalist enterprises failed to meet the needs of workers. Since early in the twentieth century, Mondragon was dominated by a large foundry and metalworking company, closely held by family and friends. Others outside the circle could not rise above a first-line supervisory position (Whyte and Whyte 1988: 25). The kibbutzim began developing industries to employ workers displaced by technological advances in their traditional agricultural industries. The enterprise structure consistent with their values was kibbutz-controlled industries that incorporated managerial practices based on principles of workers' participation in decision making (Leviatan 1976: 525).

Although examples exist of other successful industrial cooperative startups in Europe and North America, the more common avenue for developing industrial cooperatives in rural areas has been buyouts or conversions of existing or closed plants. There are examples of cooperatives that have retained jobs, and in some cases created additional jobs, in areas often dominated by single industries, but the overall performance of worker buyouts has been uneven.[16]

Service Cooperatives

Rural worker cooperatives in the service sector have tended to concentrate in low profit businesses, employing unskilled people. Yet, even these cooperatives have the potential to provide comparable or higher wages, prospects for profit sharing (although limited), skill training in management, and a better quality of work life than comparable private sector firms.

Worker's Owned Network (WON)[17] in Athens, Ohio, has assisted in forming several cooperative retail businesses and services meeting local needs. One reason WON has been relatively successful with both service cooperatives and other small worker cooperatives is the strong community bonds and extended family networks in this rural area.[18] Perhaps the most successful service cooperative is Casa Nueva, a Mexican restaurant operating since 1985 and employing thirty-two people. The $7 hourly wage is higher than comparable work in the area. The cooperative is now assessing the feasibility of diversifying into marketing its sauces. Another cooperative cleaning business employs five to eight workers, depending on the season. After a year the cooperative began paying health benefits and recently bought out a profitable carpet cleaning company, with hopes of making more money for raises, paid vacations, better health insurance, and more paid hours rather than sweat equity. A home health care cooperative, however, had more problems operating efficiently in a rural setting. Dispersed clients and high transportation costs made it difficult to achieve economies of scale. Many people in the area were not covered by insurance and were reluctant to pay the true cost of care. At affordable prices, the cooperative could not cover its managerial costs and reverted to a privately owned, mother-daughter firm, operating on a smaller scale.

Worker cooperatives have also been able to improve job quality and extend the length of the work year in the tourist industry. The Nantahala Outdoor Center in Swain County of western North Carolina, started in 1972 as a private company, has become a leader in the white water rafting industry. The company's founder from Atlanta, Payson Kennedy, believed in employee ownership and control and first introduced profit sharing. In 1989 he restructured the company as a KESOP, an employee stock ownership plan in which both the company and workers contribute to purchase of the company's stock for each employee's stock account.[19] Through this plan, workers now have majority control of the company. Nantahala employs eighty people year round and 375 in the summer season. Of these, fifty are local people who tend to work in mainstream service jobs rather than as rafting or kayaking guides or trainers. One hundred and fifty workers are members of the KESOP, which requires at least six months' employment in a year.

Nantahala has diversified in order to extend the work season. So far, it has started a store, three restaurants, a child-care center, vacation houses, a motel/lodge, a gas station, an adventure travel program off season, and a mail order catalog for outdoor equipment.

Entry-level workers earn about the same salaries as those at private rafting companies; the middle-level workers earn more than those at private companies; and top managers earn far less, no more than three times the lowest-paid person. Salaries are an issue, and all workers want to earn more. The company offers health insurance, which is not common in the tourist industry, and opportunities for upward mobility. More than twenty department managers have been promoted internally. Despite low salaries, the lifestyle has attracted top outside managers even though they do not necessarily stay. Seven recruits have left to start their own companies in the area. Nantahala may not be building a cooperative economy, but it is spinning off a community of entrepreneurs and providing important entrepreneurial role models in a rural area. Nantahala's development of the white water rafting industry has also increased local real estate values and the tax base. The downside is that their own workers have difficulty purchasing housing, a common problem in tourist areas.[20]

Summary and Conclusions

Empirical evidence of rural worker cooperatives indicates that they can create and retain local jobs. In the cooperatives that innovated new products and services or served an export market, the jobs created have been net gains and have not simply displaced private sector jobs in local markets. The Mondragon cooperatives, the kibbutzim, and the plywood cooperatives also have shown higher productivity than comparable private sector firms, freeing more resources for alternative uses and development.

Rural cooperatives have important equity impacts. They have employed young people and disadvantaged groups in areas with few other employment options. By diversifying their products and markets, they have extended the length of the work season and provided more work stability. Successful cooperatives have redistributed wealth from owners to workers in the form of higher wages, benefits, and profit sharing.

The most important impact of cooperatives is the institutional change that alters ownership and control of production. To varying degrees, cooperative development has been responsible for a different quality of job and work environment, greater learning and skill development of members, and an ability to secure jobs and control economic decisions within the constraints of wider economic trends and markets. Even the well established cooperative systems, however, have not been able to insulate themselves totally from environmental forces. There may be an inherent contradiction between cooperative enterprise and increasingly open, competitive economies requiring advanced technologies, large capital investments, and rapid decision making.

The Mondragon cooperatives and kibbutzim proved to be dynamic enterprises capable of innovation, growth, and export from rural regions. Although the degree of economic development in Mondragon and the kibbutzim was exceptional, growth of cooperatives and integration of the cooperatives into the local economy occurred to a lesser extent in the Pacific Northwest, Quebec, and even in western North Carolina.

Despite some success stories, barriers to cooperative formation are pervasive, particularly the ability to attract entrepreneurs and mobilize capital. Cooperatives that are formed often have difficulty surviving as cooperatives. Nonetheless, cooperatives that eventually close, sell out, or degenerate from pure cooperative principles still may create positive benefits for the community and workers, as the plywood cooperatives demonstrate.

Government can accelerate rural cooperative development by financing regional cooperative development agencies and passing favorable tax, procurement, and trade protection legislation. This favorable treatment can help the cooperative sector survive in what is essentially an alien environment for this type of enterprise development. Yet government economic assistance alone will not create viable rural cooperatives. Cooperative values must be present in a community to sustain the development process.

The key issue is how those values are created and sustained. Some observers consider cooperation a learned behavior that develops from experience in the family and other social and economic insititutions (Putterman 1982; Gamson and Levin 1984). Public leaders can influence the formation of cooperative values. Mondragon's Father Jose Arizmendi, who began a technical college, was the inspiration behind Mondragon's first cooperative entrepreneurs. Sometimes those values can be imported, as in the case of Nantahala in North Carolina. But, so far, Nantahala's example has not led to the formation of additional cooperative firms in western North Carolina.

Rural communities that are already familiar with other types of agricultural, credit, or consumer cooperatives are good candidates for forming worker cooperatives. However, under present conditions, supporting worker cooperatives can be expected to have modest local impacts at best. Even successful worker cooperatives in U.S. rural communities have only employed a fraction of the local labor force.[21] Without dramatic economic downturns or ideological shifts in the United States that are more favorable toward cooperative values and a more equitable distribution of resources, worker cooperatives should be thought of as a supplemental rural development strategy.

NOTES

1. These principles were developed by the Rochdale pioneers, who began establishing worker and consumer cooperatives in Britain in 1844.

2. Some cooperatives may also pursue other social and political goals, such as equitable pay structures, providing socially useful products and services at reasonable costs to the community, or supporting other cooperative and social change organizations. However, these goals are incidental to the main goals being examined here.

3. Despite abuses of the ESOP legislation, Ellerman (1990: 117) argues that the ESOP is an important transitional legal structure for partial worker ownership that can build to full democratic worker control.

4. For a review of the worker cooperative literature, see Dickstein (1991).

5. The common ownership cooperatives in Britain permit no equity investments of members and no participation in the growth of the cooperatives' assets. All capital raised internally from members is loan capital. Consequently these cooperatives have no equity to leverage external conventional financing.

6. For a more detailed discussion of barriers to cooperative development, see Dickstein (1991).

7. For a more thorough discussion, see Dickstein (1991).

8. Cooperatives tend to remain under one hundred workers in size, partly because of an internal constraint. If cooperatives are to be managed democratically, they should remain small (300 to 500 members at most).

9. These might include marketing, research and development, environmental scanning of future trends, and strategic planning.

10. Hired labor can also result from the need for part-time, seasonal workers in certain industries in order to remain competitive.

11. Case studies of worker cooperatives have repeatedly revealed various forms of degeneration although empirical research has not documented the extent of degeneration within the worker cooperative sector. According to Ben-Ner (1988), many qualitative observations indicate that a significant share of worker-owned firms are transformed into capitalist firms either through sale of shares to nonmembers or hiring a significant proportion of nonmembers.

12. Silviculture is the branch of forestry dealing with the development and care of forests.

13. Both Gunn (1984) and Greenberg (1984; 1986) report substantial participation of members in the policy-making process and governance of the cooperatives. Berman (1982) also notes benefits to nonmember workers. They are usually paid above union scale and benefit from the continous employment provided by the cooperatives.

14. The cooperative's manager, Alcide Bernard, gave this assessment of job quality, phone interview, May 13, 1991.

15. Using a paired sample of six conventional firms and six kibbutz industries, Melman (1969) found that the kibbutzim had greater capital productivity, profit per worker, and labor productivity with little difference in their administrative costs. Barkai (1977: 133–37) also found kibbutz industry had greater increases in total factor productivity than the Israeli private non-dwelling economy.

16. For example, the Center for Community Self-Help and its Self-Help Credit Union, located in Durham, North Carolina, assisted in several buyouts and conversions of troubled textile plants in rural North Carolina. Only one of the plants is still operating, with marginal profitability. See

Brodie and Weiser (1988) for an evaluation of these firms' performance. However, Randolph Leisurewear, a worker buyout in Buckhaven, Scotland, grew from twenty-four workers in 1981 to over forty in 1989 to meet increased demand for their high quality industrial clothing. See Annual Report 1988–1989, Scottish Development Cooperatives Committee, Glasgow, Scotland.

17. WON has now become the Appalachian Center for Economic Networks (Acenet).

18. June Holley expressed this opinion in a talk, March 23, 1990.

19. "K" in the ESOP stands for section 401k of the Internal Revenue Code that permits employee deductions.

20. This observation was made by Mark Hunt, treasurer of Nantahala, phone interview, May 2, 1991.

21. The plywood cooperatives, which are the largest and longest surviving cooperative sector in the United States, employed only 2,597 member and nonmember workers in all of Oregon and Washington, according to a 1982 survey (Gunn 1984: 101).

REFERENCES

Arsenault, Raymond. 1988. Evangeline, Prince Edward Island, the Uncontested Co-op Capital. *Worker Co-ops* (Winter) 7,3: 7–10.

Barkai, Haim. 1977. *Growth Patterns of the Kibbutz Economy*. Amsterdam: North-Holland.

Ben-ner, Avner. 1988. Comparative Empirical Observations on Worker-Owned and Capitalist Firms. *International Journal of Industrial Organization* 6: 7–31.

Berman, Katrina. 1967. *Worker-Owned Plywood Companies: An Economic Analysis*. Pullman: Washington State University Press.

Berman, Katrina. 1982. The Worker-Owned Plywood Cooperatives. In Frank Lindenfeld and Joyce Rothschild-Whitt, eds., *Workplace Democracy and Social Change*, 161–75. Boston: Porter Sargent.

Blasi, Joseph. 1986. *The Communal Experience of the Kibbutz*. New Brunswick, NJ: Transaction Books.

Blasi, Joseph, Perry Mehrling, and William F. Whyte. 1984. Environmental Influences in the Growth of Worker Ownership and Control. In Bernhard Wilpert and Arndt Sorge, eds., *International Yearbook of Organizational Democracy*, vol 2. New York: John Wiley & Sons.

Bradley, Keith, and Alan Gelb. 1983. *Worker Capitalism: The New Industrial Relations*. Cambridge: MIT Press.

Brodie and Wieser. 1988. Evaluation of the Center for Community Self-Help Loan Portfolio: Self-Help Ventures Fund, Englewood Investment Corporation, Self-Help Credit Union, Durham, North Carolina. New Haven, CT: Brodie & Wieser.

Clement, Michel, and Claude Martel. 1989. *Profil des Cooperatives de Travailleurs Forestier en* 1987–1988. Quebec: Gouvernement du Quebec, Ministere de l'Industrie du Commerce et dela Technologie.

Clement, Michel, and Claude Martel. 1990. *Profil des Cooperatives de Travailleurs Forestiers* 1988–1989. Quebec: Direction des Cooperatives, Gouvernement du Quebec.

Cornforth, Chris et al. 1988. *Developing Successful Worker Cooperatives.* London: Sage Publications.

Daniel, Abraham. 1982. Regional Cooperation in Israel. Cambridge, MA: Harvard Center for Jewish Studies, Project for Kibbutz Studies.

Dickstein, Carla. 1988. The Role of Cooperative Development Agencies in Developing Worker Cooperatives: Lessons from Philadelphia. *Economic and Industrial Democracy 9,2:* 197–224.

Dickstein, Carla. 1991. The Promise and Problems of Worker Cooperatives: A Survey Article. *Journal of Planning Literature 6,1:* 16–33.

Ellerman, David. 1984a. Workers' Cooperatives: The Question of Legal Structure. In Robert Jackall and Henry Levin, eds., *Worker Cooperatives in America,* 257–74. Berkeley, CA: University of California Press.

Ellerman, David. 1984b. *Management Plan with Labor as a Fixed Cost: The Mondragon Annual Business Plan Manual.* Somerville, MA: Industrial Cooperative Association.

Gamson, Zelda, and Henry Levin. 1984. Obstacles to the Survival of Democratic Workplaces. In *Worker Cooperatives in America,* Robert Jackall and Henry Levin, eds., 219–44. Berkeley: University of California Press.

Greenberg, Edward. 1984. Producer Cooperatives and Democratic Theory: The Case of the Plywood Firms. In Jackall and Levin, eds., pp. 171–214.

Greenberg, Edward. 1986. *Workplace Democracy: The Political Effects of Participation.* Ithaca, NY: Cornell University Press.

Gunn, Christopher. 1984. *Workers' Self-Management in the United States.* Ithaca, NY: Cornell University Press.

Jackall, Robert, and Henry Levin, eds. 1984. *Worker Cooperatives in America.* Berkeley, CA: University of California Press.

Jordan, John. 1983. A System of Interdependent Firms as a Development Strategy. Paper prepared for the International Seminar on Labor Ownership and Workers' Cooperatives, University of Orebro, Sweden, 13–17 June.

Leviatan, Uri. 1976. The Process of Industrialization in the Israeli kibbutzim. In *Popular Participation in Social Change: Cooperatives, Collectives, and Nationalized Industry.* June Nash, Jorge Dandler and Nicholas S. Hopkins, eds., 521–47. The Hague: Mouton Publishers.

Melman, Seymour. 1970. Industrial Efficiency Under Managerial Versus Cooperative Decision Making: A Comparative Study of Manufacturing Enterprises in Israel. *Review of Radical Political Economy 2,1:* 9–34.

Melnyk, George. 1989. Cooperative Farming: A Model for Worker Ownership in Agriculture. In Jack Quarter and George Melnyk, eds., 85–112.

Partners in Enterprise: The Worker Ownership Phenomenon. Montreal: Black Rose Press.

Morrison, Roy. 1991. *We Build the Road as We Travel.* Philadelphia: New Society Publishers.

Profile of the Kibbutz Movement. 1989. *Worker Co-ops* 9,1: 13.

Putterman, Louis. 1982. Some Behavioral Perspectives on the Dominance of Hierarchical Over Democratic Forms of Enterprise. *Journal of Economic Behavior and Organization* 3: 139–60.

Quarter, Jack. 1989. Starting Worker-Owned Enterprises: Problems and Prospects. In Jack Quarter and George Melnyk, eds., 33–58.

Talbot-Dagenais, Michele. 1986. *Worker Co-ops* 6,1: 21–24.

Tannenbaum, Arnold. 1974. *Hierarchy in Organization: An International Comparison.* San Francisco: Jossey-Bass.

Thomas, Henk, and Chris Logan. 1982. *Mondragon: An Economic Analysis.* London: Allen & Unwin.

Whyte, William F., and Kathleen Whyte. 1988. *Making Mondragon: The Growth and Dynamics of the Worker Cooperative Complex.* Ithaca, NY: ILR Press.

Wiener, Hans, and Robert Oakshott. 1987. *Worker Owners: Mondragon Revisited.* London: Anglo-German Foundation.

CHAPTER 6

Community Involvement in Education as a Rural Development Strategy
GINNY EAGER

Introduction

Forward in the Fifth was formed to channel community involvement into the effort to improve education in Kentucky's Fifth Congressional District. According to the 1980 Census, fully 62 percent of the adults in the Fifth District did not have a high school education; this was the highest percentage in the nation.[1]

A group of civic leaders convened at the Shakertown Roundtable[2] in May 1986 to discuss the problem, and asked the Mountain Association for Community Economic Development (MACED)[3] to prepare and present a report on the status of education in the District for the meeting.

MACED's education report, *Would You Like to Swing on a Star?*,[4] was based on personal interviews with a wide range of citizens—students, parents, business people, teachers, and other school personnel. The report cited the following problems as contributing to low educational attainment in the District:

- Low expectations at home and school.
- Poor communication between parents and schools.
- Loss of small "community" schools due to consolidation.
- Poor teacher education.

- Heavy influence of nepotism and patronage.
- Low funding.

Most everyone interviewed for the report recognized the poor quality of their educational system and expressed their willingness to work together to correct the problem. The report recommended the formation of an organization aimed at improving education in the District by offering programs to address the problems identified.

> The overwhelming message we heard during our interviews is that people are ready *now* for a change. Whether the issue is helping children find their place in a big world, helping parents help their children learn, or working with teenagers who can't read, our interviews showed that there are people throughout the Fifth District with ideas and energy for tackling the problem. The central issue for citizens concerned about education is how best to harness this energy and allow the people with good ideas to put their ideas to work.[5]

The Strategy

Forward in the Fifth's founders realized that these local people were ready to work to improve their local schools. It had to provide a mechanism for them to do so. This mechanism was the formation and support of county-wide organizations that would work locally to improve schools. MACED's report noted, "A Fifth District . . . education organization could . . . give legitimacy and muscle to those who want momentum for education change.[6]

Thus, Forward in the Fifth's strategy was twofold—first, it chose to harness the energy of the people in the District by forming county-wide organizations called Local Affiliates; and, second, it committed itself to provide ongoing support and assistance to enable the organizations to improve the educational attainment of the citizens in their counties.

Everyone present at Shakertown also realized that the economic benefits from this strategy would occur over the long term. "People in the Fifth District recognize how much economic opportunities are entwined with educational standing, and many are ready to break the cycle. The existence of a District-wide development and education group would be a message in itself about the willingness and readiness of the Fifth District to move ahead," stated the MACED report.

This chapter will examine the one basic strategy used by Forward in the Fifth: to improve education by harnessing the energy of local people to work toward improving education. Participants at the Shakertown Conference were well aware of the economic conditions of the region, and hoped an organization created to improve education would supplement work in the region by economic development organizations.

Those attending the Shakertown Conference also heard a report on the economic conditions of the region. This report examined the types of jobs and industries that would be suited to the region. "To become competitive in attracting such jobs, the Fifth District must overcome its weaknesses and systematically promote its strengths," stated the report. "What the people lack, on the whole however, is an adequate education."[7]

Research in other areas indicates that low educational attainment does not always hinder economic growth in rural areas. However, even these reports agree that the need to improve education and training of young people is critical.[8]

Background

The Fifth District contains twenty-seven rural counties, twenty-four of which are in Appalachia.[9] Eastern Kentucky had been economically dependent on the coal mining industry for years. Little education was needed to be a coal miner, and during the most recent industry booms in the early 1970s, the pay was very good, sometimes as high as $30,000 for entry-level positions. Hundreds of young people saw no need to obtain an education when they could go into the mines and earn that salary. Indeed, their fathers and grandfathers had done it before them.

The advent of mechanization and growing environmental concerns about clean air and land reclamation, coupled with stricter federal regulation of the mining industry in the 1980s, caused a decline in the industry—leaving thousands of unemployed and uneducated people with no other skills or major job opportunities. In 1980, per capita income in the Fifth District was $4,470, only three-quarters of the state level. Unemployment in the District fluctuates substantially from county to county. During the 1980 to 1990 decade, the average unemployment rate ranged from 5 percent in Jessamine County to 20 percent in McCreary County. In 1990, nearly 30 percent of the District's residents had incomes below the federal poverty level; and 45 percent of school children qualified for free or reduced-price lunch.

There are several groups working on economic development issues in the region; however, their efforts have been impeded by the lack of basic skills within the work force.[10] Jobs in most industries now require not only basic skills such as reading and simple math, but also increasing technical skills such as computers and algebra—and many industries will not locate in areas without an educated work force. Those civic leaders at the 1986 Shakertown meeting realized that to improve the economic conditions of the area, the educational attainment of its citizens would have to be improved. The MACED report demonstrated that the citizens of the District were ready to help.

Forward in the Fifth was formed as a nonprofit entity. The founders asked MACED to staff the new organization. The organization has three full-time staff, its Executive Director and two Local Affiliate Coordinators who are all MACED employees leased to Forward in the Fifth. Administrative support is provided by MACED staff on an as-needed basis.

Starting with those interviewed for the report, the staff began to organize citizens in each county to form Local Affiliates. Existing groups in three counties became Affiliates, and new groups were formed in the other twenty-four counties. The District contains thirty-eight school systems—twenty-seven county systems and eleven independent systems. Staff originally anticipated having to form a Local Affiliate for each school system in those counties with more than one. However, the very first Affiliate quickly proved this to be unnecessary, as the academic booster clubs of two school systems in one county voluntarily banded together to become Forward in the Fifth's first Local Affiliate. Shortly after that, a single new organization was formed as the Affiliate in a county with three school systems.

There were only two basic requirements for an organization to become an Affiliate of Forward in the Fifth: it had to have a letter of support from the school superintendent of each school system in the county, and it had to be composed of a cross-section of the community: educators, business people, civic leaders, and parents. The support of local school administrators was critical. Prior to 1986, so-called "education improvement groups" had formed in many counties with the express purpose of ousting a superintendent or other school personnel. This caused many superintendents to be immediately suspicious of any "education improvement" organization.

Forward in the Fifth board members met with school superintendents during the organizational period and asked how an organization could help them improve their schools. Many of Forward in the Fifth's early programs and activities were developed in response to advice those superintendents provided. This helped allay many fears and suspicions on the part of superintendents.

Starting in 1987, Forward in the Fifth encouraged its Affiliates to work with, not against, existing school administrations. This nonadversarial approach was critical if Affiliates were to obtain the support of superintendents. Staff occasionally hears from Affiliate leaders about a superintendent who has not wholeheartedly embraced Forward in the Fifth's programs and activities. But even in those counties, the Affiliates have been able to function effectively. At worst, the Affiliates are tolerated by these superintendents. No superintendent has tried to hinder any Affiliate programs or activities.

Affiliates are comprised of a broad range of citizens. All of them have teachers and school administrators actively involved. Parents also make up a big proportion of Affiliate membership. Some of the groups have a better record of business involvement than others, but all of them have some business representation. All twenty-seven Affiliates are staffed by volunteers. In many cases, a local business person or the school system provides services such as copying, postage, and clerical support at no cost to the Affiliate.

Local Affiliate Support

From the beginning, Forward in the Fifth staff provided the Affiliates several kinds of support. It immediately offered to match up to $1,500 in funds raised locally by Affiliates, and has continued to do so each year. Having money in hand has motivated the Affiliates to find innovative ways to improve their local schools. Forward in the Fifth has matched nearly $300,000 during the past eight years.[11] Forward in the Fifth developed and funded a few "ready-made" projects for Affiliates to implement; these were projects that could get Affiliates started with little effort and give them an early sense of accomplishment. In addition, it has helped Affiliates develop their own "home-grown" programs, or adapt those begun in other Fifth District counties.

The District-wide "ready-made" programs developed by Forward in the Fifth are detailed below:

- *Attendance Improvement Program.* At the suggestion of school superintendents within the region, Forward in the Fifth implemented a program to reward schools that improved their attendance, maintained high attendance, or had the best overall attendance in the District. Both school systems and individual schools were eligible for the prizes. In 1991, Forward in the Fifth altered this program to place more responsibility for improving attendance with Local Affiliates. The organization now awards $500 grants to each Affiliate to develop and implement its own attendance program.

- *Rolling Classroom Field Trip Project.* Many children living in the Fifth District seldom have the opportunity to travel outside their own small communities. As children are more prone to drop out of school if there is nothing to interest them, a trip outside their small world can excite them and pique their interest in the learning process. Forward in the Fifth sponsored field trips for fifth-grade students for five years. Prior to that, schools in the District seldom allowed, let alone funded, field trips for students.

- *Learning Skills Program.* A University of Kentucky professor of developmental education spent a sabbatical in a Fifth District school system testing her theory that students who were taught how to study would have a better chance of success in college. Her years at the University had shown her that many bright students begin college, only to fail because of poor study skills. She taught study skills—note taking, speed reading, memorization techniques—to students, while instructing classroom teachers on how to incorporate study skills into the regular curriculum. Forward in the Fifth formed a partnership with the University to expand this program and offer it to all Fifth District schools.

- *Parental Volunteer Reading Project.* Students whose parents are actively involved in their education have a much greater chance of succeeding in school. In an effort to promote a higher level of parental involvement, Forward in the Fifth designed this project that brings parents into first- and second-grade classrooms to read out loud. Besides increasing parental involvement, the program helps students obtain a strong grasp of critical language arts skills that are crucial to successful learning. The project also places more resources into Fifth District classrooms because each participating teacher receives a set of books.

The above programs are multi-year offerings; other programs, however, are offered one time only, or for a limited time. Some of these programs are discussed below:

- During the 1987–88 school year, Forward in the Fifth brought the NASA Community Involvement Program to the District.

Officials from NASA visited schools, made presentations to students, and conducted in-service workshops for teachers.

- In September 1987, Forward in the Fifth sponsored a two-day conference on math and science activities for 250 teachers. An Alliance of Math and Science Teachers was formed by those attending the conference and now functions as an independent organization.
- Forward in the Fifth brought the Blue Apple Players to the District in the spring of 1989. The Players are a professional drama troupe from Louisville; they write, produce, and perform musicals about social problems affecting today's young people. They performed *Down From the Sky*, which dealt with drug and alcohol abuse, in each county in the District.
- During the 1989–1990 and the 1990–1991 school years, Forward in the Fifth and the Kentucky Department of Education's Space Education Program jointly offered "Space Science You Can Teach" workshops for 200 elementary teachers.
- In a joint venture with the Appalachian Regional Commission (ARC) and IBM, Forward in the Fifth placed 40 Writing to Read labs in Fifth District elementary schools. IBM donated the equipment, ARC provided funding for training, and Forward in the Fifth coordinated the logistical arrangements.

Another major part of the support strategy has been to develop a network among Affiliate leaders to stimulate their calling upon one another for advice and assistance. Twice a year representatives from all the Affiliates meet to share their success stories and problem-solving techniques. Forward in the Fifth staff regularly visits and phones Affiliate leaders to learn of their new initiatives, discuss problems, put them in touch with other Affiliates who have solved similar problems, give them "pats on the back," and make them feel that they are an important part of a movement. One Affiliate leader spoke of the value of this assistance when she said:

> I worked on education in this county for 10 years before Forward in the Fifth was created. Five of us did everything. We couldn't get anyone else to help. The work we are now doing is snowballing beyond my wildest dreams. The difference is the credibility and visibility we get from being part of the big Forward in the Fifth.

Forward in the Fifth also produces and mails a monthly news-letter to Affiliate members and other people associated with or in-terested in the program as an additional networking tool. It contains stories on different ways Affiliates are increasing their membership, involving more business leaders in their programs, raising funds, working to support school administrators and teachers, and enriching the education of children.

The original mailing list for the newsletter was composed of the people interviewed for the 1986 MACED report, plus all school superintendents, instructional supervisors, directors of pupil personnel (truant officers), and principals. The list totaled just over 700 for the first issue, which was published in November 1986. As Affiliates were organized, members were added to the list. By August 1994, it was being mailed to more than 8,000 people; this demonstrates the interest of Fifth District residents, and of others outside the District, in Forward in the Fifth's activities and programs.

Progress

Since its creation, Forward in the Fifth has contributed to an improvement in dropout rates, graduation rates, attendance, and test scores, and has encouraged more Fifth District citizens to be supportive of education as an investment in their communities.

Attendance and dropout rates have improved slightly in the District since 1986—attendance from 94.5 percent in 1985–1986 to 95.0 percent in 1991–1992, and the annual percentage of dropouts has fallen sharply from 2.9 to 1.0 percent during the same period. There has been a dramatic improvement in the proportion of high school graduates attending college, moving from 38 percent in 1984 to 48 percent in 1990, compared to the national increase from 34 percent in 1984 to 39 percent in 1989. Most impressive is the percentage of adults with a high school education that has risen from 38 percent in 1980 to 50 percent in 1990.

Attitudes in the District have also changed. For example, a teacher who participated in the Learning Skills Program told staff, "I meant to retire until all this got started. Now it's just too interesting. I wouldn't miss being here for the world." A Fifth District superintendent explained his views about Forward in the Fifth: "Forward in the Fifth is there when we need them. It's a welcome relief. It's not threatening. Forward in the Fifth helps build up our self-confidence, so we can open up and talk about our concerns."

Forward in the Fifth's Rolling Classroom Project, described above, also demonstrates a drastic change in attitudes on the part of school administrators. In speaking with students across the District in 1986, Forward in the Fifth staff discovered that very few of them had ever taken a field trip. In 1991, the fifth year of Forward in the

Fifth's Rolling Classroom project, people began telling staff that teachers, principals, and superintendents were not only encouraging field trips for all grade levels, but also were fully funding them. Forward in the Fifth demonstrated to the schools that field trips were an effective dropout prevention tool and educational experience.

Superintendents, many of whom had viewed educational improvement groups as only "out to get them," now make comments like, "When I think of Forward in the Fifth I think of these words: supportive, sincere, positive and child-centered," and "These experiences [the Rolling Classroom field trips and teacher mini-grants] could not be made available to our students without the help, support and backing of the Forward in the Fifth organization."

Evaluation

Forward in the Fifth's strategy of channeling community involvement to improve education has been successful. The organization reached its initial goal of forming Local Affiliates in each of the twenty-seven counties in the District during its first two years, and all are still operational in 1991. Each of them has incorporated, and several have achieved their own tax-exempt, nonprofit status. It may be several more years before improvements in the District's economic conditions will be visible.

A closer look reveals a mixed level of success. Some of the Affiliates are conducting only a bare minimum of education improvement activities, while others have prospered and grown and conduct a level of activities rivaling that of the parent organization.

During the spring of 1991, Forward in the Fifth contracted with Sandra Miller of Winrock International to carry out an organizational evaluation. Ms. Miller and Forward in the Fifth staff developed a method of measuring the effectiveness of Affiliates. The organizations were evaluated on the number and quality of programs offered, participation in District-wide workshops and conferences, attendance at sharing sessions, and fundraising results. The evaluator found eleven very active Affiliates, five moderately active, four slightly active, and seven not very active.

There are eighteen school districts in the eleven counties with very active Affiliates. In three of those school districts the percentage of ninth graders graduating increased by more than ten percentage points from 1984 to 1992; in three systems the rate increased by five percentage points or more. The remaining districts increased by two points. The percentage of graduates attending college increased in all eighteen school districts between 1984 and 1992.[12]

Ms. Miller and Forward in the Fifth staff determined that several factors contribute to the success of an Affiliate. These include: strong internal leadership, support of the Affiliate by local businesses, economic vitality of the community, a strong relationship between Affiliate membership and the local school administration, and an appropriate organizational structure. All Affiliates with strength in all of these areas fell into the very active category; those with none of these strengths fell into the not very active category.

An examination of several specific Local Affiliates will illustrate this point. One of the very active Affiliates is located in Farm County.[13] The county's economic base is predominantly agricultural, but it also has several agricultural satellite businesses (such as gate manufacturers) that contribute to an economic climate slightly healthier than in most Fifth District counties. The Affiliate formed in May 1987 and has a broad-based membership of local business leaders, school personnel, parents, and civic leaders. It meets once a year. Any resident of the county can join the Affiliate for a small fee. The organization has a board of directors that meets monthly and is the primary decision-making body. The board developed a strong committee structure and delegates work to those committees. Committee chairs attend monthly board meetings to provide progress reports. The members of these committees carry out the work, but are not expected to attend the board meetings. To allow for continuity within the leadership, each chair of the board is elected for a two-year term, after which he or she continues to serve as a member of the board. This Affiliate has been fortunate in that all three of the Chairs to date have been strong, dedicated leaders in spite of the fact that they were also very busy business people.

The Affiliate has participated in every District-wide program offered by Forward in the Fifth, and has also developed many of its own programs and activities. These local programs include academic and attendance incentive programs (one of which has been replicated in six other counties in the District), mini-grants for teachers that fund innovative and creative classroom activities that teachers would not be able to otherwise do (which they award twice a year), a solid fund-raising plan, an annual membership drive, and a scholarship program for graduating seniors.

It also has the strong support of the local school system. The superintendent is a nonvoting, ex officio member of the board of directors and regularly attends meetings. He fully supports the Affiliate and the programs it offers to his schools.

The Farm County Affiliate has achieved its own tax-exempt, nonprofit status. It has an annual budget of about $30,000, and has received its full $1,500 match from Forward in the Fifth each year. It conducts several different fund-raising activities, including an annual membership drive, a truck raffle, and operation of food booths at a local community festival. The funds for its scholarship program come from soft drink machines and memorial donations solicited at local funeral homes. The organization is considered to be the most successful Local Affiliate by Forward in the Fifth staff. Even without continuing support from Forward in the Fifth, this organization will continue to prosper.

One of the "not very active" Affiliates is in Mountain County, which has a very small population and a depressed economy. The economy immediately presents a fund-raising problem that this group has not been able to overcome. The group affiliated in July 1987 with the strong support of the local school administration and support from the small business sector. The first president was a local minister who was very active in community affairs and was instrumental in helping to organize the group. It started out small, participating only in the District-wide programs developed and offered by Forward in the Fifth, and has never progressed beyond this stage.

Early in the group's second year of operation, the founding president relocated to another county, and the Affiliate virtually died. The local school superintendent did not want to see the organization fold, so he single-handedly kept it going, although for nearly a year it participated in no activities. The group received a full Forward in the Fifth match for two years (1989 and 1990) and about one-third of the match it was eligible to receive in 1991.

Obviously, the Mountain County Affiliate did not have, or lost, strength in most of the factors viewed as necessary for success. Even with the poor economic situation of the community, with a strong leader the organization could have been more active (there are more active Affiliates in counties that are nearly as economically depressed). In addition, this organization has never participated in any of the District-wide meetings and, as a result, has not been able to learn from personal contact with other Affiliates.

Just recently it has shown signs of "revitalizing," and initiated a mini-grants program for teachers in the 1991–1992 school year. The new president is planning to attend the next District-wide meeting. Although it is considered to be the least successful Affiliate, if the new leadership is strong enough, Forward in the Fifth staff thinks it can still become an effective education support group in its county.

These two extremes of Forward in the Fifth Affiliates demonstrate that the strategy of channeling local involvement has worked, albeit in varying degrees. The Farm County Local Affiliate is obviously successful, and Forward in the Fifth staff view the Mountain County Affiliate as successful in that it is slowly pulling itself out of obscurity and becoming a viable education support group in its county.

A quick look at some Local Affiliates who fall in between these two extremes will demonstrate how strength in just one or two of the factors mentioned above can also lead to a successful organization, and how failure in just one or two factors can be a major deterrent to the organizations.

An Affiliate in Coal County—another Fifth District county with a depressed economy—is one of the very active groups. It participates in District-wide offerings. It develops and implements its own programs locally. Representatives attend District-wide meetings, and it has the strong support of the local school administration and the small business sector in the community.

The key to Coal County's success has been a very strong, dedicated leader. A strong relationship with school officials has been another key factor. The local school board gave the Affiliate leader a desk and use of the phone in their offices for Affiliate activity. Although they have not had nearly the financial resources of the Farm County Affiliate, this organization has still received its full $1,500 match for each of the past four years (1988–1991). Its annual budget may never be as high as Farm County's, but it is involved in a wide variety of projects and it could survive on its own without Forward in the Fifth.

Another Affiliate—in Ridge County—was very active and successful until its founding president relocated to another county in 1990. All the factors for success were present—a strong economy, support of the local school administration, participation in District-wide meetings, implementation of both District-wide programs and programs developed locally, and a very strong president. Unfortunately, this Affiliate did not allow for continuity in its leadership position and when the founding president left, the Affiliate floundered.

The Ridge County organization is still minimally active. The leader who stepped into the presidency is an employee in the school system and does not have sufficient time to devote to the organization. The group occasionally sends representatives to District-wide meetings, but has not developed any new programs since the first president left. It has also been forced to drop some activities that it had sponsored for two or three years because no one was willing to devote the time and energy to carry them out. This group has its own tax-exempt nonprofit status and has received its full match for each of the four years since its inception. Forward in the Fifth staff believes the Ridge County Affiliate will probably be able to continue functioning on its own, but not at the level of activity of 1989 or 1990.

Conclusion

Overall, Forward in the Fifth's strategy of channeling local involvement into the effort to improve schools was a successful endeavor. The formation of an Affiliate in each county was the first indication of success. Of those twenty-seven Local Affiliates, staff believes that eleven of them are very strong, viable players in the education improvement movement and that each of these groups could continue if the parent organization was dissolved. Affiliates in six other counties could probably continue for a few more years, and the remaining ten organizations would probably cease operations within a few months of Forward in the Fifth's demise, should that occur.

Statistics for school systems in counties with strong Affiliates show that the local efforts are paying off. The continued growth of even the most successful organizations, and the revitalization of the weaker ones, demonstrate that Forward in the Fifth's strategy is working locally. The continued interest in and growth of Forward in the Fifth's newsletter further indicates the success of the organization and, thus, its strategy.

The change in attitudes toward education is perhaps the hardest indicator to measure. However, Forward in the Fifth staff senses an improvement in attitudes from personal contacts throughout the District who say again and again what a difference Forward in the Fifth and the Local Affiliate has made in their county. An Affiliate leader summed it up best at a District-wide meeting when discussing an academic incentive program that the organization was sponsoring: "Because of positive attitudes, praise and recognition of students, it is now the 'IN' thing to be a good student! And believe me, that's a change. That's progress."

Forward in the Fifth needs to devote more time and resources to assist Affiliates that are undergoing leadership transitions. In some cases, assistance is needed in identifying new leaders who can be an asset to some of the organizations. Although developed specifically for Kentucky's Fifth Congressional District, Forward in the Fifth staff and its founders believe that the strategy of channeling community involvement to improve education could work in other rural areas of the nation.

NOTES

1. Bureau of the Census, *1980 Census of Population and Housing, Congressional Districts of the 98th Congress, Kentucky* (Washington, DC: U.S. Department of Commerce, Bureau of the Census).

2. The Shakertown Roundtable is an educational conference activity of Shakertown at Pleasant Hill, Kentucky, a nonprofit organization. It meets several times a year to discuss various issues affecting the state of Kentucky.

3. The Mountain Association for Community Economic Development (MACED) is a private nonprofit economic development organization working in Central Appalachia. MACED receives funds from private foundations and government agencies.

4. *Would You Like to Swing on a Star?*, A Report to the Shakertown Roundtable Conference on Economic Development and Education in Kentucky's Fifth Congressional District (Berea, KY: Mountain Association for Community Economic Development) May 1986.

5. MACED, *Swing*, p. 65.

6. MACED, *Swing*, p. 67.

7. *Two Days that Moved a Generation to Action*, the Charge from the May 1986 Meeting of the Shakertown Roundtable (Harrrodsburg, KY: Shakertown) 1986.

8. *Education and Rural Economic Development: Strategies for the 1990's*, Economic Research Service (Washington, DC: U.S. Department of Agriculture) September 1991.

9. Kentucky lost a congressional seat after the 1990 Census. The state was redistricted in December 1991, and the Fifth District is now different. Forward in the Fifth continues to work in its original twenty-seven counties, and is currently organizing Affiliates in the twelve new counties.

10. The mountainous terrain and lack of basic infrastructure, such as good roads and a plentitul water supply, have also impeded development of the region.

11. Forward in the Fifth has received funding from the following sources: the Appalachian Regional Commission, the Ford Foundation, the Mary Reynolds Babcock Foundation, the Hazen Foundation, the James Graham Brown Foundation, the Kentucky Department of Education, the Knight Foundation, the Christian Appalachian Project, and Fifth District businesses and individuals.

12. "Evaluation of Forward in the Fifth," Sandra Miller, internal document (Berea, KY: Forward in the Fifth) June 1991.

13. The county names have been changed.

PART III

Standard Development Techniques

CHAPTER 7

Manufacturing Recruitment as a Rural Development Strategy

KEVIN T. McNAMARA, WARREN KRIESEL, AND DANIEL V. RAINEY

Manufacturing recruitment remains a primary local economic development strategy throughout the United States. While this strategy was successful for many rural communities throughout the 1960s and 1970s, researchers Rosenfeld, Bergman, and Rubin (1985) have suggested that rural communities will be unable to attract new manufacturing investment in the future because of a structural change in the U.S. economy. This change has resulted from the migration of many low-skill, cheap-wage employers to Third World countries and a shift to service employment in the U.S. economy (Johnson 1984; Deaton and Weber 1986). It is hypothesized that manufacturing firms that maintain American operations will seek the labor, capital, transportation, and other resources found only in and around metropolitan areas. Researchers therefore suggest that rural communities, once prime locations for firms seeking low-skill, low-wage labor, are left with limited opportunity to attract new manufacturing investment.

Despite this growing consensus that rural communities lack the resources to attract new manufacturing investment (Barkley 1993), state and local governments and economic development organizations continue to invest in industrial recruitment as a primary economic development strategy (Smith and Fox 1990). As the number of plants seeking domestic industrial sites declines, there has been rapid expansion in the number of communities actively recruiting new manufacturing investment (Levy 1981). Are these wise investments? What are the chances of communities' success in industrial recruitment? How can local leadership incorporate these probabilities into their assessment of the appropriate local development strategy? These questions are the focus of this chapter.

The first section of the chapter discusses a firm's industrial site location process and provides an overview of the distribution of new manufacturing investment among nine regions in the United States during the four-year period of 1986 to 1989. The second section reviews recent empirical research on regional and community attributes that impact firms' location decisions. The third section discusses the results of a recent location study for Georgia counties, and the last section describes how those results can be used by county leadership.

Overall, the results of industrial location studies show that among the factors that a county can control, investments in public services such as fire protection have a greater impact on plant location probability than investments in industrial sites. Furthermore, investments in industrial sites will yield a benefit only if they actually attract an industry, whereas improvements to fire protection will yield added benefits in the form of reduced insurance premiums paid by county residents. Based on available evidence, we encourage county leadership to be realistic in their planning for economic development. Indeed, the research results indicate that some counties face extreme location disadvantages and that they should refocus their development strategy away from industrial recruitment.

New Manufacturing Location in the United States

Concerns about the growth of new manufacturing in the United States can be eased by examining recent trends in manufacturing investment. New plant investment data from 1986 through 1989 indicate 5,824 major investments were made in the forty-eight contiguous states (Conway Data, Inc.). These data include manufacturing investments that exceeded a value of $1 million, created in excess of fifty jobs, or had a minimum of 20,000 square feet of new floor space. Table 7.1 indicates annual number of new manufacturing investments made in the United States by nine regions.[1] While all regions attracted new investment over the four-year period, the investments were concentrated in four regions: East North Central, South Atlantic, East South Central, and West South Central (see table 7.1 for states in these regions).

Table 7.1: New Manufacturing Investment in 48 Contiguous States, 1986–1989

Region[a]	1986	1987	1988	1989	Totals	1990 Population[b]	Locations Per Million Population
East South Central	166	185	209	258	818	15.2	53.8
South Atlantic	332	432	411	469	1644	43.6	37.7
West South Central	108	197	162	250	717	26.7	26.9
East North Central	369	208	173	242	992	42.0	23.6
West North Central	102	80	88	131	401	17.7	22.7
Mountain	57	59	61	62	239	13.7	17.4
Pacific	117	123	109	153	502	39.1	12.8
New England	41	33	38	43	155	13.2	11.7
Middle Atlantic	92	84	60	120	356	37.6	9.4
TOTALS	1384	1401	1311	1728	**5824**		

Source: Conway Data, Inc., 1987, 1988, 1989, 1990

a. East South Central includes Alabama, Kentucky, Mississippi, and Tennessee; South Atlantic includes Delaware, D.C., Florida, Georgia, Maryland, North Carolina, South Carolina, Virginia, and West Virginia; West South Central includes Arkansas, Louisiana, Oklahoma, and Texas; East North Central includes Illinois, Indiana, Michigan, Ohio, and Wisconsin.

b. Based on 1990 population from 1990 Census of Population, in millions.

Investments in these four regions, which comprise about 52 percent of the total United States population, accounted for 72 percent (4,171 investments) of the total 5,824 investments. On a per capita basis, the East South Central region attracted the most new firms, attracting 53.8 per million population. The New England and Middle Atlantic regions attracted the fewest firms per capita, attracting 11.7 and 9.4 firms per million population, respectively. Clearly, with more than 1,300 new major manufacturing investments made in the United States each year during the 1986–1989 period, communities can still benefit from new manufacturing investment. The critical question for rural development policy, however, is whether rural communities can compete effectively for this new manufacturing investment. If so, which communities can compete most effectively, and which type of investments are the most promising targets? The next section discusses a conceptual model for a firm's location decision process as the basis for empirical analysis of manufacturing location to address these questions.

Plant Location Decisions and Local Recruitment Strategies

A footloose[2] manufacturing firm's location decision process is a multistage process that begins when the firm decides to invest in a new manufacturing facility (Smith 1981; Schmenner, Huber, and

Cook 1987). The first stage of the firm's location process involves the selection of a geographic region that will optimize the firm's location with respect to factor supply and product markets. This region could be a state, a multistate area, or other area depending on a specific firm's location requirements. From a community perspective, until this regional location choice is made, local government policy can do little to influence the firm's site selection decision.

Once a firm has selected a specific region, it searches within the region to identify a specific site that will allow the firm to maximize profits. This search may include evaluation of a variety of sites within the identified region that meet some criterion deemed critical by the firm in influencing its cost of production. Selection of a specific site within the region is based on cost factors that include labor availability and costs, agglomeration economies, the community's eagerness for industrial development, access to input factors and product markets, and miscellaneous firm cost factors (Kriesel 1983; McNamara, Kriesel, and Deaton 1988; Kriesel and McNamara 1991b). Local quality of life factors also can influence a firm's location decision (Hekman 1982). During this site-selection stage of the search process, state and local actions can influence location decisions.

State and community development efforts that focus on attraction of new manufacturing investment attempt to convince footloose firms that the state or community offers the firm a least cost of production site, or one that will enable the firm to earn a higher return on investment than any other site. Marketing efforts focus on three main areas: factors believed to influence a firm's costs; incentives that offer benefits to specific firms identified as having a potential interest in locating in the state or community; and investments in local infrastructure that attempt to improve a state or community's competitiveness for general manufacturing vis-à-vis other locations. Research on the effectiveness of these state and local recruitment efforts is needed to quantify the benefits states or communities receive from their recruitment efforts. A lack of data systematically measuring specific state and/or local recruitment activities and investments limits researchers' ability to test the effectiveness of the activities in attracting new manufacturing plants. Determining success and whether a firm's location choice was related to local recruitment efforts is difficult to determine (Finsterbusch and Kuennen 1992). However, the importance of specific community attributes to firm locations can be examined to identify factors that influence firm location decisions. Industrial location research does not directly measure the success or failure of local government industrial recruitment programs. Information provided by the location research, however, can be used to assess a locality's attractiveness to industry and to guide formulation of policies to promote manufacturing investment.

While several attributes are associated with industrial location at the state level, research provides limited guidance for state policy attempting to attract new manufacturing investment. Carlton (1980); Bartik (1985); Wasylenko and McGuire (1985); and Schmenner, Huber, and Cook (1987) have examined factors that influence firm locations at either the state or metropolitan level. These studies found several attributes of a state's economy to be associated with the state's ability to attract new manufacturing investment. The size of the state's manufacturing base (Carlton 1980; Bartik 1985; Schmenner, Huber, and Cook 1987) and available technical expertise (Carlton 1980) had positive associations with manufacturing investment. Building costs (Bartik 1985; Schmenner, Huber, and Cook 1987), labor force unionization (Bartik 1985; Schmenner, Huber, and Cook 1987), and energy costs (Carlton 1980; Bartik 1985) were state attributes that were negatively associated with manufacturing location.

State policies, generally through tax abatement or infrastructure incentives, have not been shown to consistently have a positive association with firms' location decisions. Carlton (1980) and Schemenner, Huber, and Cook (1987) found that state tax levels and incentives did not influence firms' location decisions. Bartik's research, on the other hand, suggests that high state tax levels had a negative influence on location.

The literature on factors influencing manufacturing firm location at the county level does provide leaders with insight into local development policy options that affect the probability of a specific community attracting new manufacturing investment. They also suggest which local factors are important location determinants. A summary of the results of location studies is presented in table 7.2. The community location factors presented in the table can be divided into two types—those that cannot be locally controlled and those that can be influenced by local government policy. As leaders examine their community's potential for attracting new industry, they should consider how their community compares to other communities in regard to both types of location factors. Investments in factors that the community can influence, like industrial site quality, may be fruitless if the community lacks other attributes that are important to firms.

Agglomeration economies represent the cost savings that accrue to firms that locate in larger communities with a relatively large concentration of population and commercial/manufacturing activity.

Table 7.2: Community Location Factors[a]

A. Agglomeration factors
    population (1, 3, 5, 6)[b]
    population density (5)
    commercial employment (1)
    manufacturing employment share (7)
    number of manufacturing plants (5)
    distance to SMSA (2, 3)

B. Labor quality/cost/availability
    labor force size (2)
    unemployment rate (4, 7, 9)
    wage rate (1, 5, 7)
    percent of adult population with high school diploma (6)
    labor productivity (1)
    distance to vocational school (5)
    distance to four-year college (2, 8)

C. Transportation facilities
    interstate highway access (2, 4, 5, 7, 8)
    distance to airport (5)

D. Access to Capital
    bank assets (5)
    bond financing (2, 8)

E. Site facilities and services
    site quality (2, 8)
    public site ownership, price (2, 4, 8)
    sewer capacity (5)
    location incentives (9)
    development group (6, 7)

F. Taxes
    property tax rate (3, 7, 9)
    freeport (4)
    local income tax (7)

G. Public services
    mean years of schooling (7)
    per public school expenditures (2, 8)
    high school math achievement test score (6)
    fire protection rating (2, 4, 8)

a. Factors listed are measures that have been found to have statistically significant relationship to manu-facturing locations in cited studies.

b. Numbers in parentheses correspond to number of study in which variable was significant. Studies in-clude:
    1. Agthe and Billings (1977)
    2. Debertin, Pagoulatos, and Smith (1980)
    3. Dorf and Emerson (1978)
    4. Kriesel and McNamara (1989; 1991a; 1991b)
    5. Kuehn, Braschler, and Shonkwiler (1979)
    6. McNamara, Kriesel, and Deaton (1988)
    7. Rainey (1992)
    8. Smith, Deaton, and Kelch (1978)
    9. Walker and Calzonetti (1989)

Agglomeration influences the size and quality of the labor force, availability and cost of business, financial and capital services, and access to suppliers and consumers. The importance of these factors suggests communities with both larger populations and commercial/ manufacturing bases are in general more attractive locations for new manufacturing facilities. Small rural counties offer less attractive locations, and are at a disadvantage when competing for manufacturing investment. While the agglomeration factors are important to firms, communities can do little, if anything, to impact these factors. Depending on the size and location of a community vis à vis a metropolitan area, the community can take action that might mitigate its lack of agglomeration economies. For example, infrastructure investments that improve access to metropolitan areas, cooperation with neighboring jurisdictions to improve the level and quality of public services, or targeting industrial development efforts to industries that could be closely linked to a community's existing economic bases may increase rural communities' potential for attracting new manufacturing investment.

Labor characteristics also influence location decisions. The association of the measures presented in table 7.2 to firm location decisions suggests that communities in labor market areas with a large, well-trained, productive work force provide more attractive manufacturing locations (Rainey 1992). Access to vocational schools and colleges also seems to be important to firms. The results also suggest that firms are attracted to locations with lower wage rates. Labor factors suggest that urban communities, and rural communities located close to urban areas, offer firms location advantages. While communities can provide educational programs to improve the productivity of local labor, they cannot generally impact the size of the labor force, labor availability, and prevailing wage rates. Community leadership, therefore, cannot strongly influence local labor factors through government policy actions.

Manufacturing firms need access to transportation facilities. Both highway and air service access are important to firms seeking industrial sites. Urban communities and rural communities located near interstate highways and airports appear to be more attractive locations than remotely located communities because of firms' transportation needs. Communities have limited influence over the location and development of either interstate highways or airport facilities. These factors, therefore, are beyond any local policy options.

Industrial site quality, local taxes, and local public services are three categories of local determinants that local policy can influence. Community actions that improve industrial sites, lower property and inventory taxes, and expand local school, public safety, and fire protection services have positive impacts on their probability of attracting new manufacturing investment. Communities considering manufacturing recruitment as a strategy, however, should be aware that these investments may not help communities overcome disadvantages, such as poor highway access and a small labor force. Local leaders' expectations of the potential returns to various investments must be well thought out before any such investments are made.

A general conclusion from location studies is that a community's attributes influence location choices for new manufacturing investment. Community leaders, however, must be cautious in their interpretation of these results and their application to local development planning. Location decisions are based on firms' assessment of how well specific industrial development sites meet some minimum cost and other location criteria. Communities that offer some characteristics that firms seek, such as low property taxes and public ownership of industrial sites, may not be competitive because they lack other location factors that firms seek. Community leaders need to be able to assess their community's probability of attracting new manufacturing investment before they consider specific strategies, or investments, as part of local industrial recruitment efforts. If a specific community has a relatively high probability of attracting new manufacturing investment, community leaders need to determine which local investments would have the greatest return in terms of increasing the community's probability of attracting new manufacturing investment.

A manufacturing location model is a useful tool in evaluating the appropriateness of industrial recruitment strategies of specific communities. The model provides leaders with a method for evaluating their community's attractiveness as an industrial site compared to other communities in the region or state. The analysis does not consider a community's comparative advantage over other communities for the attraction of a specific firm or industry. Communities that are not competitive for footloose firms might attract manufacturing investment because of a specific advantage that the community offers to firms with specific location needs. Community leaders who believe that their community offers specific location advantages to firms in a particular industry may wish to analyze their community's attractiveness in comparison to other communities seeking to attract industries in that sector. For instance, a community that has a comparative advantage in transportation due to access to a deep water port facility might compare itself to other communities with a similar port facility as it analyzes its potential of attracting a firm that needs the port facility.

The next section of the chapter uses a model developed by Kriesel and McNamara (1991a) to illustrate how community leaders can assess their probability of attracting manufacturing investment and examine how their probability of attraction will change in response to local investment that improves community characteristics. This model provides leaders with information about their community's relative attractiveness to industry.

A County-Level Industrial Location Model

The authors estimated a county-level industrial location model to determine communities' probabilities of attracting new manufacturing investment and to identify community factors that impact firms' location decisions. The manufacturing location model included both community location factors that are beyond a community's ability to influence and those that communities can directly control and change through specific local investment. A county-level ordered, categorical logit model was used to estimate the probability of a Georgia county attracting a manufacturing plant. The model and complete empirical results are described in Kriesel and McNamara (1991b). The analysis was conducted on the 1986–1989 period, during which 121 of Georgia's 169 counties attracted one or more new manufacturing facilities.

Among six location factors not controlled by communities that were included in the model, three were found to be significantly different from zero in predicting plant location: the unemployment rate, mileage of interstate highway within a county, and the population's racial composition. The local unemployment rate was included in the model as a measure of labor availability. Its significance suggests that firms consider local labor availability in location decisions. The inclusion of racial composition is suggested by Till's (1986) research, where counties with a high proportion of blacks were found to attract fewer manufacturers.[4] The interstate mileage variable was included as a measure of access to transportation routes. While these variables do not measure location factors that community leadership can directly impact, they do provide information that is valuable to communities that are considering manufacturing recruitment as a local development strategy. Communities that do not have available labor, lack interstate highway access, and have a higher proportion of blacks are at a competitive disadvantage to communities not having these characteristics.

Three other variables in the model were statistically significant: passage of inventory tax relief referenda, local fire protection ratings, and the quality of local industrial development sites. These variables represent factors that can be controlled, or influenced, by local leadership. The results suggest that communities that enact inventory tax relief, which reduces a firm's local tax liability, will increase their probability of attracting manufacturing investment. The local fire protection rating also influenced location decisions. Communities that take actions to improve local fire protection will have a positive impact on their probability of attracting new manufacturing investment. The third locally-controlled variable associated with firms' location decisions was a measure of local industrial site quality.[5] The results suggest that communities can invest in one of several industrial site attributes to increase their attractiveness to firms seeking industrial sites.

Site quality is related to three site specific attributes: lot size, the site's distance to an interstate highway, and the distance to an airport with commercial air service. Community characteristics also influence the site's quality. These include the educational attainment of adult population, the size of the local manufacturing base, the civilian labor force size, and whether or not the community is in a metropolitan area. While communities can improve the quality of local industrial sites by purchasing larger tracts of land that have good highway and air service access, there are still community characteristics, such as educational attainment and labor force size, which limit the impact that communities can have on improving the quality of their industrial sites. As community leaders consider investments in site quality, fire protection, or other local factors, they should consider their community's general competitiveness against other communities to provide a realistic estimate of potential local returns from investments in industrial development.

Application of Location Model to Local Development Planning

A county's leadership can use the results of a manufacturing location model to evaluate (1) their chances of attracting a manufacturing plant to their county, and (b) alternative strategies for attracting a plant. For example, with an estimate of a Georgia county's probability of attracting new manufacturing investment, leaders from that county can consider the expected returns from various recruitment investments. They can make an estimate of the local tax revenue cost that would result from passage of a local inventory tax relief ordinance and compare it with costs of other development options such as further development of an industrial site or improvement of the local fire protection rating. Comparing the probability increases with the associated costs will indicate which investment is the most cost effective.

An analysis of the thirty-four Georgia counties with an estimated probability of a new plant location less than 50 percent indicates that passage of a freeport referendum (estimation of local inventory taxes), improving the county's fire protection rating, and increasing the quality of a local industrial site would increase the county's probability of attracting a new plant (Kriesel and McNamara 1991a). Substantial improvements in existing industrial sites (approaching $1 million) would be needed to increase their probability an additional 5 percent. Improving the fire protection by one rating point in the same community increases probability of attracting new manufacturing investment by nearly 8 percent. Therefore, if a county can achieve the one point improvement in its fire protection for less than $1 million, then investments in fire protection (and similar public services) would be a more cost effective strategy than investing in industrial site improvements for increasing the community's probability of attracting a new firm. Adopting local inventory tax relief, by removing local personal property tax liability on business inventories, increases the county's probability of attracting a firm by about 8 percent. The cost associated with this policy option can be estimated with local tax records and compared to the costs of other strategies aimed at improving the community's attractiveness to industry.

It is important for a county's leadership to realize a vital distinction between investing in industry-specific items versus public services that impact firms' costs. A speculative shell building, paved access roads, or industrial tax breaks yield benefits *only if* the county actually attracts a new plant that uses those investments. On the other hand, local investment in public services, such as police and fire protection, schools, and public utilities, provides benefits to a county's residents even if it does not attract a plant. In the case of improved fire protection, for instance, residents benefit immediately by paying lower insurance premiums. These community benefits should be considered when leaders examine different strategies for improving their community's attractiveness to industry.

Counties in Georgia have been successful in industrial recruitment efforts during the 1980s. About 58 percent (ninety-two counties) of Georgia's 159 counties attracted at least one new manufacturing plant during 1987–1989. The large share of counties with new manufacturing plants suggests that industry recruitment is a good strategy for Georgia counties. State industrial developers indicate that all Georgia counties are involved in industry recruitment efforts, although some are more active than others. No data on local development organizations, strategies, budgets, or other characteristics are available. The Georgia results of counties' probabilities of attracting new plants are not easily transferable to localities in other states or regions because of variations in the general attractiveness of regions to industry, and in the types of and number of firms locating in different states or regions. The importance of specific community attributes in attracting firms, however, does provide insight into which local policies have the greatest impact on a community's attractiveness to industry. It also suggests which types of communities have higher probabilities of attracting new manufacturing plants.

In order to gain more general information about local recruitment prospects, probabilities were computed using the mean values of county factors for Georgia counties grouped by the Economic Research Service's (ERS) county classification code's urban-rural continuum (Butler 1990). Location probabilities estimated are presented in table 7.3. The number of counties in each category is reported along with the estimated probabilities of attracting one new manufacturing facility (probability 1) and two new facilities (probability 2).

In Georgia, a state that has been among the leaders in attracting new manufacturing investment throughout the past thirty years, even the most remote, rural type of county has a probability of attracting new industry that is greater than 50 percent. The results, however, do suggest that industries have a strong urban bias in selecting sites. County codes 6 and 7, representing the forty-four most rural counties, had probabilities of thirty-seven to forty percentage points lower than the code with the highest probability of attracting a new plant (code 1—urban counties) and fifteen to eighteen percentage points lower than code 5, the next less remote group of rural counties. The differences for probability 2 was forty-nine to sixty-eight percentage points for code 1 and seventeen to thirty-six percentage points for code 5. These estimates suggest that rural communities are at a disadvantage in competing with urban communities for new manufacturing investment. The more remote and smaller the rural county, the greater the disadvantage. These counties should be cautious in recruitment efforts, especially in states that are not attracting a large number of new plants (see table 7.1).

Summary and Conclusions

Location trends (table 7.1) and recent location research (table 7.2) provide general insight into a specific community's potential for attracting new manufacturing investment. An agglomeration of population and economic activity, labor availability and quality, air and highway transportation facilities, industrial site quality, and local public services were important location factors in most of the research cited. In general, communities with larger economies and populations are more attractive for manufacturing firms because many firms can operate at a lower cost of production at these sites.

Table 7.3: Probability of Attracting New Manufacturing Investment[a] for Georgia Counties by County Type[b]

County Type	Number of Counties	Probability 1[c]	Probability 2[d]
Code 0,1	18	.93	.86
Code 2,3	20	.81	.70
Code 4,5	8	.90	.82
Code 6	27	.73	.57
Code 7	42	.71	.54
Code 8	21	.56	.37
Code 9	23	.53	.18

Ten county types are based on ERS urban-rural continuum code presented by Butler. Classification codes were collapsed into seven groups because three codes had less than five observations each.

Code	Metro Counties
0	Central counties of metro areas of 1 million population or more
1	Fringe counties of metro areas of 1 million population or more
2	Counties in metro areas of 250,000 to 1 million population
3	Counties in metro areas of fewer than 250,000 population

	Nonmetro Counties
4	Urban population of 20,000 or more, adjacent to a metro area
5	Urban population of 20,000 or more, not adjacent to a metro area
6	Urban population of 2,500 to 19,999, adjacent to a metro area
7	Urban population of 2,500 to 19,999, not adjacent to a metro area
8	Completely rural or fewer than 2,500 urban population, adjacent to a metro area
9	Completely rural or fewer than 2,500 urban population, not adjacent to a metro area

a. Probabilities based on analysis of manufacturing locations in Georgia during the 1987–1989 period.
b. Probability of attracting at least one new manufacturing plant, computed.
c. Probability of attracting one new manufacturing facility.
d. Probability of attracting two new facilities.

These communities should consider industrial recruitment options as part of their local development strategy. Local policy can influence a community's probability of attracting new manufacturing investment and its ability to compete with other communities for manufacturing investment. Analysis of a community's location attributes can help local leaders target industrial recruitment spending to get the greatest increase in the community's location probability per local dollar spent.

Rural communities are often less attractive to industry than urban counties (Barkley 1993). Rural communities in some regions of the United States, however, successfully attracted manufacturing plants in the late 1980s. Two factors that are beyond local control, interstate highway access and available labor, tend to be key factors in these plant locations. Rural communities in the four regions that have attracted 72 percent of total new plants in the United States over the 1986–1989 period (table 7.1) could be successful in manufacturing recruitment efforts. In Georgia, which is in one of these regions, for instance, rural communities have done quite well as indicated above. Rural leaders in these regions should carefully assess their community's probability of attracting a new manufacturing plant. Many rural communities will find it difficult to attract new manufacturing investment in the 1990s (Barkley and Hinschberger 1992; Testa 1992). If their community is competitive, they should make investments in local factors that will result in the greatest increase in the community's probability of attracting a manufacturing facility. If their community has a low probability of attracting manufacturing investment, they should consider other development strategies. Leaders in rural communities outside of these four regions should be very cautious about investing in manufacturing recruitment. Industrial location research reviewed above evaluates community characteristics associated with successfully attracting new manufacturing investment. The range of attributes of the firms making the investments, both within sectors and across sectors, may vary greatly. Certainly some communities with a low estimated probability of attracting a new manufacturing facility have successfully attracted new investment. These communities might have targeted specific sectors or firms that would benefit from specific local attributes. Community leaders, however, should be cautious with investments as competition for most types of new manufacturing investment will be keen through the 1990s.

If a specific community's probability for success in attracting new manufacturing investment is low, the community's leaders might promote more local growth through policies to stimulate expansion of existing manufacturing firms or in nonmanufacturing sectors. These rural communities should consider self-development (Green et al. 1990) strategies that might offer their communities greater potential for local economic growth.

This chapter has examined manufacturing recruitment as a rural development strategy by focusing on community factors that influence plant location decisions. The chapter does not address the broader social, environmental, and economic implications of a new manufacturing facility on a community. These issues are important, and difficult to address. Small communities experience less indirect income and employment growth from new manufacturing investment than large communities because large communities provide more opportunities for backward and forward linkages between the new firm and the local economy (Shaffer and Fernstrom 1973; Shahidsaless, Gillis, and Shaffer 1983). State and local policymakers should consider the broader impacts that manufacturing growth will have on a community in their assessment investment in specific recruitment strategies. Assessment of the success or failure of industrial recruitment programs is often based on whether or not new industry was attracted and how many jobs were created by the new industry. Examining the economic development impacts of industrial recruitment should include a more comprehensive examination of the total income and employment impacts, as well as the social and environmental impacts, of the new investment. Community leadership investing local resources in recruitment and providing large location incentives could leave a community and its economy worse off than it would have been had it not invested in recruitment efforts and attracted the new plant. The long-run implications of recruitment for the community's development and quality of life must be carefully considered.

NOTES

1. Data on the urban-rural distribution and on the state level distribution by standard industrial classification code are not available.

2. A footloose firm is one that is not restricted to a specific location because of supply- or demand-related constraints.

3. The focus of these studies has been community or state factors that influence firms' location decisions. The analysis has not considered specific needs of firms by industry or type, such as by standard industrial classification (SIC) code. The limited number of location observations of any particular SIC code are not sufficient in any one state to permit cross-sectional analysis.

4. This negative association between the proportion of minority population and industry location could be due to several factors such as racial discrimination, a perceived higher propensity among blacks than whites to unionize, or perceptions of areas with high minority populations as poor because of the lack of skilled and educated workers.

5. The measure was derived from a hedonic price analysis of industrial sites throughout the state.

REFERENCES

Agthe, D.E., and Bruce, R.B. 1977. "The Importance of Community Economic Factors in the Success of Public Industrial Parks: A Case Study of the Southeast." *Business and Economic Review* 24: 3–6.

Barkley, David L. 1993. "Manufacturing Decentralization: Has the Filtering-Down Process Fizzled Out?" Ch. 2 in *Economic Adaptation*, David L. Barkley, editor. Westview Press: Boulder.

Barkley, David L., and Hinschberger, Sylvain. 1992. "Industrial Restructuring: Implications for the Decentralization of Manufacturing to Nonmetropolitan Areas." Economic Development Quarterly 6(1): 64–79.

Bartik, T.J. 1985. "Business Location Decisions: Estimates of the Effects of Unionization, Taxes, and Other Characteristics of States." *Journal of Business and Economic Statistics* 3(1): 14–22.

Butler, M.A. 1990. *Continuum Codes for Metro and Nonmetro Counties* (Staff Report No. 9028). Agriculture and Rural Economy Division, Economic Research Service, U.S.D.A., April.

Carlton, D.W. 1980. "The Location and Employment Choices of New Firms: An Econometric Model With Discrete and Continuous Endogenous Variables." *Review of Economics and Statistics* 47: 574–82.

Conway Data Inc. *Industrial Development and Site Selection Handbook* Vol 32(1) 1987; Vol 33(1) 1988; Vol 34(1) 1989; Vol 35(1) 1990.

Deaton, B.J., and Gunter, D. 1974. "The Influence of Community Characteristic on Industrial Plant Location and Expansion: A Preliminary View." *Tennessee Home and Science* (July).

Deaton, B.J., and Weber, B.A. 1986. *The Changing Rural Economy of the United States*. Department of Agricultural Economics, Virginia Polytechnic Institute, Blacksburg, Virginia.

Debertin, D.L., Pagoulatos, A., and Smith, E.M. 1980. "Estimating Linear Probability Functions: A Comparison of Approaches." *Southern Journal of Agricultural Economics* 11: 65–69.

Dorf, R.J., and Emerson, M. 1978. "Determinants of Manufacturing Plant Location for Nonmetropolitan Communities in the West North Central Region of the United States." *Journal of Regional Science* 18: 109–20.

Epping, G.M. 1982. "Important Factors in Plant Location in 1980." *Growth and Change* 13: 47–51.

Finsterbusch, K., and Kuennen, D. 1992. "A Look at Business Recruitment as a Rural Development Strategy: Some Previous Findings on Business Recruitment in Rural Areas." *Policy Studies Journal* 20(2): 218–29.

Florida, R., Kenney, M., and Mair, A. 1988. "The Transplant Phenomenon." *Commentary* (Winter).

Green, G.P., Flora, J.L., Flora, C., and Schmidt, F.E. 1990. "Local Self-Development Strategies: National Survey Results." *Journal of the Community Development Society* 21(2): 55–73.

Hekman, J.S. 1982. "What Are Businesses Looking For?" *Economic Review*, Federal Reserve Bank of Atlanta, June.

Johnson, T.G. 1984. "Off-Farm Employment of Small-Farm Operators: A Strategy For Survival." *Proceedings of the Forty-Second Professional Agricultural Workers Conference*, Tuskegee, Alabama, December 2–4.

Kriesel, W. 1983. *The Estimation of Benefits, Costs, and Probabilities of Manufacturing Plant Location in Rural Virginia*. Unpublished Master's Thesis, Blacksburg, Virginia, Virginia Polytechnic Institute.

Kriesel, W., Deaton, B., and Johnson, T. 1984. "Industrial Development As a Community Investment Decision." *Selected Paper*, American Agricultural Economics Association, August.

Kriesel, W., and McNamara, K.T. 1991a. *A Guide for Improving Industrial Development Prospects*. Georgia Cooperative Extension Service, University of Georgia, Athens, Georgia.

Kriesel, W., and McNamara, K.T. 1991b. "A County-Level Model of Manufacturing Plant Recruitment with Improved Industrial Site Quality Measurement."*Southern Journal Of Agricultural Economics* 23(1): 121–27.

Kriesel, W., and McNamara, K.T. 1989. *An Implicit Pricing Model for Characteristics of Industrial Sites*. Faculty Series 89–59, Department of Agricultural Economics, University of Georgia, November.

Kuehn, J.A., Braschler, C., and Shonkwiler, J. S. 1979. "Rural Industrialization and Community Action: New Plant Locations among Missouri's Small Towns." *Journal of the Community Development Society* 10: 95–107.

Levy, J.M. 1981. *Economic Development Programs for Cities, Counties and Towns*. New York: McGraw-Hill.

McNamara, K.T., Kriesel, W., and Deaton, B. 1988. "Manufacturing Location: The Impact of Human Capital Stocks and Flows." *Review of Regional Studies* 18(1 Winter): 42–48.

Rainey, D.V. 1992. *Manufacturing Location: The Importance of Local Taxes and Labor Market Areas*. Unpublished Masters Thesis, Department of Agricultural Economics, Purdue University, West Lafayette, Indiana.

Rosenfeld, Stuart A., Bergman, Edward M., and Rubin, Sarah. 1985. *After the Factories: Changing Employment Patterns in the Rural South*. Research Triangle Park, NC: Southern Growth Policies Board.

Schmenner, R.W. 1982. *Making Business Location Decisions*. Englewood Cliffs, NJ: Prentice-Hall, Inc.

Schmenner, R.W., Huber, J. C., and Cook, R. L. 1987. "Geographic Differences and the Location of New Manufacturing Facilities." *Journal of Urban Economics* 21: 83–104.

Shadows in the Sunbelt. 1986. MDC, Chapel Hill, North Carolina.

Shaffer, R., and Fernstrom, J.R. 1973. "Selling a Community on Industry." In *Bringing in the Sheaves*. Oregon State University Extension Service, Oregon State University.

Shahidsaless, S., Gillis, W., and Shaffer, R. 1983. "Community Characteristics and Employment Multipliers in Nonmetropolitan Counties 1950–1970." *Land Economics* 59(1): 85–95.

Smith, D.M. 1981. *Industrial Location*. New York: John Wiley and Sons.

Smith, E.D., Deaton, B.J., and Kelch, D.R. 1978. "Location Determinants of Manufacturing Industry in Rural Areas." *Southern Journal of Agricultural Economics* 10: 23–32.

Smith, T.R., and Fox, W.F. 1990. "Economic Development Programs for States in the 1990s." *Economic Review,* Federal Reserve Bank of Kansas City (July/August): pp. 25–35.

Testa, William A. "Trends and Prospects for Rural Manufacturing" *Economic Perspectives* March/April 1993.

Till, T. 1986. "The Share of Southeastern Black Counties in the Southern Rural Renaissance." *Growth and Change* 17: 44–55.

Walker, R., and Calzonetti, F. 1989. "Searching for New Manufacturing Plant Locations: A Study of Location Decisions in Central Appalachia." *Regional Studies* 23: 15–30.

Wasylenko, M., and McGuire, T. 1985. "Jobs and Taxes: The Effect of Business Climate on States' Employment Growth Rates." *National Tax Journal* 38(4): 497–512.

CHAPTER 8

Volunteer Visitor Business Retention and Expansion Programs

SCOTT LOVERIDGE, THOMAS R. SMITH, AND
GEORGE W. MORSE

Business retention and expansion programs have typically been used in rural towns[1] to help communities encourage growth of local businesses by providing a means for firms to express their problems and concerns. The programs also connect firms to individuals who can suggest or provide solutions to selected obstacles to firm growth and stability. Encouraging local businesses to remain and grow helps generate new jobs and local economic activity (Bozeman and Boseman 1987: 538–53; Miller 1990: 17–31). Business retention and expansion programs gained popularity in the 1980s, and now over twenty states employ some form of retention and expansion program. The rapid adoption of business retention and expansion programs by so many states is probably also due in part to increasing layoffs and plant shutdowns as the United States struggled to beat international competition in manufacturing, to a growing recognition in the 1980s that more communities were chasing fewer firms in industrial attraction programs, and to a well-publicized study by Birch (1979) showing that existing firms account for the majority of new jobs in the local economy. The Birch study also provided support for the idea of encouraging business formation as part of a community's economic development strategy. Effort in the area of entrepreneurship is needed, but development of local entrepreneurial capacity is usually a long-term process. Industrial attraction and business formation efforts are more likely to be successful if existing businesses are thriving. Thus, business retention and expansion efforts can provide a good foundation for business formation and attraction efforts.

Most business retention and expansion programs rely on face-to-face interviews with local businesses as a means of collecting data on firm problems and concerns. Two major approaches have evolved. "Lone Ranger" business retention and expansion programs rely on paid professional visitors who are able to provide immediate technical assistance to firms with problems. This chapter focuses on Volunteer Visitor Business Retention and Expansion (VVR&E) programs, which depend on local citizens to visit firms and prescribe solutions to problems. While immediate, firm-specific problems do receive attention as part of a typical VVR&E program, *the program emphasizes developing local strategic planning capacities* to create a climate for continuing, positive dialogue between local businesses and community leaders. The VVR&E concept has proven popular with state sponsors because it is a low-cost program that teaches local leaders how to promote long-term economic growth in small communities. The business visitation approach also scores well in comparison to other development strategies in surveys of local economic development groups (Finsterbusch et al. 1992).

The principal goal of VVR&E is a stable, strong local economy developed through improving the competitiveness or efficiency of local firms.[2] The program addresses this objective by enhancing communications and strategic planning among businesses, community leaders, larger units of government, and citizens. The program works through or catalyzes the formation of a group of citizens concerned with community development, and the immediate employment effects of such a group are likely to be dwarfed by normal fluctuations of the business cycle (Humphrey et al. 1988: 1–21). Even in the long run, the change in local employment after a successful VVR&E program could be negative, if an uncompetitive firm uses the resources it learns about through the program to become more capital-intensive in its method of production. In this scenario, the program prevents the firm from going out of business, but some jobs are lost after the plant is retooled. Thus, use of secondary employment or income data to evaluate VVR&E is not straightforward. This chapter reports on the resources required to support a VVR&E program at the state level, and on results of two surveys undertaken to evaluate VVR&E programs.

Basics of VVR&E

The objectives of a VVR&E program are to increase incomes, employment, and the quality of life for community citizens. Volunteer visitor retention and expansion programs achieve these objectives by fostering an action-oriented strategic planning process for leaders of rural counties or communities. The strategic planning process seeks to build a broad-based coalition for economic development that will continue to operate after the formal end of the program. The immediate goals of the program are to demonstrate a pro-business attitude within the community; help firms solve local problems; help firms use state development programs; and provide data for economic development. These goals and the extent to which they are attained are discussed in detail in the results section of this chapter.

A statewide organization usually provides assistance in the process, with the local program being organized and led by a local coordinator who spends an average of eighty-nine hours on the program over roughly eight months. The number of firms contacted during the program is determined locally, with the average program visiting thirty-nine firms. Two-thirds of these are manufacturing firms. Typically, teams of two community leaders visit local firms and fill out a questionnaire on the business's attitudes about the community. These visits usually last about an hour. The average program recruits twenty-four volunteer visitors to interview firms—volunteers are usually asked to visit firms within a month of their training. After the interview is completed, a task force composed of an average of eleven local leaders reviews the questionnaire and responds to any firm-specific issues within their power and resources. Loveridge et al. (1991) provide discussion of the local resources required to implement a VVR&E program.

The state sponsor tabulates the data and provides an overview of community-wide business concerns. The task force is urged to develop a set of community-wide strategic plans and recommendations aimed at improving the business climate for existing local firms.[3] These recommendations often include programs to help firms become more competitive, to improve the quality and availability of the local labor pool, and to improve the quality of life in the community. A community meeting is typically held to share the recommendations with a broader range of concerned citizens, with attendance averaging about 100 people. Throughout the process, interactions among the task force members, and between the task force and the business community, help develop and strengthen a local "network for development" and thereby improve communications between businesses and leaders. This network often continues to function for months or years after its initial creation. For detailed steps on conducting a local VVR&E program, see Phillips et al. (1993).

State Support of VVR&E

Twenty-six states currently support local VVR&E programs, with state governments, universities, and/or utilities involved, depending on the state. Table 8.1 summarizes the type of educational/technical assistance offered by three well-established state programs, and presents the costs per community associated with each of the programs. These three programs were selected as representative because they provide three distinct models of the VVR&E process, and because most programs in other states have borrowed from one or more of these three states.

Table 8.1: Characteristics of VVR&E Programs—Three State Models, 1986–1987

Characteristic	New Jersey	Georgia	Ohio
Principal Sponsors	Utilities, State Government	State Government, Utilities	University, State Government
Training Staff (FTE)			
State staff	1	1	1
Regional staff	0	0	1
Report Generation Staff (FTE)	1	1	2
Communities Participating in 1986–1987	12	8	14
Average Number of Firms/Visited per Community	58	15	55
Components of Report			
Employment trends	No	No	Yes
Survey results	Yes	Yes	Yes
Locally written recommendations	Yes	No	Yes
Report Transmission			
Number of copies to community	30	1	25
Summary report	None	25 copies	250 copies
Cost per Program	$18,000	$10,500	$ 9,500
Participation Fee Paid by Community	None	None	$ 500

Source: Adapted from Otto, Morse, and Hagey 1990: 40.

The state sponsor's roles are to recruit communities; help community leaders understand the mechanics of the program; provide information on development assistance; analyze the data collected on firm visits; and advise community leaders on action plans based on the local data. Within those roles, however, specific means of supporting VVR&E vary. Some state sponsors limit their activities to providing short written instructions, computerizing the data, and developing written and graphic descriptions of the results. At the opposite end of the spectrum, other state sponsors provide training programs for the local VVR&E leadership team; conduct training for volunteer visitors; develop written reports that include secondary data on the community's economic trends; furnish "tentative recommendations" based on the firm survey data and secondary data; brief the task force on the results and recommendations; and solicit task force feedback recommendations to be included in a final report.

Program Structure and Employment Impacts

As stated above, immediate employment effects are not the principal focus of VVR&E programs. Nonetheless, any job created or saved by addressing a firm-specific problem uncovered by the program does indirectly help assure success on other objectives. At the community level, these immediate "success stories" provide the citizens who have donated their time to VVR&E with evidence that the program does provide benefits to their community, encouraging them to continue their involvement in local strategic planning and networking activities. Similarly, at the state level, immediate successes translate into higher enthusiasm for the program, simplifying the task of convincing uninitiated communities to try VVR&E. Since immediate job creation and job saving can have such influence on overall program outcomes, it is worthwhile to investigate differences between programs that did and did not report success in this area. A survey of local coordinators is used here to explore such differences.

The coordinator is a member of the community who organizes the local VVR&E effort with support from the state government, the extension service, or a local utility company. Major coordinator functions include: learning about the program; recruiting a task force and volunteers; identifying firms to be interviewed; assisting with volunteer training; helping firms solve problems; and working with the task force to develop and disseminate communitywide recommendations. Of all the program participants, coordinators are the most aware of communitywide program benefit.[4] For example, a program that keeps one 300-employee plant from closing, but which

Table 8.2: Firms Interviewed and Volunteer Visitors by Immediate Employment Impacts

Coordinator Reported Immediate Employment Impact?	Average Number of:	
	Firms Visited	Volunteer Visitors
Yes	40	28
No	36	19

Source: Coordinator survey by authors (see pp. 139–41)

has little immediate impact on other firms in the community, is likely to receive high marks from the coordinator, but only mediocre marks from all but one of the firms contacted as part of the program.

In 1989, 158 VVR&E coordinators in six states who had participated in programs between 1986 and 1989 were mailed questionnaires.[5] Eighty-one responses were received, for a 51 percent response rate. Eighty percent of the respondents had served as coordinator as a relatively small part of their job; the rest were volunteers—thus the respondents had little reason to inflate their evaluations of program effectiveness.

Twenty-five percent of the coordinators reported some immediate employment effects, while 54 percent said they had not observed any job saving or creation as a result of the program.[6] Job saving ranged from ten to 250 employees, while job creation effects ranged from eight to 500 employees. To examine how program structure might influence performance in this area, the sample was divided into those that did and did not report immediate effects, and selected means were calculated.

Programs with immediate employment effects interviewed slightly more firms, had more volunteer visitors, and had a lower number of firms per volunteer than other programs (table 8.2). Average volunteer training time was two hours for both groups, but the survey showed that programs with immediate employment effects were more likely to have engaged their volunteers in participatory rather than passive training activities. These program differences indicate that volunteer recruitment and training are important in identifying firms with immediate problems.

The average program uncovered thirty-eight local problems and had fifteen requests for information on state development programs. Once firms with immediate problems are identified, someone must take charge of providing assistance. Coordinators reporting immediate employment effects reported spending an average of over three times as much effort on this activity than less successful coordinators (twenty-eight versus nine hours), as well as additional time providing information to firms (averages of nine versus six hours). Survey results also show that the additional time providing information to firms was likely to be spent in active, personalized contact with firms requesting information on state and federal programs. In addition to their higher overall time commitment to follow-up activities, coordinators reporting immediate employment effects were more likely to have acted in conjunction with others—rather than alone—to solve firms' problems.

Success on Program Objectives

Some conceptual problems with using secondary income or employment data to evaluate VVR&E were discussed above. An alternative to secondary measures of the effect of a program is to solicit evaluations from program participants. In using such a strategy, it is necessary to examine specific program objectives, capturing participants' perceptions of how well the program worked in each area. Four objectives are common to VVR&E programs. These are: (1) demonstrate a pro-business attitude, (2) help firms use state development programs, (3) assist firms in solving local problems, and (4) provide data for economic development. Survey results relating to these four objectives are discussed below.

Data on achievement of these objectives were collected from the firms visited and from the local VVR&E program coordinator.[7] Basic characteristics of the coordinator survey were described in a preceding section. For information on firms' response to VVR&E, firms in Ohio that had participated in the program were surveyed. Seventy-seven survey responses from rural Ohio firms were matched with questionnaires filled out as part of the original VVR&E programs.[8] Both coordinators and firms were asked to rank the VVR&E program on a 1 to 10 scale for each objective. Median ranks are reported in table 8.3. Firms ranked the program lower on all objectives than did coordinators, which was expected since not all firms are helped by the program, and some firms may not associate the program with the communitywide benefits it generates. However, firms and coordinators did track each other reasonably well in terms of the ranking given each objective. For each objective, respondents to both surveys were categorized as ranking the program "low" if they gave the program a below median rank, and "high" if they ranked the program at or above the median. These categories were then used to

Table 8.3: VVR&E Achievement of Four Objectives: Median Rating by Local Coordinators and Firms

	Coordinator Rating	Firm Rating
Demonstrate Pro-Business Attitude	9	7
Help Firms Solve Local Problems	7	5
Help Firms Use State Development Programs	5	6
Provide Data for Economic Development	8	7

Sources: Coordinator and firm surveys by authors (see pp. 139–41 and note 8). A scale of 1 to 10 was used in both surveys, with 10 indicating a high degree of success. The wording of the questions varied slightly between the firm and coordinator program evaluation surveys, reflecting the different perspectives of the respondents. Rounding mean responses to the nearest integer yielded values identical to the median responses. Roughly 9 percent of the coordinators did not respond to these questions, while about 6 percent of the firms did not answer these questions.

develop tables relating to other responses given by the firms and coordinators, as discussed below.

Coordinator Responses

Program Objective 1: Demonstration of a Pro-Business Attitude. Through visits to businesses, and by developing a community action plan to address concerns raised by local businesses, a successful program shows firms that the community views them as a valuable asset. This can help overcome firms' reluctance to share their problems with local leaders, ultimately shortening the time between emergence of a problem and its resolution.

Coordinators gave the program the highest scores in achieving this objective (table 8.3). In contrast to the finding for immediate employment effects, programs that were the most successful in demonstrating a pro-business attitude in the community interviewed *fewer* firms than did less successful programs (table 8.4). Coordinators from the programs that worked best also spent more time on immediate follow-up assistance to firms (table 8.4). Interviewing fewer firms may free coordinator time, allowing more attention to those firms interviewed, a better focus on overall survey results, and the development of recommendations that help the entire business community rather than just the firms interviewed. Successful programs were much more likely to have produced a written report and to have developed written recommendations for community action as part of the report. Analysis of the survey revealed that coordinators who ranked the program low and who did develop written recommendations worked alone to write the recommendations more frequently than other coordinators. Thus, a combination of individualized attention to firms and building a consensus for economic development appears to be characteristics of programs that work.

Table 8.4: Resources Committed to VVR&E Program and Coordinators' Pro-Business Ranking

Coordinator Ranking of Program Success in Demonstrating Community's Pro-Business Attitude	Average Number of Firms Interviewed	Written Report	Written Recommendations	Average Hours Coordinators Spent on Follow up
High (9 or above)	36	93%	76%	33
Low (8 or below)	50	75%	50%	21

Source: Coordinator survey by authors (see pp. 139–41). Percentages represent percent of programs. High and low categories determined by the median value (9 out a maximum of 10) of coordinator's responses to a question on program success in solving local problems.

Program Objective 2: Help Firms Use State Development Programs. State development programs are constantly changing, and it is difficult for firm managers to keep updating their information. Further, most firms use these programs infrequently, reducing their incentive to learn about the programs. The VVR&E program attempts to overcome this difficulty by asking firms whether they could use information on state business assistance programs during the volunteer visit to the firm. Firms are provided with information as part of program follow-up activities. Some programs designate a community member who has some familiarity with state programs to serve as the "State Development Consultant." The person serving in this volunteer role has the responsibility of facilitating firms' contacts with state development programs.

Coordinators gave this objective the lowest average ranking (table 8.3). Possible explanations for the low ranking include: (1) unrealistic expectations on the level and types of programs available; (2) an expectation of preferential treatment from state agencies for program participants; and (3) inadequate training and/or background of the volunteer "consultant" used to facilitate contact with state programs.

The more successful coordinators were more likely to have used a "consultant" to facilitate distribution of information on state programs, used more volunteers, spent many more hours assisting firms than other coordinators, and more hours providing information to firms. (These "consultants" may or may not be paid professionals.) The overall picture that emerges here is that the program works best when resources are put into giving firms more individualized attention, both in collecting information on their situations and in trying to connect firms to appropriate state assistance.

Table 8.5: Initial Review of Completed Surveys to Identify Problems and Successes in Solving Local Problems

Coordinator Ranking of Program Success in Solving Local Business Problems	Initial Review of Completed Surveys Done by:			
	Coordinator	Task Force	Other	Total
High (7 or above)	51	46	3	100%
Low (6 or below)	79	21		100%

Source: Coordinator survey by authors (see pp. 139–41). Cells represent percent of programs. High and low categories determined by the median value (7 out of a maximum of 10) of coordinator's responses to a question on program success in solving local problems.

Program Objective 3: Assist Firms in Solving Local Problems. While the major goal of the program is strategic planning, political support for the program is built by addressing the immediate concerns of firms whenever possible. Moving a light pole to better illuminate a firm's entrance or getting a city to improve its water purification facilities would both be categorized as solving local problems. Thus, a local problem solved by the program might relate to a specific firm (i.e., the light pole) or many firms (i.e., poor water quality). Success on this objective leads to greater firm efficiency, which in turn translates into higher profits, greater market share, or both. Increased market share or profits increases the likelihood that the firm will remain in business or expand.

Program success on this objective ranked third best (table 8.3). Programs that worked the best on this objective were more likely to rely on a task force review of the questionnaire to identify and resolve local problems (table 8.5), and had coordinators that averaged nearly twice as many hours assisting firms. The best programs were also more likely to develop written recommendations for community action (77 percent versus 56 percent) Here again, programs that put the most attention on individualized responses to firms and on developing broad-based solutions to local problems appear to work the best. Involving the task force in the process brings not only greater creativity but also a greater range of resources to bear in problem-solving activities.

Program Objective 4: Provide Data for Economic Development. A key objective of the program is to help local leaders develop a picture of the needs and condition of the local economy and enable them to formulate better strategic plans for community development. The information used in their planning comes from responses to the survey administered by the volunteer visitors, and is supplemented with industrial outlooks pertinent to the local economy supplied by the state sponsor.

Coordinators reported that this was the second most successful objective (table 8.3). Some measure of success on this objective is not difficult to achieve because the process of getting volunteers to conduct a face-to-face business survey assures provision of current data on local economic climate. To be truly useful to the community, however, the data must be used to assess the community and develop action plans.

Coordinators ranking the program high on this objective averaged twenty-one *fewer* total hours on the program than did other coordinators, and an average of fourteen hours less time examining the data and developing recommendations for strategic plans. Qualitative differences in state sponsors' presentation of the data to communities after processing is a potential explanation for this finding.[9] Coordinators ranking the program below the median were less likely to have written a report than other coordinators (79 percent versus 92 percent).

Firm Responses

On all four objectives, firms ranking the program above the median averaged a smaller number of employees than those with a lower appreciation of the program. Firms ranking the program above the median on the "help firms solve local problems" objective had also been in business an average of twenty years less than the other group, while for the other three objectives, the average starting year was roughly equal between those that ranked the program above and below the median. The program evidently works best for small, young firms because these firms are more likely to have the most limited management resources to solve their problems.

Summary and Conclusions

The evidence presented in this chapter has clearly demonstrated that a business retention and expansion program can be an effective economic development tool if local coordinators put their time and volunteer resources to appropriate uses. The survey results show that:

1. Carefully developed training programs involving larger numbers of volunteer visitors lead to better immediate and long-term result.
2. Coordinators that spend more time on immediate follow-up to individual firm problems are more likely to have programs that work.

3. The most effective programs get local leaders actively involved on the task force both in working on firms' immediate concerns and in developing final recommendations.
4. Coordinators that spend less time on developing recommendations have programs that work better—this may be related to the level of assistance provided by state sponsors in analyzing results and report writing.
5. Firms that reported that the program worked to solve local problems tend to be smaller and younger than other firms.

Through training, orientation, and provision of technical support, state sponsors of business retention and expansion programs can have considerable influence over how local programs are run, although local people have ultimate control over how they structure their programs. Hopefully publication and dissemination of these results will convince state and local program leaders to alter their programs, thereby increasing their probability of success.

As state and local leaders strive for improved economic growth in their communities, they should consider that a successful business retention and expansion program can be effective not only in achieving growth and stability of existing businesses, but also as a springboard for other economic development programs such as industrial attraction or business formation. The data collected by the community in the course of a business retention and expansion program can easily be repackaged into information for businesses considering locating in the area. Communities are often dropped from businesses' prospective site lists because of a lack of data (Phillips 1991). Such an information package can emphasize local strengths and community plans for dealing with weaknesses. More importantly, the improved communications between business, education, and local government resulting from an effective VVR&E program are likely to translate into a positive feeling about the area in the business community. This positive feeling is likely to be communicated either directly or indirectly to prospective businesses visiting the area. Attitudes of existing businesses about the local business climate can be an important factor in the final stages of site selection (Phillips 1991).

Improving prospects for existing businesses by linking them with state programs and solving local problems should increase the rate of new businesses formation for several reasons. First, growing businesses are more likely to generate spinoffs and create new input markets than are declining businesses. Second, an area with a reputation for successful businesses will likely be able to attract capital more cheaply and easily than an area with an unstable economy. This will reduce the financial and non-financial costs of obtaining start-up capital, thereby increasing the odds of successful business formation. Third, an area with a sound local economic base will be better able to finance adequate training for the local labor force, increasing the probability of successful new start-ups.

The premise that a good business climate affects the potential for business attraction and formation is consistent with the "growth promotes growth" or hysteresis phenomenon described by Bartik (1991). Putting existing businesses first makes good sense not only because the probability of success is likely higher than with other economic development methods, but also because it can improve the odds of success if communities choose to expand their economic development efforts to other methods.

NOTES

1. Of the eighty-one communities surveyed as part of this research, only two have populations of more than 30,000, and both of them are suburban counties rather than urban cities.

2. Morse (1990: 3–12) suggests several other goals, but the major focus of most programs relates to efficiency.

3. Some state sponsors provide suggested plans and recommendations as part of their report to the task force. In these instances, the task force selects, modifies, and/or supplements the suggestions.

4. For a discussion of response validity and informant estimates, see Deaux and Callaghan (1985: 365–68).

5. Roughly twenty states sponsored VVR&E programs at the time of the survey. All of them were invited to collaborate in the evaluation research. State program leaders in Indiana, Minnesota, Nebraska, North Dakota, Ohio, and Wisconsin chose to participate.

6. Seventeen coordinators did not respond to this question.

7. The local coordinators served as volunteers or had this task added to their regular job assignment. Consequently there is little reason for them to inflate their ratings as might be the case if their employment depended on performance. Another safeguard against coordinator bias was that results were not reported by individual communities. The variability in evaluations between objectives suggests that coordinators responded frankly.

8. Forty-one Ohio VVR&E programs were conducted between 1986 and February 1989. Twenty-eight of the communities had completed the program by the summer of 1988, and were believed to have had sufficient time to act upon community-wide action plans made as part of the program. Out of the twenty-eight communities targeted to be surveyed, eleven permitted Ohio State University to mail a survey to VVR&E

program task force members and firms. The eleven communities constituted a population of 734 participants from which a random sample of 310
participants, stratified by firm size, was drawn. The survey was fielded in
the summer of 1989. The aggregate response rate was 47.4 percent, or 147
usable questionnaires returned. Sixty-six percent of the responses were
from firm managers or owners, and 34 percent from task force members.
Of the ninety-seven questionnaires returned by firms, seventy-seven
could be linked to the firms' responses to visitors' questions during the
VVR&E program. The original identification codes were missing or
unavailable for the remaining twenty firms. It is the information from the
seventy-seven matched firms that is discussed in this document.

9. Some states gave communities only a computer-generated print-
out with little or no explanatory text, while other states provided a draft
final report that the coordinator and task force could modify before
presentation to the community. States following the former strategy shift
much of the burden of making sense of the raw data to the task force
and/or local coordinator. Since these groups usually have little or no
experience in working with the type of data supplied, development of
recommendations under these circumstances is likely to be time-con-
suming and frustrating.

REFERENCES

Bartik, Timothy J. 1991. *Who Benefits from State and Local Economic Development
    Policies?* Kalamazoo, MI: The W.E. Upjohn Institute for Employment
    Research.
Birch, David L. 1979. *The Job Generation Process.* Research report prepared for
    the Economic Development Administration, U.S. Dept. of Commerce.
    Cambridge, MA: Massachusetts Institute of Technology Program on
    Neighborhood and Regional Change.
Birch, David L. 1987. *Job Creation in America: How Our Smallest Companies Put
    the Most People to Work.* New York: The Free Press.
Bozeman, B., and J. Boseman. 1987. "Manufacturing Firm's Views of
    Government Activity and Commitment to Site: Implications for Busi-
    ness Retention Policy," *Policy Studies Review* 6: 538–53.
Deaux, Edward, and John W. Callaghan. 1985. "Key Informant Versus
    Self-report Estimates of Health-risk Behavior." *Evaluation Review* 9(3):
    365–68.
Finsterbusch, Kurt, Cecelia Formichella, Daniel Kuennen, and Meredith S.
    Ramsay. 1992. "Evaluation of a Wide Range of Job-Generating Activi-
    ties for Rural Counties," *Journal of the Community Development Society*
    23(1): 103–21.
Humphrey, Craig R., Rodney A. Erickson, and Edward J. Ottensmeyer.
    1988. "Industrial Development Groups, Organizational Resources, and
    the Prospects for Effecting Growth in Local Economies." *Growth and
    Change* 19(3): 1–21.

Loveridge, Scott, Thomas R. Smith, and George W. Morse. 1991. "What Does it Take to Run a Local Business Retention and Expansion Program? A Six State Survey," *Economic Development Review*, 9(1): 12–15.

Miller, J. 1990. "Business Retention and Expansion in the Great Lake States, 1976–1980." In G. Morse, ed., *The Retention and Expansion of Existing Businesses: Theory and Practice in Business Visitation Programs*, pp. 17–31. Ames, IA: Iowa State University Press.

Morse, George. 1990. "A Conceptual Model of Retention and Expansion Visitation Programs." In G. Morse, ed., *The Retention and Expansion of Existing Businesses: Theory and Practice in Business Visitation Programs*, pp. 3–12, Ames, IA: Iowa State University Press.

Otto, Daniel, George Morse, and Ellen Hagey. 1990. State Educational/ Technical Assistance Programs. In G. Morse, ed., *The Retention and Expansion of Existing Businesses: Theory and Practice in Business Visitation Programs*, pp. 35–43. Ames, IA: Iowa State University Press.

Phillips, Phillip D. 1991. Site Selection: Corporate Perspective and Community Response." *Economic Development Review* (Spring): 4–11.

Phillips, Phillip D., Greg Nieman, Ray Rakers, Jerry W. Robinson Jr., and Anne Heinze Silvis. 1993. *Retaining and Expanding Local Business and Industry*, Cooperative Extension Service, University of Illinois at Urbana-Champaign. 80 pages plus appendices.

CHAPTER 9

Technical Assistance Services and Rural Business Startups: A Four-State Study

TERRY F. BUSS AND MARK G. POPOVICH[1]

New business development and entrepreneurship is being promoted as an important element of a comprehensive rural revitalization strategy (Coffey and Polese 1985; Prestwich 1988; Popovich 1988). Many communities and states see it as an alternative, or at least a complement, to the more traditional practice of recruiting large corporations and branch plants through the use of tax abatements and other inducements (Popovich, 1988; Hobbs, 1987). Rural areas are developing public and private programs to help new business owners start up and succeed. These include small business development centers, entrepreneurship training, business incubators, small business advocates, economic development corporations, self-help groups, and technical assistance from extension agents, community colleges and universities, Private Industry Councils, business organizations, and private sector providers (General Accounting Office 1989; Frederick 1988; Boyle 1987). If programs associated with financial management and capital formation are included, even more sources of assistance are available.

Evaluation research has lagged behind the proliferation of programs for rural business development (Eisinger 1988). The central question is: Is technical assistance important in stimulating rural business development? Related and relevant questions include: Who uses technical assistance? Do new business owners who use these services differ from those who do not? What kinds of services are most in demand? Who are the most effective providers of technical assistance? (Corporation for Enterprise Development, 1993).

This chapter provides preliminary insights into what kinds of technical assistance services—not including financial management or raising capital—work for new business owners in rural economies. Results are important to not only those starting new businesses but also investors, potential employees, business service providers, and public policymakers concerned with rural development. Interviews with over 1,100 owners of new businesses started in rural areas of Arkansas, Maine, Michigan, and North Dakota are the basis for the study that we focus on in this chapter.

Hypotheses

The impact and value of technical assistance services to new rural business owners has not been extensively studied. Literature reviews conducted by numerous researchers suggest that most of what is known comes from program descriptions, case studies, anecdotes, or extrapolation from studies of urban areas (e.g., Frederick and Long 1989). For example, Zupnick and Katz (1981) describe several rural new enterprise development programs offering technical assistance. Hoy (1983), after undertaking a case study of Texas entrepreneurs, helped develop a pilot program for rural development by the Texas Agricultural Extension Service. Schwartz (1985) built technical assistance into a state economic development strategy, based on interviews with public officials and business people in Iowa. And Thompson (1965) developed a model of regional science extrapolating rural economic shortcomings from urban ones. But even this knowledge is sparse.

Although little social science or policy research studies exist for rural areas, at least to our knowledge, it is possible to develop some hypotheses based upon the general literature on entrepreneurship. It seems reasonable to assume that services are more likely to be consumed when new rural business owners and/or their businesses are at risk of failure or likely to experience severe problems (see Buss, Popovich, and Gemmel, 1991, for a detailed review of the literature). The characteristics examined below offer a place to begin exploring the relationship between technical assistance and entrepreneurship.

Characteristics of New Rural Business Owners

In order to consume services, a new business owner must know about the service, perceive a need for the service, feel comfortable asking for help, and lack alternative sources for obtaining help. Those who would consume services under these conditions would be educated, higher income, majority populations, and older people. Those experiencing trouble or expecting trouble in their business also may seek assistance, including those who have no business experience, are working long hours during a week, rely on the business as their sole source of income, encounter startup problems, could not work full time on startup, started business for negative reasons, are outsiders (born outside the county), or are displaced workers.

New Rural Business Characteristics

Some new rural businesses might have a greater need for these services. These might include businesses that are larger, started from scratch, involved in the takeover of failed firms, experiencing rapid growth, newer startups, employing larger capital commitments, relying on bank loans, expanding to regional markets, operated outside the home, and operated on a seasonal basis.

Methodology. This study is part of a larger study of rural entrepreneurship and new businesses in rural areas of five states. Iowa was not included in this study. A detailed discussion of the methodology for each state and the entire project has been reported elsewhere (Popovich 1988).

The study consisted of over 1,100 telephone interviews with a random sample of the owners of new businesses started in the 1980s that were in operation at the time of the interview. Sample sizes and years covered by this study for each state are: Arkansas (n = 300; 1/80 to 12/87), Maine (n = 310; 1/82 to 9/88), Michigan (n = 203; 1/82 to 12/88), and North Dakota (n = 315, 1/80 to 7/88). Analysis of variance showed that there were no major differences in findings across states.

Technical assistance was measured by asking new rural business owners if they had participated in any university, public, or private program offering workshops in starting a business, specialized business training, help in preparing a business plan, help in preparing a marketing plan, training for employees, or help in finding workers.[2] These items were scored "1" if they received assistance and "0" if they did not. The items were added to yield an *index* of technical assistance usage. A score of "0" indicates that no technical assistance services were used. A score of "6" indicates that all six service types were used.

Findings

Who Uses Technical Assistance?

In the rural areas analyzed, the characteristics of owners and their new businesses were not associated with the consumption of technical assistance services (see table 9.1). Stated differently, knowing the characteristics of either owners or their businesses did not help predict who is likely to use technical assistance.

In all, twenty-four correlations (Kendall's tau)[3] were included in the analysis. Only four correlations proved to be statistically signif-

Table 9.1: Correlates of Technical Assistance

	Kendall's Tau	Statistical significance
Characteristics of Firm		
Failing	.03	.180
Growth	.06	.007
Age of Firm	.02	.157
Start up Capital	.01	.347
Bank Loan	.04	.084
Local Market	.03	.095
Size of Firm	.05	.008
Started from Scratch	−.03	.167
Operated in Home	−.03	.149
Seasonal Business	−.03	.126
Characteristics of Entrepreneur		
Marital Status	.01	.395
Born in County	−.02	.203
Education	.13	.001
Poverty Status	−.03	.083
Sex	−.04	.064
Prior Business Experience	.02	.201
Hours per Week Worked	.02	.178
Percent Business Contributes to Income	−.04	.095
Race	.00	.319
Had Problems at Startup	.03	.065
Worked Full Time at Startup	.00	.444
Displaced Worker	−.02	.167
Age	−.08	.001
Started for Negative Reason	−.01	.279

Table 9.2: Technical Assistance Sought

Type of Assistance:	Percentage of Those Seeking Assistance
Workshop in starting a business	11.4%
Specialized training in business	18.3
Help in preparing a business plan	10.1
Help in preparing a marketing plan	7.5
Training employees	6.8
Help in finding workers	11.1

Note: percentages are not cumulative; some respondents participated in more than one program.

icant—firm growth, size of the firm, and the education level and age of the owner. Although these correlations were significant, they were so weak—.13 or smaller—as to be meaningless for policy purposes.

What Kinds of Services Are Most in Demand?

Thirty-six percent of those surveyed used some form of technical assistance. Of those using services, 19 percent used only one, but 11 percent used two and 7 percent used three services. For about one-tenth of those seeking some assistance, all six forms of technical assistance were used (see services listed in table 9.2).

A wide variety of technical assistance services were consumed. The most common service sought was specialized training related to the owner's business. This training was dominated by workshops, seminars, or courses—usually offered at a community college. Much of the training included topics in small business management and license credentialing (e.g., real estate).

Services in three areas are available in most communities, including starting a business, developing a business plan, and preparing a marketing plan. These were used by some of those surveyed, as were work force training and assistance in obtaining workers.

In Arkansas and Maine, technical assistance providers mentioned by entrepreneurs were classified as public or private. Surprisingly, one-half of the services were provided by the public sector. For example, suppliers helped some entrepreneurs get started so that they would be able to sell their products. In other cases, accountants and attorneys offered services.

Why Were Technical Assistance Services Not Used?

Sixty-four percent of those studied did not use technical assistance services—although most services were available to the busi-

Table 9.3: Why Technical Assistance Was Not Used

Reason	Percentage of all respondents having a problem
Not available locally	9.3%
Did not need	46.3
Unaware of program	25.2
Did not believe programs would be helpful	5.6
Objected to government interference	4.1
Heard bad things about program	2.0
Wrong kinds of program offered	2.4
Bad previous experience	0.1
Did not have time	8.5

Note: percentages are not cumulative. Some respondents offered more than one reason for not consuming technical assistance.

Table 9.4: Evaluation of Services Used (percent)

Opinion:	Strongly Agree	Agree	Disagree	Strongly Disagree	Missing
Program essential	16.5%	29.7%	29.2%	6.7%	18.0%
Would use again	15.2	45.4	17.0	3.2	19.2
Would recommend to others	21.2	47.4	10.5	2.2	18.7

nesses surveyed. Almost half (46 percent) of those not using services reported that they did not need the assistance offered. About one-third (35 percent) were either unaware of services available locally (25 percent) or claimed that services were not available locally (9 percent). An inventory of local services conducted as part of the project suggested that these claims were generally false. Negative perceptions of the quality or usefulness of the services offered were rare (see table 9.3).

What Kinds of Services Are Most Effective?

Technical assistance services were highly valued by participants. The overwhelming majority of those who used services considered them essential in their startup (46.2 percent) and/or would use them again (60.6 percent). They also would recommend them (68.6 percent) to others (see table 9.4). About one-fifth reported no opinion, leaving only a small minority who were dissatisfied.

Variables measuring the value of technical assistance to entrepreneurs—assistance was essential, would be useful in the future, and would be recommended to others—were correlated (using Kendall's tau) with all independent variables reflecting characteristics of the firm and the entrepreneur.[4] The three measures of value were highly correlated, suggesting that entrepreneurs were either entirely satisfied or dissatisfied with technical assistance received. As was the case in table 9.1, about one-third of the correlations (21 of 72) were statistically significant and among these, coefficients were quite low—not exceeding .13. Although low in magnitude, correlations were consistent with hypotheses: those who valued assistance most were likely to be poor, educated, larger employers, experiencing problems in starting up, older, and recipients of bank loans.

Policy Implications

The idea that technical assistance services of many kinds can play a role in facilitating the startup and success of rural businesses seems to pass the market test. Substantial numbers of new rural business owners consume services, and most highly value the services received. More importantly, entrepreneurs not only consumed public services that were provided gratis but also paid private venders for assistance. We conclude that technical assistance services should be viewed as an important component of a rural economic development strategy.

Technical assistance services have a good reputation among those who have accessed them. Nevertheless, there are some disgruntled participants—enough to cause problems for some programs. Business owners may be as much at fault as the service providers, however. Some have unrealistic expectations about their business and about the impact these services can have. Either too much or the wrong things are expected. Service providers should do everything possible to ensure that their customers have more realistic ideas about the nature, role, and potential impact of these services.

There are also concerns over whether disadvantaged groups—particularly the poor, minorities, or women—are receiving technical assistance services that will facilitate their efforts to develop new rural businesses. Our data, which include only those who successfully developed new businesses, suggested that these disadvantaged groups do access services at about the same rate as the population as a whole. However, the real concern is low rates of new rural business formation and/or success by some groups. For example, while women were represented among the new rural businesses in about the same proportion as in the general population, the poor and minority groups were not. One means of assisting these groups to become more economically successful would be to support and encourage entrepreneurial inclinations (e.g., O'Neil 1988). Technical assistance could play a role in this.

Not all entrepreneurs who need technical assistance obtain it. Significant numbers do not know about these services, or do not know that they are available locally. This suggests that efforts to broadly disseminate information, including case examples, could spur additional owners to seek services. Service providers should review their marketing strategies to make sure that more of those who could use assistance are aware of the technical assistance services available.

Many provider organizations, however, appear to have a limited ability to meet increased demand for services. Since public information efforts may increase demand, policymakers must consider whether additional resources should be allocated to build the institutional capacities of providers to meet demand.

Three important caveats regarding our study should be noted. First, we were unable to incorporate experimental design methodology into our study; that is, entrepreneurs were not randomly assigned to one group receiving and another not receiving technical assistance in order to determine the effectiveness of local programs. In other words, we cannot determine whether service consumers would have succeeded in business without assistance. But we do know that those who received services appeared to value them highly. And many were willing to spend not only their valuable time but also their money.

Second, because the study dealt only with new successful firms, we have no data on the long-term benefits of receiving technical assistance. We do know that new successful firms account for at least 20 percent of all jobs in the labor force in the four states under study and that the age of the new firm—from birth to a high of 5 years—was not correlated either with use of technical assistance or with its value. It appears, then, that technical assistance is likely appropriate for all firms, not just new ones.

Third, the study did not address two important groups: those who failed in business and those who did not get very far in starting up. These groups have been important targets of public policy and programs, the former in retention strategies and the latter in prospective entrepreneur activities (e.g., "entrepreneurial prospecting") (Bernier and McKemey 1987). These groups should be the focus of future studies.

NOTES

1. The authors would like to thank Barbara Henrie of the Northwest Area Foundation, Susan Sechler of the Rural Economic Development Program of the Aspen Institute and the Ford Foundation, Richard Hage of the U.S. Economic Development Administration, and Barbara Dyer of the Council of State Planning Agencies for their financial support and encouragement. Special thanks are extended to Dick Gross and Governor George Sinner of North Dakota, Steve Adams and Richard Silkman of the Governor's Office in Maine, Bob Nash and Governor Bill Clinton of Arkansas, and Richard Anderson, Ken Voytek, and Hal Wolman in Michigan.

2. Our study did not include issues of business finance or management under technical assistance. The complexity of these issues was beyond the scope of this chapter. A paper analyzing the sources and amounts of capital obtained is in preparation by the authors. In addition, the authors have completed a major study of entrepreneurial finance and technical assistance in Montana and Idaho in cooperation with the Corporation for Enterprise Development of Washington, D.C. (see Buss 1994; Corporation for Enterprise Development 1993).

3. Kendall's tau is an ordinal measure whose coefficient ranges in value from $+1.0$ to -1.0. It can be interpreted in the same way as Pearson's correlation coefficient.

4. Because the results of this analysis were not significant for policy purposes, and in order to save space, tabular data was not reported here but is available from the authors.

REFERENCES

Boyle, M. Ross. 1987. *Developing Strategies for Economic Stability and Growth.* Washington, DC: Council for Urban Economic Development.

Buss, Terry F. 1994. "Technical Assistance to Business in Small Western Cities." *Economic Development Commentary* 18: 25−28.

Buss, Terry F., Popovich, Mark G., and Gemmel, David. 1991. "Problems in Starting New Businesses in Rural America: A Four State Study." *Government and Policy* 9: 371−81.

Bernier, Robert E., and McKemey, Dale R. 1987. "Entrepreneurial Excavating." Paper presented at the National Rural Entrepreneurship Symposium, Knoxville, Tennessee, February 10−12.

Coffey, W. J., and Polese, M. 1985. "Local Development: Conceptual Bases and Policy Implications." *Regional Studies* 19: 85−93.

Corporation for Enterprise Development. 1993. *Entrepreneurial Action Handbook.* Washington, DC: CFED.

Eisinger, Peter. 1988. *The Rise of the Entrepreneurial State.* Madison, WI: University of Wisconsin Press.

Frederick, Martha. 1988. "Directions in Rural Entrepreneurship." Paper presented at the Annual Meeting of the Southern Regional Science Association, Morgantown, West Virginia, April 14 – 16.

Frederick, Martha, and Long, Celeste A. 1989. *Entrepreneurship Theories and Their Use in Rural Development: An Annotated Bibliography.* Agriculture and Rural Economy Division, Economic Research Service, U.S. Department of Agriculture.

General Accounting Office (GAO). 1989. *Rural Development: Federal Programs that Focus on Rural America and Its Economic Development.* Washington, DC: GAO.

Hobbs, Daryl. 1987. "Enterprise Development: Is It a Viable Goal for Rural Communities?" Paper presented at the National Rural Entrepreneurship Symposium, Knoxville, Tennessee. February 10 – 12.

Hoy, Frank. 1983. "A Program for Rural Development from Inception through Implementation." *Journal of Community Development.* 14: 33 – 48.

O'Neil, Hugh. 1988. *Creating Opportunity.* Washington, DC: Council of State Policy and Planning Advisors.

Popovich, Mark. 1988. *New Business, Entrepreneurship, and Rural Development: Building a State Strategy.* Washington, DC: National Governors' Association.

Prestwich, Roger. 1988. "A Guide to Studies and Programs Relevant to Small Business Development and Rural Revitalization." Spring Hill, MN: Regional Issues Forum.

Schwartz, Gail. 1985. *Rebuilding Iowa's Economy.* Legislative Study Committee on Economic Development, State of Iowa, July.

Thompson, Wilbur. 1965. *Preface to Urban Economic Development.* Baltimore: Johns Hopkins University Press.

Zupnick, Jan, and Katz, Stacy. 1981. "Profiles in New Enterprise and Economic Development." In Robert Friedman and William Schweke, eds., *Expanding the Opportunity to Produce.* Washington, DC: Corporation for Enterprise Development.

CHAPTER 10

The Importance of Local Airports to Rural Businesses

RICHARD J. REEDER AND CORY WANEK[1]

Introduction

Today's increasingly global and high-tech economy is placing new demands on transportation systems in rural America. These demands call for more efficient intermodal systems, with the local airport serving as a key transportation link for many rural businesses. Airport improvements, rather than new airports, may be required if rural communities are to make the most of their economic potential, but not all rural communities can make effective use of such improvements. This chapter summarizes recent research on this topic and supplements this with insights gained from interviews of selected economic development experts in rural Wisconsin. The findings should assist federal, state, and local policymakers in assessing the potential economic development consequences of upgrading rural airports.

Much of the literature on airports and airlines over the last ten years has been concerned with deregulation and its effect on airline passenger and freight service. (Recent research that addresses this problem in rural or small communities includes Due et al. 1990; U.S. General Accounting Office 1990; Forkenbrock et al. 1990; and Stommes 1989.) The recession and slow growth during the early 1990s, however, has directed more attention to airport construction and improvements as a form of infrastructure investment to stimulate the economy in the short run and to promote the growth of globally competitive industries in the long run.

Of particular interest is the growth of high-tech businesses that produce high-value, lightweight products and "just in time" components that require timely air transport. These firms have grown rapidly in recent years, providing the kind of quality, high-wage jobs that are fast disappearing in other industries. In an attempt to attract and stimulate the growth of such air-dependent businesses, several states have begun building specialized air-cargo airports with industrial parks (Pearl 1992). Some of these, such as the Global Transpark project in North Carolina, could have a major long-term development impact on rural areas. Other ambitious projects, such as the construction of passenger "way ports" that would serve as hubs to facilitate passenger air travel, might also significantly benefit rural economies (Corporation for Enterprise Development 1990). The greatest benefit, however, might come from the improvement of many of the smaller, existing local airports that currently serve rural areas and might further the growth of high-tech development in rural America.

Economic development officials in rural America are particularly interested in this topic because of the difficult restructuring that the rural economy experienced during the 1980s, when many of the traditional rural industries, such as farming, mining, and low-tech manufacturing, experienced slow growth or decline due in large part to increased competition in the global economy. This has caused rural development experts to emphasize the need to diversify rural economies. Fast growing, high-wage, high-tech firms rank high on the list of firms rural development officials want to attract. Many people believe good air transportation is essential for thriving high-tech firms.

The importance of airports to rural businesses is also a topic of concern for transportation officials. The Intermodal Surface Transportation Efficiency Act of 1991 (ISTEA) "encourages States to link economic development and [the] evolving global economy with business logistics improvements" (Hansen 1992). Airports, one of the key intermodal links in the global economy, are being emphasized in this program.[2] ISTEA also requires that states begin "a continuous statewide multi-modal transportation planning process which takes into account international border crossings and access to ports, airports, national parks, recreation and scenic areas, monuments and historic sites, recreation travel and tourism land use, and economic development" (Hansen 1992). When considering proposals to fund airport projects in rural areas, states will have to take into account the economic development implications for rural businesses. Hence, there is a need for information on how airports affect rural businesses, what aspects of airports are important, and what firms or places will benefit most from airport development.

This chapter reviews recent research on the importance of airports for businesses, with a particular emphasis on small towns and rural areas. First, we examine the literature on business location decisions; this generally consists of surveys of businesspeople about the importance of airports in their location decisions. Next we review the empirical literature identifying statistical relationships between airports and rural economic development. Because relatively few researchers have focused on the many smaller local airports serving rural areas, we conducted interviews of selected rural economic development officials in Wisconsin to help fill this void in the literature. Our findings and policy implications are summarized in the last section.

The Literature on Business Location Decisions

On first sight, the literature on the influence of airports on business location decisions presents a paradox. On the one hand, the Aviation Advisory Commission (AAC) has argued that few businesses today would consider locating where there is no airport service (Cooper 1990). This claim seems to be supported by studies showing that practically all businesses are located within an hour or two travel distance to an airport.[3] On the other hand, surveys of businesses often find that airports are among the least significant factors influencing business location decisions. Much more important in the opinion of businesspeople are availability of a skilled labor force and proximity to markets. For example, one survey of Nebraska industrial plants found air freight and air transportation ranked thirty-third and thirty-sixth in importance among forty-three factors (Shively 1974). Along similar lines, a recent survey in North Carolina found that only 2 percent of the inputs and 3 percent of the outputs of manufacturing firms were transported by air (Hartgen et al. 1991).

What are we to make of these paradoxical findings? One possible answer to this question is that most firms may find access to airports necessary, but airport access is not in itself sufficient to dictate business locations.[4] AAC's claim that airports are necessary for business location is not inconsistent with most firms ranking airport access relatively low in business location decisions, because firms may simply take as a "given" the fact that they will have access to airports. The proliferation of airports—virtually all communities in the continental United States are within thirty minutes of an airport (U.S. Department of Transportation 1987)—almost guarantees that firm location decisions are seldom decided by whether or not the location has access to an airport. Other factors, including the characteristics of the local airport, vary more from place to place, and these generally take precedence in determining which site is ultimately selected.

Another possibility is that airports may be more important to the growth of firms than to their initial site selection. For example, the Shively (1974) study that found airports were relatively unimportant for site location also found more dissatisfaction with air freight and passenger services than with any other factor (except taxes), suggesting that firms could benefit a lot from improved air service.

Another possible explanation for this paradox is that some of the more positive studies examine only those firms that are presently using airports as part of their normal business activities, while the more negative studies examine all businesses. A recent survey of firms with private planes at general aviation airports (civilian airports with private planes and no scheduled passenger or freight service) found that, in the absence of the local airport, 19 percent of these firms would relocate, 7 percent would go out of business, and 30 percent would continue operating locally but expected their sales volume to decrease 15 percent or more (Weisbrod 1990). Although this demonstrates that the airport has importance for firms currently using the airport, clearly a less dramatic impact would have been found had all firms in the area been surveyed rather than just those that used the airport.

Another study emphasizing the wide variations in how firms view airports is Barkley and McNamara's (1993) survey of 108 nonmetropolitan branch plants in Georgia and South Carolina. They found twenty-three ranked proximity to airport unimportant, thirty-six below average importance, thirty-three above average importance, and sixteen very important. Furthermore, these answers were empirically linked to the actual firm locations. Firms that said airport proximity was important were actually located, on average, only 2 miles from a metro area, implying they were close to a major airport.

Airport Use by High-Tech Firms

It is important to recognize that airports can have a significant economic impact on the local economy even if only a minority of firms use the local airports, especially if this minority of firms represents an important and growing segment of the local economy. This may be the case for those rural communities that are trying to gain or retain a link with today's global, high-tech economy.

Many surveys have found that high-tech and research and development firms use airports extensively and rank airports among the top five or six factors influencing their location (Norris and Golaszewski 1990). Air cargo transporation is a key for many high-tech industries. For example, a survey in Pennsylvania (DeAngelis et al. 1986) found that high-technology firms shipped an average of 9 percent of their products and services by air compared with only 1 percent for other firms.

Leeper et al.'s (1989) extensive study of the air cargo industry claimed that deregulation of the air cargo industry in 1977 was responsible for the dramatic improvements in air cargo service through the emergence of express air cargo services like Federal Express. According to the Leeper et al. (1989: 3–9–3–10) study:

> Service of the air cargo/express industry have been a major factor in bringing small communities and rural America into the mainstream of economic growth. New manufacturing and high technology plants, along with medical and research centers, are being attracted to low capital/production cost areas of the country, at least in part, because they are being provided regular express transportation access to every other corner of America, and most parts of the world.

Leeper et al.'s nationwide study found that in 1987 there were 72 million total U.S. air cargo shipments valued at $183 billion; about 20 percent of these shipments—worth $36 billion—came from their "all other" category (that is, not from the fifty-four major markets they examined). This "all other"category included about 2,000 counties—mostly nonmetropolitan areas. The average value per pound shipped was $32 for the U.S total and $29 for the "all other." Trends from 1983 to 1987 indicate rapid growth in the value of cargo shipments. The total number of shipments grew more rapidly in the United States as a whole (United States, 100 percent; all other, 85 percent), but, more important, the total value shipped grew more rapidly in the "all other" category (United States, 57 percent; all other, 67 percent), as did the value-per-pound shipped (United States, 7 percent; all other, 16 percent).

The more rapid growth in high-value-per-pound shipments from places outside of major markets in the mid-1980s supports the claim that recent growth in air cargo transportation has benefitted small cities or rural areas more than large and medium-sized cities, particularly in terms of stimulating high-value shipments. Leeper et al. also looked at plant location growth for the top seventy-six air freight-producing industries over 1981–1985 and found similar results. During this period, there was a 10 percent increase in air freight-producing plants in the United States, and a 13 percent increase for such plants in the "all other" category.

All of the top manufacturing industries in value of air freight shipped in 1987 produced products that rely on high-technology manufacturing. The top five, ranked by total value of shipments, were: (1) computers and computer equipment; (2) aerospace engines, parts, and vehicle equipment; (3) radio and TV communication equipment; (4) semiconductors and related devices; and (5) electronic components. The top five ranked by percentage growth of total pounds shipped from 1983 to 1987 were (1) semiconductors and related devices; (2) computers and computing equipment; (3) agricultural chemicals; (4) telephone equipment; and (5) medical/surgical appliances and supplies. All five increased their air cargo by more than 30 percent over this four-year period. These are the type of high-value, high-tech industries that many rural areas seek (Leeper et al. 1989).

Leeper et al. claimed that the emergence of "just in time" manufacturing has led to more extensive use of air cargo service. This claim was supported by a 1988 study (Lieb and Miller) that found 38 percent of the Fortune 500 manufacturers had "just in time" programs, while another 20 percent were considering such programs. Many retailers were also using "just in time." "Just in time" puts a premium on service reliability and nighttime air cargo operations to assure next day delivery (Leeper et al. 1989). This may mean that some rural airports may need to be upgraded to provide for all-weather, nighttime operations to service such companies.

Cargo transportation is not the only function airports provide to high-tech or high-wage firms. Local development officials claim that proximity to a major airport is very important for the location of company headquarters and producer services businesses (Boyle 1992a). This claim is supported by DeAngeles et al. (1986), whose survey of firms showed that high-tech firms in Pennsylvania were more likely to use air transportation for business trips than were other firms (48 percent versus 18 percent). Leistritz's (1993) in-depth study of telecommunications establishments in North Dakota found air service was important as a means for headquarters personnel and telemarketing clients to travel to business locations.

Although these studies all support the notion that air transportation is important for high-tech development in rural areas, it is important to keep in mind that high-tech industry still accounts for a relatively small percentage of total employment in rural, as well as urban, America. Phillips et al. (1991) found that only 5 percent of rural (nonmetro) jobs were in high-tech firms in 1986, and only 4 percent of rural job growth over the period 1976–1986 came from high-tech firms. High-tech industry was more important for metro areas, but it still accounted for only 9 percent of total metro employment in 1986 and 11 percent of total metro employment growth from 1976 to 1986.

Glasmeier (1991) and Phillips et al. (1991) found that nonmetro areas have been receiving less than 15 percent of the total high-tech job growth.[5] This relatively small share of total high-tech employment growth supports the conventional wisdom that few rural areas have the skilled labor force required by high-tech or high-wage industries, and that many such firms prefer to locate in or near urban areas to benefit from the agglomeration effects of close association with similar firms. If one looks at high-tech plant locations, however, rural areas have significantly surpassed metro areas in their rate of increase, suggesting that a decentralization process may be occurring in which rural areas may ultimately gain a larger share of total high-tech employment than they have now (Glasmeier 1991).[6]

Other Industries That Use Airports

For rural areas that have difficulty attracting high-tech firms, airports may still provide economic benefits, because some traditional rural industries are dependent on airports to a relatively high degree. Among these are industries that make lightweight, high-value products like leather gloves and mittens, apparel, tobacco products, and drugs; industries that make high-value machinery, such as machine shops, refrigerator and heating equipment, and farm machinery; and industries that require quick product delivery, such as newspapers and periodicals (Boyle 1992b).

Almost any kind of rural community can benefit from general aviation airports.[7] Weisbrod's (1990) survey of businesses using general aviation airports notes that these airports make important contributions to agriculture, utilities, finance, fishing, and real estate industries by providing such services as crop-dusting; transportation of staff, visitors, and clients; and aerial surveys and photographs. In addition, general aviation airports are the location of flight training services, aircraft charter services, and other aviation-related industries.[8]

Rural areas with recreational or cultural amenities might benefit most from one of the larger regional airports with regularly scheduled passenger service. Many such areas have significant potential for developing the tourism or retirement sectors of their economies. Proximity to airports can be very important for such places, especially where long-distance travel is involved. For example, the Yampa Valley Regional Airport in Colorado has been credited with reviving a depressed coal-dependent economy through conversion to a tourist-dependent ski resort economy (Cooper 1990).

Regional airports usually have direct ties to a variety of on- and off-airport firms. On-airport businesses include passenger and cargo airlines, airline suppliers, airport concessions, and government agencies. Off-airport businesses—those located nearby in the local community—include hotels, travel agencies, regional airline headquarters and ticket offices, car rental operations, and ground transportation agencies (Norris and Golaszewski 1990). Thus, without even counting businesses that use airports to transport inputs or outputs, regional airports can provide millions of dollars and hundreds of jobs to a local economy (Stommes 1989).

Empirical Studies Identifying Airport Impacts on Growth

Cooper's (1990) review of the literature on airports and economic development concluded that most studies found "that airports do contribute significantly to, or at least influence, the economic activity beyond the airport site itself." Kusmin (1994), however, reviewed several studies that found insignificant relationships. For example, Dorf and Emerson (1978) found no significant relationship between distance to regularly scheduled airline service and several measures of manufacturing business growth in nonmetropolitan areas in the West North Central region. Fox and Murray's (1990) study found no significant relationship between distance to a major airport and new business establishments in Tennessee counties.[9]

Kusmin's own empirical analysis (Kusmin et al. 1994) used multiple regression to explain nonmetro county earnings growth in the United States from 1979 to 1988. In this, one of the most comprehensive empirical studies undertaken to determine the factors associated with rural economic growth, Kusmin used eight different models (or methods) and over forty explanatory variables, plus various control variables for industry and region. He concluded that proximity to an airport with regularly scheduled passenger service was one of only nine variables that significantly contributed to county earnings growth in the majority of the models tested, including his "preferred" or final model.

The mixed findings of these studies are not particularly surprising. Airports are not the focus of the analysis in most studies attempting to explain economic development. Many such studies involve only the simplest of specification forms for airports, such as a dummy variable for the presence of a major commercial airport with regularly scheduled service or a measure of the distance to this airport. They usually ignore the presence of the smaller airports that are more common in rural areas (general aviation airports), and they often do not do a good job in measuring the characteristics of the airport.

When local airports are the focus of the analysis, including both small and large airports and the characteristics of airports, it should be easier to establish an empirical relationship between airports and economic growth. For example, Martin's (1972) assessment of airport impacts in North Carolina counties used a detailed specification of airport-related factors. Martin found that county economic growth (change in retail sales per capita from 1958 to 1970) was significantly related to his three primary airport variables: incremental airport investment, feet of paved runways, and number of aircraft based at the airport. Martin performed regression analysis separately for North Carolina's urban counties (over 50,000 population) and rural counties (under 50,000 population).[10] For urban counties, incremental airport investment was more consistently significant than feet of paved runways. For rural counties, feet of paved runways was more consistently significant.

A more recent example of the advantages of identifying airport characteristics is Rosenfeld et al. (1989), which examined nonmetro employment growth in twelve southern states over the period from 1977 to 1984. This study found that having an airport facility had no significant effect on local employment growth, but when airline service was measured as scheduled airline operations per thousand county employees, they found a noticeable expansionary effect. Goode and Hastings (1989) used a similar measure of the quality of local air service (number of airlines with scheduled stops in a community) and found that air service was a significant and positive factor in explaining whether nonmetro communities in the Northeast and Mid Atlantic region had successfully attracted a manufacturing plant over the 1970 to 1978 period.

Effects on High-Tech and High-Pay Industries

According to Norris and Golaszewski (1990), "numerous studies have indicated that the location of high-technology and research and development (R&D) firms shows a strong and positive association with the presence of airports." Whereas most of the studies they cite do not pertain specifically to nonmetro areas, two recent studies, by Porterfield (1990) and Glasmeier (1991), have found air services to be significant factors in explaining high-tech growth in nonmetro areas.

Porterfield's (1990) nationwide study focused on producer services industries; these might be viewed as including the kind of high-tech industries that require good air services. Porterfield also examined manufacturing industries, which in general are not high-tech. The quality of airport variable in Porterfield's analysis was the number of takeoffs and landings of commercial flights at the busiest airport within fifty miles of the county. Porterfield found quality of air service was associated with both manufacturing and producer service employment growth in metro counties, but it was associated only with producer services employment growth in nonmetro areas, and this was only true for remote nonmetro counties. This finding supports the notion that high-tech industries are particularly affected by air service in nonmetro areas, and implies the benefits are greatest in the more remote areas.

Glasmeier's (1991) study of metropolitan areas surrounded by rural high-tech firms found that access to good air service was the major explanatory variable determining high-tech firm plant locations, with plants concentrated near cities with large airports. Rural high-tech plant expansions were also associated with metro areas that had good air service.

Among the high-pay businesses sought by rural communities are industries with headquarters or multiple branches. Goode and Hastings (1989) disaggregated by industry when they estimated the importance of air service on a community's ability to attract manufacturing plants. They found quality of air service was positively associated with the location of nine industries and negatively associated with five other industries. Among the group of industries positively affected by airports were industries with corporate headquarters and multiple branches, suggesting that airports are particularly important for the location of these industries.

Promising Directions for Future Research

More research is needed along these lines to identify the impacts of airports on other specific industries. Not only do different industries rely on air service to different degrees (as was found by Porterfield), but also different industries probably require different types of air service. When one begins to disaggregate industrial impacts of airports in this fashion, however, one must recognize that air services are not really "independent factors" whose contribution to a local industry can be measured as a simple additive or multiplicative increment. In some cases, air service may constitute only one of a group of factors that can stimulate development only when they are all present in an industrial location. Most empirical models ignore this interdependency of development factors and hence they inaccurately measure the empirical relationships between airports and individual industries. Thus, more care is needed in the construction of empirical models that focus on particular industries. Hopefully, such research will not only provide a better assessment of the value of airports but also identify those factors that must go along with airports for industrial development policies to succeed.

Although quality air service appears to be significantly associated with economic growth, particularly with growth of high-tech-manufacturing (Glasmeier 1991) and producer services industries (Porterfield 1990), it is sometimes difficult to separate out cause and effect. While airports can generate business employment growth, local employment growth can also generate demand for airports. Thus, while the research suggests a causal effect of airports on development, more research is needed to identify the extent and nature of airports' causal effect on the growth of local businesses and vice-versa.[11]

In addition, more research is needed to enable local development officials to estimate the expected benefits of building or expanding an airport in a specific location or region as a way to guide policies for future airport construction or improvements. Two kinds of information are required. First, one must have a good idea of the amount of usage an airport will generate. This must be based on surveys of local businesses and citizens and requires a sound economic assessment of the proposed airport's viability. Second, one must be able to project local economic impacts using input-output models. Available research on this topic includes the "User's Guide" developed by the Wyoming Aeronautics Commission (1985) to assist local officials in conducting airport economic impact assessments. Dunbar's (1990) analysis of airport impacts in North Central Texas provides a good example of how local impacts (direct, indirect, and induced) can be estimated and then compared among various airports within a region.

Additional research is also needed to assess the importance of the many smaller, general aviation airports that serve rural communities. Most empirical studies focus on the availability of regularly scheduled air service at a major airport in a nearby metropolitan airport, and ignore the importance of the smaller airports located in nonmetro areas.[12] These local airports can be a significant factor to many rural businesses and deserve more attention from researchers.

Interviews on the Importance of Local Airports

To get a better understanding of how these smaller, local airports contribute to rural businesses and which factors are associated with significant airport effects, we interviewed knowledgeable development experts from six nonmetropolitan counties in Wisconsin during the summer of 1992 (figure 10.1). In some cases, we supplemented these interviews with calls to other knowledgeable local officials. The counties were not selected randomly, but we believe these counties vary enough to provide some useful insights on the importance of factors such as type of airport; local economic base; the level of income; highway access; and proximity to metro areas and to airports with regularly scheduled commercial service, which might affect the importance that rural businesses place on having a local airport.

Table 10.1 provides a brief summary of background data on these counties. Four of the counties were manufacturing-dependent (manufacturing contributed 30 percent or more of total labor and proprietor income in 1986). Several counties had tourist destinations such as ski resorts, lakes, and forests; and one was a retirement-destination county (net inmigration during the 1970s of 15 percent or more of people aged sixty or older). All but one of the counties had over half of its population located in rural areas (places other than communities with 2,500 population or more). Although all six counties shared a border with a metro area, two were remote enough that there was little commuting to the metro area, hence they were defined as "nonadjacent" for our purposes.[13] In 1987, three of the counties had incomes from $11,000 to $12,000 per capita, while the other three had somewhat higher incomes from $13,000 to $15,000 (close to the national average). Population remained almost constant in most of these counties during the 1980s, with the biggest changes being in Sauk (an 8 percent increase) and Taylor (a 5 percent increase). Three of the counties experienced close to the national average (12 percent increase) in real per capita income growth from 1979 to 1987: Taylor county's economic growth (18 percent) was well above average, while Dodge (8 percent) and Lincoln (5 percent) were well below average.

In each county, we asked local development officials how important the principal local airport was to local businesses and economic development, and why. In addition, we asked questions about the characteristics of the airport, including the availability of

instrument landing and takeoff capabilities. This is important because airports with the capacity to use Instrument Flight Rules (IFR)
provide more reliable air service in bad weather than those that rely
on Visual Flight Rules (VFR). We also asked whether airport improvements were needed or planned for the future. We summarize
our findings beginning first with the more rural and remote counties
and proceeding to the more urban and metro-adjacent counties.

Taylor County

Taylor County was the most rural of the counties we examined;
79 percent of its population was located in the rural portion of the

FIGURE 10.1: Study Areas in Wisconsin

Table 10.1: Background on Selected Nonmetro Wisconsin Counties

County	1990 Population	1980–1990 Population Change	1980 Rural Population	1987 Income Per Capita	1977–1987 Income Change Per Capita	Adjacent to Metro County[a]	Type of Economic Base[a]
Dodge	76,600	2%	55%	$13,197	8%	yes	Manufacturing
Langlade	19,500	-3	57	11,202	13	yes	Retirement
Lincoln	27,000	2	51	11,470	6	yes	Manufacturing
Sauk	47,000	8	63	13,359	12	yes	Unclassified
Taylor	18,900	5	79	11,752	18	no	Manufacturing
Wood	73,600	1	47	14,167	11	no	Manufacturing
Nonmetro Average	23,000	1%	72%	$11,822	12%	NA	NA

a. Adjacency and economic base typology developed by the U.S. Department of Agriculture, Economic Research Service (Butler 1990; Bender et al. 1985). As of 1983, 39 percent of all U.S. nonmetro counties were adjacent to metro areas; 28 percent were manufacturing-dependent; 21 percent were retirement destinations; 15 percent were unclassified. Other types of counties identified by the Economic Research Service include farming, mining, government, poverty, and federal lands counties.

Source: U.S. Department of Commerce, Bureau of the Census, and Bureau of Economic Analysis.

county, and the county was not adjacent (in a commuting sense) to any metro county. It was a relatively low-income, manufacturing-dependent county that benefitted significantly from economic development in the form of substantial increases in both population and real per capita income during the 1980s. The railroads abandoned the area, and there were no four-lane highways in the county, but there was still quite a bit of trucking. The closest airport with scheduled air service was about 70 miles away from Medford, Taylor's largest town.

A local economic development official in the county claimed the airport in Medford was very important to the local business. Corporate and commuter jets used it regularly. At the time of our interview, three relatively large companies were located in Medford; one was characterized as high-tech, and another had its headquarters in Medford. In the opinion of this local official, all three companies had grown because of the airport. Airport expansion (the addition of another runway) was viewed as necessary for further business development and this project has begun, but there has been difficulty raising funds to complete it. Converting to an instrument landing system (the airport was closed fifteen days a year because of bad weather) was one of the improvements planned over the next five years.

Sauk County

Among the six counties we examined, Sauk ranked second (just behind Taylor) in percentage of rural population and first (just ahead of Taylor) in population growth rate. Sauk's real per capita income also increased at the national average rate during the 1980s. Unlike Taylor, Sauk County had a more diverse, higher-income economy that was not particularly dependent on manufacturing. Sauk County also had the advantage of being adjacent to a metro area and had access to several major highways.

Sauk had three general aviation airports—all eligible for upgrading in the next five years—and was within forty-five minutes of an airport with regularly scheduled commercial air service. A former economic development official in the county viewed air transportation as one of many issues important in site location, but did not see it as critical for most firms in this county.

Langlade County

Langlade was a retirement destination county containing various amenities such as lakes, national forests, and a ski resort, but it was fairly distant from major population centers. It was a relatively low-income area, having fewer than 20,000 residents, with over half living in rural portions of the county. Railroad service ended ten years ago. During the 1980s, its population declined slightly, while its real per capita income increased slightly above the national average rate of increase.

A former director of economic development for Langlade County said that the county's IFR general aviation airport in Antigo had a lot of private and commuter service, and identified a firm that had expanded there because of the airport. The airport was also used a lot for emergency ambulance service. An official of the airport committee said that some firms were interested in locating in the area, but the airport runway was too short and the closest airport that met their needs was too far away—about 45 miles. One firm left the area because of this problem. Plans called for airport improvements over the next five years to provide more runway length and capacity to attract more business.

Dodge County

This manufacturing-dependent county was adjacent to the Milwaukee metro area and its per capita income was relatively high. It was the most populous (76,600) of the counties we examined, though over half of its population was rural. Its economy had suffered in the 1980s; population grew slightly and real per capita income grew slowly.

A local extension agent said the county's general aviation (VFR) airport in Juneau was very important for John Deere-Horicon Works which used "just-in-time" manufacturing in its production. Lately, the company had been complaining that it needed an all-weather service (IFR) and that airports in the southern states looked better. The airport was scheduled for improvements over the next five years, but, in the view of this official, this may not be soon enough to hold onto this high-tech business. The closest airport with regular commercial air service was about 60 miles away.

Wood County

Almost as populous as Dodge County, Wood was the least rural (47 percent rural) of the six counties, and had the highest per capita income ($14,167). Its economy was manufacturing-dependent. Located in the center of the state, it was not adjacent (in the commuting sense) to any metro area and no four-lane highways went into the main town of Marshfield. Although its population was stagnant, the county benefitted from an average increase in real per capita income during the 1980s.

A local economic development expert in Marshfield said that the town's general aviation (IFR) airport was very important in retaining and expanding local businesses. An airline (Midstate Airline) started there in the early 1980s but only lasted a few years. The airport's main contribution was to local businesses that used an industrial park near the airport. It also helped stimulate business for the local health care facility. In addition to using the Marshfield airport, local businesses had access to the county's Wisconsin Rapids airport, which had commercial air service and was located only about 35 miles away. The Marshfield airport was also scheduled for improvements over the next five years.

Lincoln County

Like Wood County, Lincoln's population was about half rural and half urban, but Lincoln had a much smaller population (27,000) and was located adjacent to a metro area. Although it was located near lakes, forests, and ski areas, its economy was manufacturing-dependent with relatively low income per capita. Its population and income were relatively stagnant during the 1980s.

A local official in Tomahawk, a small town in the center of the county on the Wisconsin River and Mohawksin Lake, did not view the county's airport (IFR general aviation) as a major selling point for the community. Most businesses used the larger airport in Rhinelander, which had commercial service and was only 20 miles away (in Oneida County), or the airport in Mosinee, which also had commercial air service and was only 22 miles away.[14] The Tomahawk airport was eligible for modest upgrading over the next five years.

Discussion

Keeping in mind that our survey was limited to only six nonmetro counties in one state (Wisconsin), our findings can be viewed as consistent with recent studies that have found local airports important for the development of rural areas, but not necessarily for all rural areas. In four of the six counties (Taylor, Langlade, Dodge, and Wood), local airports were viewed as very important contributors to the local economy. In the other two counties (Sauk and Lincoln), the local airport was viewed as less important.

Both Sauk and Lincoln were adjacent to metropolitan areas, and both had good access to alternative air and ground transportation that may have diminished the value of their counties' main local airport. In the case of Sauk, there were three general aviation airports in the county, regularly scheduled commercial air service was a reasonable 45 minutes away, and the county had access to good highways to markets. The center of Lincoln county was only twenty minutes from regularly scheduled commercial air service, which significantly reduced the importance of Lincoln's local airport.

The counties where local airports were viewed as very important to the local economy had less convenient access to alternatives, such as quality air service or highway transportation.[15] In other respects, however, they did not fall into any one single category. Three were manufacturing-dependent counties and one was a retirement-tourism destination area. One of the manufacturing-dependent counties (Dodge) was a relatively high-income county adjacent to a metropolitan area that had high-tech, just-in-time manufacturing firms. The other two manufacturing-dependent counties (Taylor and Wood) were more remote and not adjacent to any metro area. No evidence was provided to indicate that either county had concentrations in high-tech manufacturing. However, Taylor County was the location of several large firms—one with company headquarters, and Wood County had an airpark (i.e., an industrial park adjacent to the airport) that appeared to have attracted airport-intensive businesses to the area.

The degree of rurality or remoteness of the nonmetro counties we examined appeared to make little difference in the economic importance of their local airports, but it did appear to be related to the need for airport improvements and the difficulty of funding those improvements. Taylor county, the most rural county we examined, had to add another runway and switch to an IFR landing system to meet the needs of further development, but was having difficulty raising funds for these improvements. Langlade, a heavily rural county that was remote from major population areas, had an airport with runways that were too short for jet planes and was desperate for airport improvements, having already lost one firm due to this shortcoming. Dodge, another heavily rural county, had high-tech "just-in-time" manufacturing, but its airport facilities allowed only visual landing and takeoffs, and officials feared that planned improvements might not come in time to avoid the loss of some high-tech firms to places with better airport facilities. All three of these counties viewed their airports as very important to local development.

Conclusions and Implications

The conventional wisdom has been that airports may contribute to rural businesses, but they are not really decisive in rural business location decisions and will not make or break a rural community's economic well-being. This review of the literature suggests that the conventional wisdom may be in need of some revision, as it ignores important new developments with respect to the growth of high-tech industries that require improved air transportation. Recent industrial location studies show that high-tech industries rank airports among the most important location factors, and recent empirical studies have shown that these industries do in fact locate and grow fastest in rural and urban areas with access to good airports.

Not all rural areas can expect to attract or nurture the growth of high-tech industries. High-tech industries generally require things more common in urban areas, such as a highly educated and skilled labor force and a conglomeration of other high-technology businesses and research facilities. But many high-tech firms can get by in places without such characteristics, and may prefer lower-cost, higher-amenity rural locations. Recent research suggests that rural communities that want to attract or hold onto such firms will need good airports to remain competitive. This doesn't necessarily mean that new airports must be built, or that rural areas must regain regularly scheduled commercial passenger and freight service that were lost as a result of deregulation. Rather, what seems to be needed most are improvements for some general aviation airports, including lengthening their runways to accommodate jets and upgrading them to enable all-weather instrument landings and take-offs.

The importance of these general aviation airports to rural businesses of all kinds should not be underemphasized. Our interviews of selected rural Wisconsin development officials were consistent with other research suggesting that many rural communities could suffer significant economic difficulties if the activities at these airports were eliminated or reduced. The importance of these airports increases as the availability of substitute modes of transportation, such as larger airports in nearby communities or good highway and rail access to markets, declines. Many manufacturing industries, both in the high-tech and the low-tech category, use these airports for transporting staff, clients, and high-value, low-weight products. These airports also make valuable contributions to producer services, agriculture, real estate, and recreation industries.

The larger, regional nonmetro airports with regularly scheduled commercial air service appear to be particularly important to remote rural areas with substantial tourism and retiree attraction potential that target populations outside the area, state, or nation. These airports may also have the most significant local economic impacts directly related to firms based on or near the airport, such as airlines, airport hotels, and airport transportation services.

In the next few years, federal, state, and local policymakers are likely to confront two important policy issues related to rural airports. One involves funding decisions for airport construction and improvements, and the other involves how to deal with congestion at large urban airports.

Proposals for major new airports, whether they be hubs for passengers or for air cargo industrial complexes, are likely to attract much attention from the media. These projects are highly visible, and may have the potential for large payoffs, but they are for the most part unproven and may be very risky investments. Policymakers should not overlook the importance of upgrading the many smaller local airports that are struggling to maintain and encourage business development. With limited federal and state funding available, efforts should be made to identify those areas that would benefit most from airport improvements, and those places that have the greatest need for fiscal assistance. Coordination between transportation agencies that fund these projects and economic agencies that monitor and evaluate development in rural areas is important in targeting such assistance. Significant payoffs could result from investments that are targeted in an efficient and timely way so as to maintain or improve the competitiveness of rural industry in the global economy.

The other policy issue involves efforts that might be made to reduce congestion at major airports by restricting smaller aircraft from these airports. This could cut the link between the global economy and many rural communities that rely on small planes that transport goods from the local airport to major airports. Research indicates that rural economic development, and high-tech development in particular, depends on access to busy airports—that is, to airports with many airlines and regularly scheduled flights. Significant negative economic consequences could result in rural areas if a policy of restricting small plane use of large airports were adopted. Rural economic problems have a tendency of transforming into urban problems, such as when unemployed, low-skill workers migrate into cities. Thus, the adverse economic consequences of such a policy would be felt in both urban and rural America.

NOTES

1. The authors wish to thank James Peoples of the University of Wisconsin-Milwaukee and J. Norman Reid, David Sears, and Lorin Kusmin of the U.S. Department of Agriculture for their thoughtful comments.

2. Federal investments in air transportation, including construction, rehabilitation, and equipment purchases, amounted to $3.7 billion in outlays in 1992 (Office of Management and Budget, 1993). In 1985, rural (nonmetro) areas got about 16 percent of Federal airport improvement program expenditures (Dubin, 1989).

3. One survey of manufacturing firms in North Carolina found "three quarters are within 1 hr and 15 minutes" from one of North Carolina's hub airports with scheduled commercial service (Hartgen, et al. 1990). Access to general aviation airports with or without scheduled service is even more common.

4. The same may be said for the role of infrastructure in general in the rural development process: infrastructure is necessary but not sufficient for development (Sears et al. 1990).

5. Glasmeier's study covered the period from 1972 to 1982; Phillips et al. covered the period from 1976 to 1986.

6. Historically, a disproportionate share of nonmetro high-tech employment has located in places adjacent to metro areas, where about half of nonmetro area population and about 60 percent of the nonmetro high-tech employment are located. Nonadjacent places, however, captured about half of the nonmetro gain in high-tech employment during the 1970s (Glasmeier 1991). It is conceivable that these trends reversed again in the 1980s as adjacent places have grown more than nonadjacent places.

7. The exceptions are small towns that are unlikely, under any foreseeable circumstances, to have enough aircraft so that the benefits justify the costs of maintaining the airport.

8. See case studies in New York (Kulka 1985) and West Virginia (Castro 1993) for examples of the economic significance of such aviation-related industries in rural areas.

9. New establishments were defined as establishments entering into the Tennessee Department of Employment Security Master Employer and 202 Files during the years 1980 to 1986.

10. Two other variables representing "itinerant operations" of air carriers and general aviation were generally insignificant.

11. Most of the studies reviewed here, with the exception of Porterfield (1990), do not test for simultaneous causality.

12. Many federally- and state-funded studies have estimated economic impacts of local airports. For example, Michigan Department of Transportation (1989) provides impact estimates for a cross-section of thirty-two airports in the state; it also contains a good bibliography of similar studies in other

states. Whereas the Michigan study includes some small airports in rural areas, most studies focus on the larger, metropolitan-area airports.

13. We used the Beale code definition of adjacency, which requires both physical adjacency and at least 2 percent of the labor force commuting to a metro area (Butler 1990).

14. Dahl (1993) credits the Rhinelander airport with stimulating significant economic growth in the region. It is a "state of the art" facility that handles jet planes with regular service to Chicago, Milwaukee, and Minneapolis/St. Paul. An industrial park is located next to the airport. Rather than attracting high-tech firms, however, this airport has attracted other forms of high-value manufacturing firms and has facilitated tourism development to this amenity-rich area.

15. The distance to an airport with regularly scheduled commercial air service ranged from 35 to 70 miles.

REFERENCES

Barkley, D.L., and K.T. McNamara. 1993. "Industry Location Decisions: Looking Inside Location Surveys For Clues." *Issues in Community and Economic Development* 4(1): 1–4.

Bender, L.D., B.L. Green, T.F. Hady, J.A. Kuehn, M.K. Nelson, L.B. Perkinson, and P.J. Ross. 1985. *The Diverse Social and Economic Structure of Nonmetropolitan America.* Rural Development Research Report No. 49. U.S. Department of Agriculture, Economic Research Service, September.

Boyle, M.R. 1992a. *Economic and Demographic Trends Newsletter* (June): 16.

Boyle, M.R. 1992b. *Economic and Demographic Trends Newsletter* (October): 12–15.

Butler, M.A. 1990. *Rural-Urban Continuum Codes for Metro and Nonmetro Counties.* Staff Report No. 9028. U.S. Department of Agriculture, Economic Research Service, April.

Castro, J.E. 1993. "Aerospace Takeoff in West Virginia." *Appalachia* (Journal of the Appalachian Regional Commission) 26 (2: Spring): 14–20.

Cooper, R. 1990. "Airports and Economic Development: An Overview." *Transportation and Economic Development 1990.* Transportation Research Record No. 1274. National Research Council, Transportation Research Board, pp. 125–33.

Corporation for Enterprise Development. 1990. *Building Competitive Rural Communities: Lessons From Mississippi.* Washington, DC: Corporation for Enterprise Development, September.

Dahl, D.S. 1993. "Boom in the North Woods: Rhinelander, Wis." *Fedgazette* (Federal Reserve Bank of Minneapolis) 5(3, July): 12–14.

DeAngelis, J.P., A.G.R. Bullin, N.P. Hummon, and S. Manners. 1986. *Transportation Access and the Location of Advanced Technology Firms in Pennsylvania.* Final Report, Vol. I. University of Pittsburgh, Center for Social and Urban Research, June.

Dorf, R.J., and M.J. Emerson. 1978. "Determinants of Manufacturing Plant Location For Non-Metropolitan Communities in the West North Central Region of the United States." *Journal of Regional Science* 18(1): 109–20.

Dubin, E.J. 1989. *Geographic Distribution of Federal Funds in 1985.* Staff Report No. AGES89-7. U.S. Department of Agriculture, Economic Research Service, March.

Due, J.F., B.J. Allen, M.R. Kihl, and M.R. Crum. 1990. *Transportation Service to Small Rural Communities: Effects of Deregulation.* Ames, IA: Iowa State University Press.

Dunbar, J.K.P. 1990. "Economic Impacts of Aviation on North Central Texas." *Transportation and Economic Development 1990.* Transportation Research Record No. 1274. National Research Council, Transportation Research Board, pp. 223–31.

Forkenbrock, D.J., T.F. Pogue, D.J. Finnegan, and N.S.J. Foster. 1990. "Transportation Investment to Promote Economic Development." In *Infrastructure Investment and Economic Development: Rural Strategies for the 1990's.* Staff Report No. AGES 9069. U.S. Department of Agriculture, Economic Research Service, November, pp. 19–42.

Fox, W.F., and M.N. Murray. 1990. "Local Public Policies and Interregional Business Development." *Southern Economic Journal* (Fall): 413–27.

Glasmeier, A.K. 1991. *The High-Tech Potential.* New Brunswick, NJ: Center for Urban Policy Research, pp. 171–89.

Goode, F.M., and S.E. Hastings. 1989. "The Effect of Transportation Service on the Location of Manufacturing Plants in Nonmetropolitan and Small Metropolitan Communities." In W. R. Gillis, ed., *Profitability and Mobility in Rural America.* Penn State University Press, pp. 95–116.

Hansen, P. 1992. "Transportation: The Vital Link in the Rural Economy." Speech to the Rural Development Brownbag group. Washington, DC, March 18.

Hartgen, D.T, A.W. Stuart, and K.E. Sickles. 1991. "Manufacturers' Views of Transportation's Role in Site Satisfaction." *Finance, Planning, Programming, Economic Analysis, and Land Development 1991.* Transportation Research Record No. 1305. National Research Council, Transportation Research Board, pp. 313–25.

Kasarda, J.D. 1991. "Global Air Cargo-Industrial Complexes as Development Tools." *Economic Development Quarterly* 5(3): 187–96.

Kulka, F.P. 1985. "The Impact of the Genesee County Airport on Genesee County," *Transportation Research Record 1025.* The Transportation Research Board.

Kusmin, L.D. 1994. *Factors Associated with the Growth of Local and Regional Economies: A Review of the Selected Empirical Literature.* ERS Staff Report No. AGES 9405. U.S. Department of Agriculture, Economic Research Service, March.

Kusmin, L.D., J. Redman, and D. Sears. 1994. *Rural Economic Growth in the 1980's: A look at Factors Associated with Earnings Growth.* Rural Development Research Report. U.S. Department of Agriculture, Economic Research Service.

Leeper, Cambridge, and Campbell, Inc. with the Colography Group, Inc., Shannon Engineering, Inc. and Synergetic Enterprises. 1989. *The All Cargo Air Industry: Its Economic Impact and Future Needs.* Washington DC: Air Freight Association, April.

Leistritz, F.L. 1993. "Telecommunications Spur North Dakota's Rural Economy." *Rural Development Perspectives* 8(10): 7–11.

Lieb, R.C., and R.A. Miller. 1988. "JIT and Corporate Transportation Requirements." *Transportation Journal* 27(3).

Martin, J.N. 1972. "Economic Impact of Airport Investment and Use in North Carolina." *Transportation Journal* 11(3, Spring): 46–52.

Michigan Department of Transportation. 1989. *Value of Airports to Their Communities—Economic Benefits of Aviation Study.* Bureau of Transportation Planning. Lansing, Michigan, August.

Norris, B.B., and R. Golaszewski. 1990. "Economic Development Impact of Airports: A Cross-Sectional Analysis of Consumer Surplus." *Transportation and Economic Development 1990.* Transportation Research Record No. 1274. National Research Council, Transportation Research Board, pp. 82–88.

Office of Management and Budget. 1993. *The Budget of the U.S. Government: Fiscal Year 1994,* April 8.

Pearl, D. 1992. "Field of Dreams: All-Freight Airports Touted as Way to Lure Firms, Pose Big Risks." *Wall Street Journal* 120(109, December 2): A1–A2.

Phillips, B., B. Kirchoff, and H.S. Brown. 1991. "Formation, Growth, and Mobility of Technology-Based Firms in the U.S. Economy." *Entrepreneurship & Regional Development* 3: 129–44.

Porterfield, S.L. 1990. "Producer Services: A Viable Option for Rural Economic Development." Paper prepared for the Southern Regional Science Association Meetings in Washington, DC, March.

Rosenfeld, S.A., E.M. Bergman, and S. Rubin. 1989. *Making Connections: After the Factories Revisited.* Southern Growth Policies Board, February.

Sears, D.W., T.D. Rowley, and J.N. Reid. 1990. "Infrastructure Investment and Economic Development: An Overview." *Infrastructure Investment and Economic Development: Rural Strategies for the 1990's.* Staff Report AGES 9069. U.S. Dept. of Agriculture, Economic Research Service, December, pp. 1–18.

Shively, R. 1974. "Decision Making for Locating Industry." In L. Whiting, ed., *Rural Industrialization: Problems and Potentials.* Ames, IA: Iowa State University Press.

Stommes, E.S. 1989. *Reconnecting Rural America: Report on Rural Intercity Passenger Transportation.* Office of Transportation, U.S. Department of Agriculture, July.

U.S. Department of Transportation. 1987. "National Plan of Integrated Airport Systems." Federal Aviation Administration, November.

U.S. General Accounting Office. 1990. *Airline Deregulation: Trends in Airfares at Airports in Small and Medium-Sized Communities.* GAO/RCED-91-13, November.

Weisbrod, G. 1990. "Economic Impacts of Improving General Aviation Airports." *Transportation and Economic Development 1990.* Transportation Research Record No. 1274. National Research Council, Transportation Research Board, pp. 134–41.

Wyoming Aeronautics Commission. 1985. *Wyoming Airport System Plan Update 1985, Volume IV, Estimating the Economic Benefits of Airports: A User's Guide.* Cheyenne, WY.

PART IV

Targeting Special Opportunities for Development

Prisons and Rural Communities: Making the Most and Losing the Least from a Growth Industry

KATHERINE A. CARLSON[1]

Prisons as Rural Industries

In 1991, the population of America's prisons reached its sixteenth year of record highs, a growth that is expected to continue. Existing prison facilities are severely overcrowded and an unprecedented building program of new prison construction is underway or planned in a majority of states (DeWitt 1991). Prisons have been traditionally identified by the general public as undesirable industries, with their siting frequently greeted by a NIMBY ("Not in My Back Yard") response. In a practice that has fit the politics of least resistance, they have traditionally been located in rural areas (Beale 1993; Nagel 1973).

Today, the economic climate in rural America is such that this once undesirable industry has become increasingly attractive to many communities. Many states are now siting prisons by soliciting bids from interested hosts, a process that often results in more towns seeking prisons than there are prisons to site (Pagel 1988). Such places are usually suffering economic problems and decline, and for various reasons have found themselves unable to attract other industries offering comparable numbers of jobs and prospects for economic growth. Few urban areas pursue a prison.

Is getting a prison a successful rural economic development strategy? The answer in some senses is certainly yes. Prisons are a source of many jobs, a majority of which are entry-level. These jobs are part of the state or federal bureaucracy that governs them, offering competitive salaries, good benefits, and a career track. New prisons are seldom less than 500 beds, with a staff of at least 300 and an annual payroll of several million dollars.[2] The industry has minimal environmental effects and, unlike those industries it often is intended to replace, such as timber, mining, or agriculture, it seems immune to recession or declines.

In addition to the payroll, prisons can provide other direct economic benefits to their host areas. While their governmental status means they will not pay taxes, there may be return of various types of tax receipts to the local jurisdictions based on the inmate population. These institutions will pay fees for use of local services, and payments for items such as utilities, medical, and educational services may be substantial. In some areas, local criminal justice agencies will be compensated for work involving inmates. Inmates themselves may make contributions to the local economy through work on public service projects both inside and outside the facility. Finally, prisons need to make continual purchases of items such as food and office and other supplies, as well as occasional purchases of equipment and furnishings. While many institutional purchases are likely to be centralized and made elsewhere, some local contracting is possible.

The benefits of a prison are not solely economic. For communities that have lost residents because of a poor economy, new employment and economic improvements may represent a source of new residents to restore community vitality. Local institutions such as schools, medical services, and churches and other voluntary organizations can be strengthened by the replacement of population and the resultant increase in service use and participation.

All effects of a prison in a rural area will not necessarily be beneficial; prisons do have some potential negatives inherent in their operation. Inmates may escape and present risks for local residents; merely living with these risks can mean adverse changes in lifestyle and community satisfaction.[3] Inmate family members and associates may move into the area to be closer to the prison, and bring with them increased crime and social service needs. Prison employment itself has been associated with high stress, and is cited as a contributor to increased strain, substance abuse, and other problems for employees and their families.

Despite these, the most likely negatives associated with prisons have more to do with location than with the characteristics of the industry itself. Like other rural industries, a prison's benefits are often dispersed throughout an area, and can easily end up going largely to some nearby urban center rather than the host community or the immediately surrounding small towns (Summers et al. 1976). Further, new residents brought in for prison employment also may bring different values and lifestyles, and change the local character; significant population growth can contribute to these changes and produce difficulties meeting increased demands for various public services as well.

With such a mixture of potential positives and negatives, it is clear that prisons have become strategies for rural development by default rather than choice: community leaders opt for them in the absence of other viable alternatives for economic improvement. They do so within the context of probable losses as well as gains, and some assessment of the relative weight and significance of both. Residents of prospective prison host communities are frequently divided on whether deficits or benefits are likely to predominate, and, as a consequence, prison siting is still seldom met with uniform public approval.

Strategy for Rural Development

The strategy associated with using a prison for rural economic development should be twofold. First, the community must be selected as a prison site, an outcome that requires meeting site selection criteria as well as overcoming (or overwhelming) any resident opposition. Secondly, community leaders must take steps during siting and thereafter that will help to maximize benefits from the industry and minimize or neutralize its deficits. Successful rural development in the case of this industry virtually requires actions that go beyond just getting it.

It is the second step of this strategy that is the primary focus of this chapter, but since this is dependent on accomplishing the first, a few words about siting and opposition are in order. Getting a prison is more difficult than it was just a few years ago because of increased competition from other, similarly desirous communities. Successful communities are those that best meet a mixture of usually formal, weighted criteria, and also do well according to other, less predictable factors: despite real consideration of such multiple factors as identified below, siting a prison remains predominantly a political process.

Formal criteria give priority to availability of essential services such as utilities, fire and law enforcement protection, and medical care. Other priorities are housing, educational, and recreational opportunities sufficient to attract and retain both line and professional staff. Optimal access to both is likely to be more readily found in larger communities or places with proximity to these. Correctional philosophy also argues for the value of incarceration close to an inmate's origins and usual release locale, adding to the weight accorded to more urban locations. For less populous and more rural prospective prison sites, these relative shortcomings are often countered by other factors not usually present in cities. Rural areas improve their prospects for selection as prison sites by having inexpensive land, property already owned by the government, and/or buildings such as hospitals or other institutions suitable for conversion to a corrections facility. They also might offer reduced costs for services and utilities, and in some areas, lower labor costs during construction and for some contracted outside services.

The primary factor adding favor to rural locations is community support. Community support derives from the potential for benefitting economically from a prison and the belief that benefits outweigh deficits; such support may be based less on facts than on severity of local needs, unfounded optimism, and forceful personalities (Carlson 1988; 1991). In urban areas, any probable prison benefits are proportionately less significant to the local economy, but the perceptions of risk and threats to community services and lifestyle are similar to those felt by rural residents (Lidman 1988). Thus, despite the rational arguments in favor of urban prison locales, without strong perceived benefits there is little to offset a prison's presumed deficits for residents of cities, and consequently little chance to generate community support for prison siting (Abrams and Lyons 1987).

Research on Prison Impacts

Among the most consistent findings of the research on prison impacts are that prisons do indeed provide considerable economic benefits to their host communities and surrounding areas (Lidman 1988; Abrams and Lyons 1987). These in turn tend to stimulate and contribute to other positive economic consequences (Smykla et al. 1984). The significance of these benefits is a product of the size of the prison relative to its host area. Prisons generally have not been found to deter location or adversely affect operations of other industries, reduce property values, or create a predominantly negative community image for other development (Hodge and Staeheli 1988; Hawes 1985; Stanley 1978).

In some prison sites studied, criminal behavior and need for social services increased (Farrington and Parcells 1991; 1989; Callier and Versteeg 1988); in others, there appeared to be no significant adverse criminal justice or social service consequences (Hawes 1985; Abrams and Lyons 1987). Resident perceptions of such problems, however, do not always match reality, and prisons do seem to produce insecurity and unease among those living nearby (Carlson 1990a; Zarchikoff et al. 1981). For the most part, inmate family members do not move to the host community; inmates themselves seldom escape and, when they do, are unlikely to victimize local residents (Lidman 1988; Abrams et al. 1985).

The prisons included in these studies have been located in both urban and rural locales. A recently concluded multi-year examination of a new, 500-bed medium security prison in a remote, rural location provides the most detailed information about prison effects and how they can be manipulated for local benefit (Carlson 1990b). The prison is located in the unincorporated town of Clallam Bay, Washington, and was solicited by community residents to reverse a decline brought about by the loss of a major employer. A substantial minority of residents opposed the prison's siting.

During its first two years of operation, the Clallam Bay Corrections Center produced more pluses than minuses for its host community and the surrounding county. In Clallam Bay itself, business revenues and the viability of local services improved substantially, a closed supermarket re-opened, and the prison helped stabilize what had been a markedly seasonal economy. There also was some new construction of housing and businesses, and the population of the community and school enrollment increased. Elsewhere in the county, local businesses and suppliers benefitted from prison purchases and many area residents were hired for prison jobs; other county communities also benefitted from new residents and the purchases made by these and other prison employees.

Most negatives associated with the prison were limited to Clallam Bay proper. These included some unwanted lifestyle changes in the community due to newcomers with different views and values, and stresses in the school from new service demands and uneven enrollment growth. Heightened wariness and insecurity were associated with the risk of escapes (there were several during the first two years of operation), and there was an increased incidence of crimes involving interpersonal violence. Few inmate family members moved to the community or the area, but some of these were involved in criminal activity and social service abuses. Their perceived significance was much greater than their actual effects, and on the whole, the community benefitted from purchases made by transient prison visitors.

Despite the preponderance of positive over negative effects associated with the Clallam Bay prison, the beneficial effects of this prison were nonetheless less favorable than they could have been and the deficits greater (Carlson 1992). Neither the community nor the county had any general plan or organized program to gain benefits and ameliorate likely problems; rather, opportunities and difficulties were handled individually (if at all), as they arose. Clallam Bay's actions on its own behalf were limited by the presumption that the community's work was done once it was selected as a prison site. Disorganization also played a part, exacerbated by the community's unincorporated status and lack of local representative government. Indigenous action was further hindered by years of economic troubles among local businesspeople, and outside investors were put off by the physical appearance of decline and the area's remoteness, and by easier financial opportunities elsewhere.

Controlling Prison Impacts

Places vary in their capacities to maximize prison benefits and minimize prison deficits. Geography, proximity, and accessibility to other communities, and the relative size and sophistication of these communities, affect the distribution of impacts in the local area. The presence and magnitude of preexisting economic and other problems, and the skills and talents available for both local and regional development, also influence outcomes. Assessment of such local and regional capacities and planning for action needed to improve them should begin with the prison siting process. The usual environmental impact assessment is unlikely to provide the critical appraisal necessary here, and should not be relied upon as the sole guide for attempts to control impacts. Communities expecting to be affected by a prison should add their own information about things such as housing, shopping preferences, and local problems to the findings of any formal assessment as the basis for future planning.

It is especially critical that expectations of benefits and how they are distributed be realistic. Need for the facility will tend to produce an overly optimistic set of expectations for its likely returns and a rose-colored vision of the area's capacity to realize these. Officials responsible for finding a prison site are not motivated to deflate such expectations (Farrington et al. 1991; Krause 1991).

Specific examples of this prevalence of hope over reality in Clallam Bay and elsewhere often begin with prison jobs and who gets them. The prospects for hiring local residents must be measured against hiring practices that typically include competitive application, limited applicable skills and experience among existing residents, and the likelihood that those needing prison jobs at the time of siting would be unable to wait for employment until a facility was opened. Failing to consider these factors in Clallam Bay produced disappointment and anger when there were few community residents included among initial hires. It also made it difficult for the institution to fill many positions requiring specialized skills.

With the same unwarranted optimism, Clallam Bay was expected to gain new residents who would purchase the town's existing vacant houses. More careful consideration would have shown needs for different housing than was available: newcomers wanted affordable housing in good condition and most preferred to rent rather than purchase. Again, there was consequent disappointment and resentment when employees opted to live elsewhere, and frustration when Clallam Bay's actual housing shortage left them with no alternative.

The targets of rural economic development are likely to include both the area as a whole (e.g., the county or a multi-county region) and the specific host community. Clallam Bay's losses typically became gains for surrounding communities, and most prison benefits remained in the county if not in the host community. There was no such broad distribution of negatives, however, and these concentrated in Clallam Bay itself. In effect, the major drawbacks of having a prison are disproportionately and inevitably localized in the immediate vicinity of the institution (Abrams and Lyons 1987). Where available, prison benefits provide compensation for these, and make them worthwhile. The fairest distribution of prison impacts would take into account the relatively greater losses that will likely be borne by the immediate host. This may best occur with county or regional policies that explicitly favor the host community and its residents over other local communities in regard to location of and enrollment in employment training, siting of new services, and other practices likely to enhance prison benefits.

Maximizing Benefits

The benefits sought from a prison are primarily economic ones, but there are usually several routes through which these can be acquired. The contribution made by prison jobs, for example, may come through local hiring and the direct employment of unemployed area residents. Prison jobs can result as well in an influx of new residents moving to the area to work at the prison or to take other employment in the revitalized local economy. Other economic contributions to the community can come from direct prison purchases and service use. Creating good opportunities for realizing each of these is likely to require a different approach.

Local Hiring

Some communities have negotiated preferential hiring agreements favoring qualified local residents for prison jobs. In one small town where the prison was located in a remodeled mental institution, former institutional employees were given priority for the new jobs (Millay 1991). Another approach to facilitate local hiring is to provide area residents with the capacity to be more competitive for prison employment, an activity that ideally begins while the facility is still under construction. Penal institutions employ many individuals in clerical and other support positions as well as corrections officers. Local educational and training programs should incorporate requirements for these positions into their offerings, or begin new programs more specifically targeted to prison employment. In Clallam Bay, an arrangement between the prison, the local community college, and the area's Job Training Center offers preemployment training to become a corrections officer to unemployed area residents, with class completion a definite advantage for subsequent prison hiring.

Meeting the Needs of Employees and Other Residents

Attracting new residents and their investments and purchases is likely to require some investment from the community as well. Housing, shopping, recreational activities, and services may need some expansion, upgrading, or other improvements to appeal to newcomers. Unfortunately, communities that seek prisons typically are in poor economic condition, and their residents seldom are in a financial position to invest in local capacities (Shichor 1992). Outside investment will be needed, and with a recent history of economic decline, may be hard to attract. Alternatives are low-cost loans or grants, and technical assistance to take advantage of these. With the advice of some outside experts, Clallam Bay combined federal, state, and county funds to pay for a new library building, a day care center, and other improvements. Repeated efforts to attract private investment for housing were largely unsuccessful, but a public/private alliance, again with external assistance, resulted in construction of new rental housing.

Keeping prison benefits at home is a hollow victory when newcomers so dislike the community that they quit their jobs, seek early transfers elsewhere, or maintain their permanent residences and families outside of the area (Zarchikoff et al. 1981). The resultant transiency is hard on both the local community and the institution, which must constantly find and train new employees. Efforts to enhance benefits should include ways of gaining or improving resident satisfaction. In addition to structural and service improvements, communities may need to market their life-style attributes through deliberate outreach programs, a newsletter or informational pamphlet on local offerings, and joint community/prison events.

Where prison siting was disputed, there needs to be attention directed to reuniting the community. The animosity generated in these situations tends to persist, and colors attitudes toward the institution and its contributions (Abrams and Lyons 1987). Deliberate outreach efforts by prison administrators can be helpful, especially with residents who retain a commitment to the community (Hodge and Staeheli 1988). As a small community's dominant employer, a prison needs to take on the roles of local philanthropist and community booster that have been typical of private industry. Prisoners themselves can be major contributors here, giving both time and money to local causes (Abrams et al. 1985).

Institutional Purchases

Prisons need a variety of goods and services to support their operation. Arrangements for utilities and other public services are bound to occur locally, and necessity may make these services good bargaining tools: Clallam County delayed permits required to complete the prison's sewage system until the state agreed on a satisfactory level of compensation for initial prison impacts. In the process, Clallam Bay was able to reduce its bond debt for the local sewer system because of payments associated with prison use.

Contracts to provide other goods and services also will be available for bid to local vendors. As with hiring, local preference arrangements may be possible, but open, direct competition with outside bidders is more likely. Area merchants do not always fare well in such competition, often lacking capacity and volume to beat bids from larger suppliers located elsewhere. Where goods or services could be competitively priced, a formal workshop on prison contracting, a how-to manual, and technical assistance from the institution or others might give rural business owners the knowledge necessary to win prison contracts.

Some prison purchases (such as those required immediately for unanticipated needs or small quantities to fill in gaps) are made outside of the bidding process. For these, proximity and service give local suppliers a decided advantage. Exercising this advantage requires some accommodation to specific prison needs for timeliness, quantity, and characteristics of the items required. Anticipation of these through knowledge of institutional operations and advance stocking can give the edge even to a comparatively more costly small-town supplier.

Minimizing Negatives

Successful maximization of prison benefits will tend to minimize negative effects as well, and it is thus very practical to put most energies into emphasizing the positive. This is partially a matter of perception: the magnitude of prison benefits received allows area residents to discount negatives accordingly. Also, hiring exclusively from the local area precludes problems in meeting the housing, services, and other needs of newcomers. There remains the need, however, to respond to the potential negatives always associated with prison operations.

Effects from Inmates

Serious criminal offenses by prisoners require action from outside criminal justice authorities. Some jurisdictions find this extra demand reduces their capacity to provide service to the civilian population (Millay 1991). Reimbursement to compensate local law enforcement and courts for time spent on escapes and crimes committed inside the prison may be needed, and this is set in statute in Washington state. Beyond this, one Washington town obtained permanent support for additional law enforcement capacity as an exchange for resolution of a siting dispute (Hodge and Staeheli 1988).

Repeat offenses by former convicts can be a problem when released inmates relocate in the area of the prison (Clark 1991; Callier and Versteeg 1988). Inmate relocation can be reduced by policies of releasing inmates only to their community of origin (Millay 1991; Shichor 1992). Avoiding concentration of services for ex-prisoners in the vicinity of the institution also discourages continued residence by former prisoners. In Salem, Oregon, it was this concentration that was felt to contribute to both increased crime rates and high demands for social services (Seidel and Heinkel 1987; Seidel et al. 1987). It is usually not possible to prohibit ex-inmates from establishing residence wherever they wish. However, if family members have not relocated closer to the prison, as discussed below, prisoner relocation is also less likely to occur.

Despite their usual rarity and lack of consequence, inmate escapes can be of considerable concern to residents living in the area of a prison (Carlson 1990a). The prospect of risk from inmate escapes can be addressed first by institutional practices that emphasize security. Even within the limits imposed by the classification of the inmates housed in the prison, these are variable and may benefit from greater public scrutiny. Perceived security also is improved by visible and well-practiced advance preparations for search and recapture of any escapee. The opportunity to be rapidly informed of an escape also helps. After several escapes, Clallam Bay set up a phone notification system operated through the prison: residents signed up for this service through an information letter mailed to every surrounding household. The number asking for the service was small, but its availability made a big difference to residents' sense of security.

Effects from Inmates' Friends and Families

Institutional policies that restrict visiting hours to a few sequential days, incorporate periodic conjugal visits, and require inmate release in the former home community seem to reduce relocation of inmate families (Clark 1991; Carlson 1990b). When the institution is remote, these policies may encourage overnight stays by visitors and increase economic returns to the local area. At the same time, an isolated institution, inmates with lengthy sentences, and housing and services that make relocation practical may contribute to inmate families moving closer to the prison (Farrington and Parcells 1991).

Whether these families or any other newcomers or visitors present problems of any significance depends in part on the service structure and the law enforcement capacity available to aid and control them. Some host communities have private, church, or non-profit centers with the mission of aiding prisoners' families. These help relieve pressures on local services and may also reduce criminal activity and other abuses. Visits from family and friends are of considerable importance to inmates, and when these are frequent and pleasant, the institution is likely to be a better place for inmates and employees alike. Ultimately, the community also benefits from a prison with minimal disruption.

Conclusions

Prisons are often successful strategies for rural economic development, but the degree of this success is a contingent one, reduced in part by difficulties in capturing the bulk of the potential benefits and in part by the occurrence of negative outcomes likely to accompany having a prison. The degree of both benefits and negatives is subject to manipulation: residents and leaders of communities hosting new prisons can take steps to moderate adverse prison consequences and facilitate desirable ones. They are likely to need some assistance in these tasks.

State and federal divisions of corrections have traditionally had a limited role in fostering community development, usually restricting any efforts to the provision of charitable and service assistance. These do contribute to community benefits, and make for improved public relations, but they do not meet the full assistance requirements of most rural areas. It is within the scope of corrections divisions and individual institutions to sponsor various programs to improve employment potential and to similarly assist local firms in the bidding and contracting processes. More direct aid must come from somewhere else; rural development specialists from regional or state offices should take an active role in assisting new prison locales. With appropriate guidance and involvement from local residents, prospects for obtaining a sizeable portion of the potential prison benefits can be improved. Restricting deficits will require the cooperative efforts of the institution, local authorities and agencies, and residents. Prisons do pose some problems that local residents must somehow learn to live with.

It must be emphasized that prisons are very permanent institutions, and there is plenty of time for adjustment and accommodation. There is evidence that residents of prison locales come to terms with their prisons, and that those who cannot do so leave the area (Maxim and Plecas 1983). Initial negative effects of prisons may set the tone for later years, but these effects can certainly be altered by subsequent events and efforts. The Clallam Bay prison increasingly hires its new employees from the local area, and prison jobs have become a rare bright spot in the otherwise gloomy economic forecast for this timber-dependent region.

Finally, once in place, prisons also tend to grow. New prisons cannot be built fast enough to keep up with the demand for prison space, and existing facilities typically help house additional prisoners through "double bunking" or other means of adding immediate space. Expansion or co-location of another facility is the common next step. Construction of additional inmate capacity on the site of an existing facility offers operational savings through efficiencies of scale; it also usually avoids any difficulties associated with finding a new site (Sechrest 1992). Procedures for expansion may be simpler, and less subject to public control, than are those for siting new facilities.

In 1991, just five years after it opened, the Clallam Bay Corrections Center nearly doubled its inmate population and altered its custody status toward more maximum security inmates. Similar multiplications of prisoners are known to have occurred in new rural prisons in Oregon and California, and have undoubtedly happened elsewhere as well. Changes in the custody status of inmate housing are somewhat dependent on institutional security characteristics: while the Clallam Bay prison was built for high security, an institution designed for minimum security inmates is less adaptable and thus less likely to change. Still, the proportion of prisoners serving longer sentences for ever more serious crimes is increasing faster than the numbers of inmates, and custody status upgrades of existing institutions, where feasible, seem likely. Institutional size and the custody status of its inmates affect the dynamic between prison benefits and deficits, and changes in either raise the potential for increases in both.

NOTES

1. Research support provided by the National Institute of Justice, Grant #85-IJ-CX-0022, and the Clallam County Sheriff's Department. Points of view are those of the author and do not necessarily represent the position of the U.S. Department of Justice or the Clallam County Sheriff's Department.

2. One recent approach to prison operation has been privatization, with state prisons being operated on a for-profit basis by private contractors. These arrangements are still atypical for new institutions, but where they occur, are expected to make little difference for host areas and overall prison impacts.

3. Prisons can be classified according to the severity of crime and/or length of sentence of their inmates. For the general public, these classifications generally fall into three categories reflective of the security arrangements of the institution: minimum, medium, and maximum. Some institutions have mixed classes of inmates, and there are other ways of labeling as well as intermediate levels of security used in some systems. As a rule, risks of escape increase as security status decreases; conversely, the degree of danger posed by an institution's inmates corresponds to security level. Thus, maximum security prisons present the lowest probability of escape but the highest threat should an escape occur.

REFERENCES

Abrams, Kathleen S., and William Lyons. 1987. *Impact of Correctional Facilities on Land Values and Public Safety*. North Miami, FL: Florida Atlantic University/Florida International University Joint Center for Environmental and Urban Problems. National Institute of Corrections (#R-84-P-02).

Abrams, K., J. Nicholas, B. Opinate, B. McDermott, A. Deister, J. Beloit, A. Heise, and H. Gladwin. 1985. *The Socioeconomic Impacts of State Prison-Siting on the Local Community*. North Miami, FL: Florida Atlantic University/Florida International University Joint Center for Environmental and Urban Problems.

Beale, Calvin L. 1993. "Prisons, Population, and Jobs in Nonmetro America." *Rural Development Perspectives* (8)3: 16–19.

Callier, Mark W., and Karyn D. Versteeg. 1988. *Preliminary Conclusions: Correctional Institutions' Impact on the City of Salem Police Services*. Salem, OR: Operational Support Section, Salem Police Department.

Carlson, Katherine A. 1992. "Doing Good and Looking Bad: A Case Study of Prison/Community Relations." *Crime and Delinquency* 38: 56–69.

Carlson, Katherine A. 1991. "What Happens and What Counts: Resident Assessments of Prison Impacts on their Communities." *Humboldt Journal of Social Relations* 17: 211–37.

Carlson, Katherine A. 1990a. "Prison Escapes and Community Consequences: Results of a Case Study." *Federal Probation* 44: 36–42.

Carlson, Katherine A. 1990b. *The Impacts of a New Prison on a Small Town: Twice Blessed or Double Whammy?* Final report of the Clallam Bay Project, National Institute of Justice (85-IJ-CX-0022).

Carlson, Katherine A. 1988. "Understanding Community Opposition to Prison Siting: More Than Fear and Finances." *Corrections Today* 50: 84–90.

Clark, Olivia. 1991. "Salem and State Prisons: A Test Case for Community Relations." *Humboldt Journal of Social Relations* 17: 97–210.

DeWitt, Charles B. 1991. "Information Sharing: A Plus for Corrections Construction." *National Institute of Justice Reports* 223: 6–7.

Farrington, Keith, Terry Edvalson, John R. Millay, and Patricia K. Middelburg. 1991. "Community Attitudes towards a Prison-Under-Construction: The Case of Ontario, Oregon." Paper presented at the annual meeting of the Academy of Criminal Justice Sciences, Nashville, Tennessee.

Farrington, Kenneth, and R. Pete Parcells. 1991. "Correctional Facilities and Community Crime Rates: Alternative Hypotheses and Competing Explanations." *Humboldt Journal of Social Relations* 17: 17–128.

Farrington, Kenneth, and R. Pete Parcells. 1989. "Asset or Liability? The Economic and Social Impacts of the Washington State Penitentiary Upon the City and County of Walla Walla." Paper presented at the annual meeting of the American Society of Criminology, Reno, Nevada.

Hawes, Jerry A. 1985. *Cities with Prisons: Do They Have Higher or Lower Crime Rates?* Sacramento, CA: State Senate Office of Research.

Hodge, David C., and Lynn A. Staeheli. 1988. "Monroe, Snohomish County, and Three Facilities." Pp. 1–43 in *Impact of Washington State's Correctional Institutions on Communities,* edited by R. M. Lidman. Olympia, WA: Washington State Institute for Public Policy.

Krause, Jerrald D. 1991. "Community Opposition to Correctional Facility Siting: Beyond the NIMBY Explanation." *Humboldt Journal of Social Relations* 17: 239–62.

Lidman, Russell M., ed. 1988. *Impact of Washington State's Correctional Institutions on Communities.* Olympia, WA: Washington State Institute for Public Policy.

Maxim, Paul, and Darryl Plecas. 1983. "Prisons and Their Perceived Impact on the Local Community: A Case Study." *Social Indicators Research* 13: 39–58.

Millay, John R. 1991. "From Asylum to Penitentiary: The Social Impact of Eastern Oregon Corrections Institution Upon Pendleton." *Humboldt Journal of Social Relations* 17: 171–95.

Nagel, William G. 1973. *The New Red Barn: A Critical Look at the Modern American Prison.* New York: Walker & Co.

Pagel, Al. 1988. "Prejudices Set Aside . . . Communities Woo Prisons." *Corrections Compendium* 22.

Sechrest, Dale K. 1992. "Locating Prisons: Open Versus Closed Approaches to Siting." *Crime and Delinquency* 38: 88–104.

Seidel, Karen M., and Carol Heinkel. 1987. *Salem Area Institutions: Correctional and Mental Health Institutions and the Ex-Institutional Population.* Eugene, Oregon: Bureau of Governmental Research and Service, University of Oregon.

Seidel, Karen M., Kevin Knudtson, and Ken Viegas. 1987. *Salem Area Community Corrections: State Clients, Local Services, and Policy Choices.* Eugene, Oregon: Bureau of Governmental Research and Service, University of Oregon.

Shichor, David. 1992. "Myths and Realities in Prison Siting." *Crime and Delinquency* 38: 70–87.

Smykla, John O., David C. Cheng, Carl E. Gerguson, Jr., Carolyn Trent, Barbara Trench, and Annette Waters. 1984. "Effects of a Prison Facility on the Regional Economy." *Journal of Criminal Justice* 12: 521–39.

Stanley, Craig E. 1978. *The Impact of Prison Proximity on Property Values in Green Bay and Waupun, Wisconsin.* Milwaukee: Wisconsin Division of Corrections and Bureau of Facilities Management.

Summers, Gene F., Sharon Evan, Frank Clemente, Elwood M. Beck, and Jon Minkoff. 1976. *Industrial Invasion of Nonmetropolitan America: A Quarter Century of Experience.* New York: Praeger.

Zarchikoff, William W., T. J. Seeger, and Darryl B. Plecas. 1981. *An Assessment of the Social and Economic Impacts of Federal Correctional Institutions on the Communities of Agassiz, Harrison Hot Springs, and Harrison Mills, British Columbia, Canada.* Ottawa, Canada: Ministry of the Solicitor General, Evaluation and Special Projects Division.

CHAPTER 12

Mending the Circle: Peer Group Lending for Micro-Enterprise Development in Tribal Communities

SCHUYLER HOUSER[1]

Reservations as Special Cases

Indian reservations are home to approximately half of the 1.96 million Indian people in the United States. Of the 278 reservations, the great majority are located west of the Mississippi River, in isolated rural areas.[1] These reservations differ from surrounding areas in at least three major ways that affect local economic life: in social, linguistic, and cultural patterns; by economic and demographic conditions; and in legal and political institutions.

Cultural Distinctions

Non-Indian Americans have consistently underestimated the importance of the cultural, linguistic, and social distinctiveness of Indian communities.[2] Federal Indian policies have, until relatively recently, been based on the central expectations that tribal identities and tribal groups would, over time, erode and disappear.[3] But essential patterns of group identification and social connection within Indian communities have persisted and evolved. Extended families have remained intact as basic social and economic units. Indian people continue to associate and work more often with other Indian people than with non-Indians. Particularly within reservations, Indian people are each others' primary day-to-day contacts, and most frequent sources of information, ethical values, and opinion leadership. Although these communities, as social and cultural systems, are by no means closed to outside influences, they evolve at their own rates and in their own directions.

Economic and Demographic Distinctions

The economic distinctiveness of many reservation communities is unenviable; they are, materially, among the most impoverished communities in the United States. In 1986, according to a study conducted by the United Methodist Church, of the twenty-five poorest counties in the nation, ten were located on Indian reservations. Tribal communities are significantly overrepresented among the poorest of the American poor.[4]

Populations of U.S. Indian reservations, in their demographic profiles, resemble unindustrialized rural, non-agricultural, ethnically distinct communities elsewhere in the world. The residents of Indian communities, including those identified in the Methodist Church study, are youthful; median ages commonly range between nineteen and twenty-three. Education levels, though increasing, are still relatively low; school dropout rates exceeding 70 percent are still common among Indian youth, although considerable progress has been made during the last decade both in elementary/secondary and adult education. Families are larger in reservation communities than in adjacent non-Indian areas; in South Dakota, for example, non-Indian households averaged 2.6 members, and Indian households on reservations ranged from 3.1 to 4.8 members.[5]

Since the late 1960s, Indian communities throughout the nation have grown, through high birth rates and increasing longevity. In the northern Great Plains in particular, this growth has coincided with a general unraveling of existing rural economic patterns. Since the late 1950s, non-Indian farmers, ranchers, and small-town dwellers have died or steadily moved away; they have not been replaced. During the same period, in contrast, many reservation communities have grown into local centers of population, as settlements in surrounding areas have dwindled. As schools, hospitals, and drugstores close in many Great Plains towns, reservation communities, in contrast, work to recruit teachers and pharmacists and build new classrooms and hospitals.

Economic growth on many reservations has not kept pace, however, as populations have increased. In each of the reservation communities identified in the Methodist Church study, per capita income was significantly lower in 1986 than in 1981. For both the Rosebud and Oglala Sioux Tribes, the unemployment rates on their reservations (including discouraged workers not counted in state statistics) have exceeded 65 percent each year since 1980.

Those jobs that exist on these reservations are, for the most part, in the public sector. Federal and tribal governments, schools, and the U.S. Public Health Service are the major employers in most tribal communities. On the Rosebud Reservation in 1985, for example, there were 1,406 full-time and 181 part-time positions. Of these, 214 were in the private sector; the remainder, or 82.5 percent, were in the public sector.[6] Because there are few stores or shops, Rosebud reservation residents must travel outside their communities for even the most basic goods and services. Money generated by payrolls and transfer payments leaves tribal communities rapidly, and with little turnover.

To complicate the development process, federal policies restrain tribes and tribal members from using their principal assets—land—as collateral for loans. For most reservation communities, land forms the major economic asset and agriculture is the primary form of production. Indian people do not, for the most part, control their lands directly; titles to most Indian lands are held by the U.S. Department of the Interior, in trust for the owners. The Bureau of Indian Affairs regularly leases these trust lands to farmers and ranchers (predominantly non-Indian on most reservations) and distributes the rents to the Indian owners at the end of each year.[7]

The policy of entering of tribal real property into trust status was designed to slow the wholesale alienation of lands from Indian control. The policy succeeded, but at a cost—Indian owners of trust lands cannot readily convert their assets to cash. These landowners cannot borrow against their major (and often sole) assets for business, or any other, purposes.

Political Distinctions

The distinctiveness of tribal political and legal institutions likewise strongly affects local economic conditions.[8] Indian governments are unique entities within the American federal system. Indian tribes have their own independent tribal governments; reservation lands, for the most part, fall outside the jurisdiction of adjacent states.

Tribes and the federal government agree that tribal governments retain many of the powers of independent sovereign states. Tribal governments, therefore, possess authority to tax, to establish and enforce civil and criminal laws on their reservations, and to regulate commerce within their jurisdictions. Increasing numbers of tribes, over the past twenty years, have begun to exercise this authority by enacting their own laws and corporate codes and creating their own judicial systems to provide adequate civil and criminal regulation.

In addition to passing laws and policies, tribal governments must also implement and enforce them. Since the late 1960s, the federal government has directed money and responsibilities toward tribal governments, and away from the Bureau of Indian Affairs, to allow tribes to build up their own administrative staffs. Thus, most tribes (despite the fact that their historical authority precedes the establishment of the United States) are relatively young as administrations, and face many of the same challenges—particularly inexperience and instability—that beset most new governments. Many tribal governments, therefore, face exceptionally difficult problems of rural social and economic development with extremely limited administrative resources.

Further, tribal governments must often fight to exercise their own authority. Their primary adversaries, particularly in the West, have been the governments of adjacent states. These disputes have frequently been resolved only through protracted litigation. Although federal courts have regularly (though not invariably) decided such issues in favor of tribal governments, the uncertainties and animosities arising from the fights have had a marked chilling effect on outside investment and business development within many tribal communities. The battles, in addition, have consumed resources— money and staff time—that might have been redirected toward uses more productive for all parties. While political self-determination appears to be an essential prerequisite for some kinds of economic development on reservations, the struggles to obtain that self-determination may, over the short term, reinforce other constraints to economic growth.[9]

Micro-Enterprises: Businesses in the Informal Sector

On many reservations, since the mid-1970s, not much has worked to produce sustained economic development. Such conventional techniques as recruitment of established industries or small business incubation have met, at best, with limited success. A few tribes have created notable exceptions—large defense-related manufacturing plants on the Devil's Lake Sioux (North Dakota) and Fort Peck (Montana) Reservations, bingo and gaming establishments on a variety of reservations close to urban areas.

These tribes, however, remain exceptions. On the Rosebud Sioux Reservation (population 18,000), since a small, tribally-managed electronics assembly plant closed in 1983, there have been no successful new formally-organized business ventures; conditions are similar on the nearby Pine Ridge Reservation (population 26,000).

Whatever robust and vigorous business activity exists on the Rosebud and Pine Ridge Reservations is very small in scale. Hundreds of micro-enterprises create arts and crafts; prepare and serve food; repair homes and automobiles, and provide music, dance, and cultural services. The enterprises ordinarily operate out of the homes of the individual entrepreneurs, and usually employ only family members. The businesses have rarely undergone formal incorporation procedures, and may not operate all year-round. Nonetheless, these micro-enterprises are, in the aggregate, significant producers of goods and services for their communities, and of revenue and value for their owners.

On the Pine Ridge Reservation, in western South Dakota (per capita income of $3,244)[10] an extensive survey of micro-enterprises determined that 87 percent of households participated in some sort of informal-sector economic activity. Of the households surveyed, 30 percent indicated that half or more of total household income came from self-employment activity; of those, 5 percent indicated that all of their household income was generated through self-employment.[11] Anecdotal evidence from other reservations indicates that these patterns of participation and income-generation are common throughout Indian country.

The business activities of micro-enterprises on reservations are diverse, but a substantial proportion are involved in some type of manufacturing. A survey conducted in 1989 on the Rosebud Reservation interviewed the proprietors of sixty-five micro-enterprises. Over 56 percent of these manufactured some product—jewelry, traditional arts, star quilts, clothing, dolls, baked goods. Other businesses included carpentry, auto repair, catering, and mobile food stands that travel to pow-wows and recreational events during the summer months. Nearly 90 percent of these businesses operate year-round.

These businesses had substantial track records. The median age of micro-enterprises in Rosebud was ten years; nearly one third had been in operation since the 1960s, and the oldest for more than forty years. A younger group of businesses, 45 percent, had existed for less than five years. More than 90 percent were sole proprietorships; a similar percentage operated out of the home of the owner. The entrepreneurs were almost equally divided between men (thirty-two) and women (thirty-three); this distribution was similar to that at Pine Ridge. For 61 percent of the Rosebud micro-entrepreneurs, their business was their primary source of income; the remainder held an additional full- or part-time job. For 62 percent, the proprietor was the sole employee; the remainder rely heavily on family members to provide additional help.

Total household income for 79 percent of the entrepreneurs was less than $15,000; only 9 percent of the households identified had incomes above $25,000. Sales for the enterprises averaged between $4,000 and $5,000 per year. The businesses sold their products primarily to individuals; only a limited amount of sales went to other businesses or to government. Sixty-nine percent of sales were made within the local area. Ten percent of the entrepreneurs indicated that their primary customer base was out-of-state; five businesses were active in mail order activities. Many entrepreneurs mentioned, spontaneously, their concerns with quality control; the business people recognized that in a isolated and relatively closed market area, a reputation for shoddy workmanship could do their businesses serious damage.[12]

Barriers to Expansion: Why Do Micro-Enterprises Stay Micro?

On the Rosebud Reservation, most businesses surveyed indicated that the lack of access to credit was a major barrier to expansion. These entrepreneurs do not have conventional opportunities to obtain even small loans, in part because they lack collateral. Neither friends or families—common sources of start-up capital for small businesses in non-Indian comrnunities—could provide funds. Nor were banks especially interested in providing the relatively small amounts of credit needed by businesses of this scale; the processing costs of arranging small, uncollateralized loans makes them prohibitively expensive for most financial institutions. And ironically, the available guaranteed loan programs from the Small Business Administration or the Bureau of Indian Affairs offer too much money for most micro-entrepreneurs, who recognize that they need to operate on a limited scale.

In 70 percent of the cases, microentrepreneurs in Rosebud began their business using only their own personal funds; seven entrepreneurs obtained loans from banks, and an additional three received assistance from government loans or grants. Only one enterprise indicated that it had a continuing relationship with a bank for current business financing.

Since most micro-entrepreneurs face a perpetual shortage of working capital, they work only to special order, and require that customers make down payments which would cover at least the cost of materials. Eighty-six percent of the entrepreneurs surveyed indicated that because they were unable to purchase materials, develop inventories, or hire additional staff, their businesses were operating at half capacity or less. Only 14 percent indicated that their businesses were operating at or close to capacity.

Almost every entrepreneur expressed a strong interest in expanding his or her business. The proprietors were asked to estimate the costs of expansion; their responses, on average, indicated needs for $2,818 in working capital, $5,335 for tools and equipment, and $4,558 for physical improvements. In many instances, the total required was less than $10,000. (According to the Small Business Administration, banks are often reluctant to deal with small business loans, even with federal guarantees of repayment, if the amounts are less than $30,000 to $50,000; processing costs on smaller loans make them uneconomical for most banks to handle.)[13]

Economic and business conditions on Rosebud appear to be very similar to those on the Pine Ridge Reservation, and in many other U.S. and Canadian Indian communities.[14] Each community has a significant number of informal micro-enterprises. Many of those enterprises have track records of stability and success, function well below their capacity, and have clearly identifiable needs for small amounts of credit. In every Indian community, entrepreneurs themselves are highly involved in local life, with family obligations and, in many cases, jobs in the formal sector; they are, however, isolated from mainstream economic and business institutions, and have extremely limited access to sources of business information or consulting expertise. Many micro-entrepreneurs indicated that they were interested in improving some of their skills—in marketing, or financial record-keeping, for example. Few among the individuals surveyed were, however, interested in taking extensive business or entrepreneurship training courses; they were, for the most part, much too busy being entrepreneurs.

Peer Group Lending for Micro-Enterprise Development

The economic conditions of micro-enterprises on Indian reservations may be relatively uncommon in the United States. Relatively few American businesses in urban areas face the combination of barriers to small amounts of credit together with geographical, social, and informational isolation. But in less developed countries, micro-enterprises form a larger portion of total business activity in both rural and urban areas, and have therefore received comparatively more attention as bases for economic development and growth.

Several cultures have developed techniques for supplying the needs of micro-entrepreneurs for credit, information, and mutual support. Among Palestinian Arabs, and in southeast Asia, borrowers may obtain small amounts of credit from groups of friends. When these groups grant loans, they base their decisions not on the collateral that the borrower can present, but on the borrower's character, as known, through years of familiarity, by neighbors and associates. Potential borrowers who wish to use this method form a small, self-selected group; each member of the group agrees to contribute a set amount at every meeting, which may be monthly or bi-weekly. At each meeting, one of the members receives, as a loan, the entire pot for that month; the recipient may be chosen on the basis of need, or by chance. The recipient then repays the loan in small monthly installments. One of the group members is usually selected to manage the business of recording payments and disbursements. Over time, the amount available for loans can increase considerably, as repayments accumulate.[15] Since all members of a group are likely to live or work in the same neighborhood, memberships—and the use of the loan—can be screened carefully. And should problems with repayments occur, peer pressure, or peer assistance, is readily available.

The Grameen Bank, in Bangladesh, has created a formalized version of a group-lending concept, and used it as the basis for an extensive rural development institution. The economist Mohammed Yunus, professor at Chittagong University, identified a need to expand self-employment opportunities for the landless, assetless poor in small villages near the university. At first Yunus made personal small loans to individual entrepreneurs, but he moved to a group-lending system, as he recognized the social and technical needs of the borrowers—not only for continued access to credit, but also for opportunities to build their own business skills and sense of self-worth. In Yunus's design, a centralized institution, the Grameen Bank (the name means "village" in the Bengali language), provides funds for loans, which are, however, made and managed by individual peer groups of five to seven members. The groups are linked with each other in district and regional organizations; a member of the bank staff travels, usually by bicycle, to peer group meetings to pick up payments and deliver loan funds. Interest rates vary with the market rate, but average about 16 percent. The average size of each loan is about $75, the maximum loan size is $180. Most of the 800,000 borrowers are women. Since the bank was established in 1983, it has used the peer-group technique to make loans totalling half a billion dollars; the repayment rate is 98 percent.[16]

Yunus's model was first imported to North America by the Calmeadow Foundation, a Canadian philanthropic organization based in Toronto. In 1987 the foundation established pilot programs, using the Grameen Bank techniques, in three isolated Indian reserves in Ontario. All of the programs were successful, and Calmeadow expanded its micro-enterprise development operations in 1990 by founding the First Peoples Fund, to provide support for the establishment of peer group lending programs in Native communities—both rural and urban—throughout Canada. In the United States, two programs employing the Grameen Bank model have been founded on reservations: the Lakota Fund, based in Kyle, South Dakota, on the Pine Ridge Reservation (formerly affiliated with the First Nations Financial Project, Falmouth, Virginia); and the Sicangu Enterprise Center, Mission, South Dakota (affiliated with Neighborhood Reinvestment Corporation[17] and Sinte Gleska University). The policies, organizational structures, and styles of all of the North American programs vary only slightly.

The programs were established as independent, non-profit corporations. Each program operates with the knowledge and consent of the local tribal or band government, but the organizations in Rosebud and Pine Ridge, by deliberate choice, maintain some distance from the turbulence of elective tribal politics. In each case, the loan program had a parent organization, a preexisting, legally incorporated organization that sponsored the start-up work. Each program, as part of its own development, sought its own incorporation under the laws of its local jurisdiction and named its own board of directors. Membership on the board brings together individuals from important supporting organizations and key constituencies. Board members of the Sicangu Enterprise Center, for example, consist of administrators from the local tribal university (the parent institution), a member of the Rosebud Sioux Tribe's credit committee (which provided a long-term loan to the center for use as collateral), a representative of Farmers' State Bank (which holds on deposit a guarantee fund, and makes the loans), and local Indian business people. After several borrowers' circles were established, the peer groups elected several of their members to sit on the board. The center in Rosebud, established in 1990, has only one professional staff member, the director, and one support staff. The Lakota Fund, in operation for three years, has two full-time professional staff and a secretary.

The founders of each of the loan programs have, for the sake of financial stability, sought and obtained operating funds from a variety of sources. Community contributions, however, have been essential as a starting point in every case. The Calmeadow Foundation requires that if a community wants to establish a loan fund, the community or its government must raise and contribute 25 percent of the amount of the total line of credit desired. That money is deposited in a local bank to serve as a guarantee fund for the loans. After the community has reached its goal, Calmeadow will contribute an additional 50 percent to the guarantee fund. The bank is expected to carry an additional 25 percent of the exposure.

In Rosebud, Neighborhood Reinvestment Corporation provided $10,000 toward the guarantee fund, and the Credit Committee of the Rosebud Sioux Tribe made a low-interest, three-year loan of $20,000, to be placed in the guarantee fund. The participating bank, Farmers State Bank of Mission, South Dakota, agreed that if a guarantee fund of $40,000 were placed on interest-bearing deposit, the bank would make available for lending a total of $200,000 by the third year of the program. (The first year ceiling was $60,000, increasing to $120,000 in the second.) The sponsoring organization in Rosebud, Sinte Gleska University, raised $45,000 to cover operating expenses for three years; the founding director of the center raised an additional $87,000 for operations.

Informing the Public, Forming the Groups

Program staff handle two parts of the public information function—educating the local public about the programs, and orienting new members—as inseparable parts of the same process. Getting the word out in rural communities often requires innovative techniques. Both the Pine Ridge and Rosebud reservations, and the communities within them, are extremely isolated, with little access to newspaper and television coverage of local information, so the programs use local FM radio stations directed at Indian audiences, weekly regional newspapers, and, most importantly, word-of-mouth (known in most tribal communities as the moccasin telegraph).

To provide more detailed information, program staff travel to small individual communities throughout the reservation and conduct public information sessions. During these sessions, the staff explain such basic concepts as micro-enterprises, character-based lending, and borrowers' circles. The presenters stress the facts that self-selected peer groups (not individual borrowers) are the basic unit of the process, and that the amount of initial loans will be limited. (In

Rosebud these limits are set at $500 per borrower, at Pine Ridge $100, and in the Canadian programs at $1,000.) Most information sessions conclude by dividing the audience into smaller circles and conducting simulated peer group meetings to provide potential borrowers with a chance to explore the dynamics of this new kind of relationship.

Staff members encourage interested applicants to form their own peer groups, with four to seven entrepreneurs. As a matter of principle, North American programs have tried to follow Dr. Yunus's example by encouraging women to form the first group in each program. Most groups formed thereafter have (without intervention by program staff) been either exclusively male or exclusively female.

Program guidelines set some restrictions on membership: members must be at least eighteen years old; two members of the same household may not be members of the same peer group. Within those limitations, however, peer groups determine their own membership. Staff do not perform much matchmaking for potential peer group members; the nature of the process demands that micro-entrepreneurs rely on their own assessments of each other's character, integrity, and credit-worthiness. Nor do staff perform credit checks on prospective members; participation for any individual depends on the evaluations of other members of the peer group.

When a peer group has assembled itself, it notifies the program director, who then conducts four to six rigorous training sessions on matters of basic business planning.[18] All members of the group must be present at each of these sessions; if anyone is absent, the trainer departs, explaining that everyone must be present if the session is to occur. When the group reschedules the session, the trainer returns.

At the outset of the training, participants review the basic concepts of the program, and the group members examine their personal visions of their own enterprises. Group members also begin to gather information they will need to prepare their own business plans. Later sessions deal with pricing and marketing; group members identify their current customer base, and develop plans to reach new customers. Additionally, the trainer works with at least one group member to identify and determine costs for the steps in that enterprise's production process; other members then use the same techniques on their own businesses. Towards the end of the orientation, the members write their own business plans, using materials and information they have developed in the previous sessions and in homework assignments. When the group has completed all training sessions, it receives a certification from the program's board in a final session, a celebration that usually involves a meal; only then may members begin to submit loan applications to their peer group.

Each peer group, after certification, functions as its own loan committee. It selects its own chairperson from among its members, and determines the times and places of its meetings. (Customarily, a staff member from the program will attend at least the first few meetings.) At the group's first monthly meeting, it evaluates loan applications from each of its own members, and decides which two members will receive the first loans. The applications are then, in the Rosebud program, forwarded to the board of directors. The board has final approval of all loans, but this action is ordinarily a formality. If board members have serious questions about a loan, they may refer the application back to the circle from which it originated. In most cases, however, the board transmits the loan approval to the bank. The center then issues the check to the borrower. All checks are distributed at peer group meetings.

Repayment

After the first two borrowers have established a pattern of regular repayment—usually after two months—the group may approve two more loans, and so on, until each member has received a loan. Groups may make recommendations that applications be revised, or provide suggestions for alternative business practices. Once an application is approved, however, all members of the peer group then become, in effect, co-signers for those loans. If any borrower in the group fails to repay the loan, all of the peer group members are responsible for the money. Everyone in the group, therefore, has a direct stake in the success of each of the others. This stake is reflected in the active interest members take in each other's businesses, and the support and advice that they regularly provide to each other.

Borrowers make their repayments, in small amounts, directly to the group during its monthly meetings. The payments are recorded by the chairperson, and transmitted to the program staff for deposit in the bank. Every member knows the status of everyone else's loan at all times. There is no confidentiality on these matters within the peer group. In the words of Mohammed Yunus, "Confidentiality breeds lies."

The costs of money to the borrowers are not artificially lowered. In addition to repaying the amount of the principal, peer group members pay interest; in Rosebud the rate is set at the equivalent of market rate (charged by the bank) plus 2 percent (which goes to the program for operating expenses). The program is explicitly intended for those who have no other access to credit; if entrepreneurs can obtain money more cheaply elsewhere, they are encouraged to do so.

In addition to principal and interest, participants pay a surcharge with each installment. Part of this additional money goes into an enforced savings account for the individual borrower. The remainder goes toward a group reserve account. Should any member miss a payment, the group may decide to draw on its reserve funds as a cushion, to make up the total amount owed to the bank. The delinquent member must then repay the group, in addition to keeping up the regular payments. The credit-worthiness of the group as a whole, however, is not damaged so long as the total dollar amounts of its payments are met. On both Pine Ridge and Rosebud, peer groups have begun, independently, to hold lunch sales and other small-scale moneymaking activities to raise funds for their own group reserve accounts.

If a peer group senses that one of its members is headed toward default on a loan, the other members decide what action to take. In most cases, the groups will have planned for such a contingency in discussing the approval of the loan; borrowers have promised, for example, to sign over to their groups the ownership of equipment or supplies purchased with the loan money. In fact, however, the careful screening of borrowers and the strong peer pressure inherent in the organization's structure work strongly to limit the occurrence of defaults. The programs in Indian communities in the United States and Canada have replicated the experiences of the Grameen Bank, with default rates of 0 to 5 percent.

After a borrower has successfully repaid the first loan, he or she may apply for a second and larger loan if all other members of the peer group are in good standing. In each program, the amount of loans increases incrementally; borrowers in Rosebud may expand their credit, over time, to an upper limit of $10,000. In micro-enterprise development programs that have been running for several years in Latin America and Bangladesh, participants have, from time to time, "graduated," and begun to use ordinary commercial sources of credit to meet the expanded needs of their businesses.

Variations on the Theme

Participants in peer-group lending programs in Rosebud and Pine Ridge indicate that the Grameen Bank model for micro-enterprise development fits comfortably in their communities because of strong local traditions of group effort and collaboration. Other communities in the western hemisphere, however, have other cultural values, and have therefore taken somewhat different approaches to the basic task of providing assistance to micro-enterprises. The Micro Industry Credit Rural Organization (MICRO), for example, which serves a primarily Hispanic population in Arizona and California, has chosen to provide loans only to individual clients, not to borrowers' circles. In 1987, the founder of the organization, Frank Ballesteros, polled prospective borrowers; they disliked the interdependence and collaboration required by circle banking techniques, and clearly preferred individual activity and self-reliance. Potential borrowers also indicated that they were prepared to provide small amounts of collateral—a wedding ring, a television set—to secure their loans.

MICRO designed its program around these preferences, and now accepts loan applications only from individual borrowers. Each application is carefully screened by one of MICRO's professional staff, who visits the workplace (usually located in the home) of the applicant. Staff members are recruited from the communities in which they work, and thus have access to the same kinds of local, informal information about applicants' reputations and credit-worthiness as do peer-group members on reservations. MICRO provides some training seminars and training sessions on business techniques for its clients, and also refers borrowers to other local institutions—community colleges, for example—that provide training and technical assistance for small-scale business development.

Significantly, as MICRO has evolved over five years, its clients have begun to join together to form local micro-enterprise associations. Members of these associations share information on the development of their own enterprises, and support and advise each other as they solve individual business problems. The members also work together on marketing and promotional activities intended to heighten the visibility, in the community and region, of their businesses.[19] These kinds of activities strongly resemble those undertaken by peer groups in Pine Ridge and Rosebud. Group actions and interactions—including the exchange of information and the social reinforcement of good business values and careful business practices—appear to be an important ingredient of successful micro-enterprise development programs in a variety of cultures.

Micro-enterprise development programs are widespread in Latin America. In at least twelve Central and South American nations, non-governmental organizations affiliated with ACCION International (Cambridge, Massachusetts) sponsor loan programs to provide small amounts of credit and training to micro-entrepreneurs. ACCION provides technical support and some fund-raising and financial services for its affiliate organizations, but policy and operational decisions are made by the national organizations themselves. As a result, the policies and approaches of each program are tailored to reflect local conditions and local preferences.

Three of these organizations—Genesis in Guatemala, ADEMI in the Dominican Republic, and the Association for Solidarity Groups in Colombia—use the Grameen Bank methodology. Both Genesis and ADEMI, however, also make loans to individuals. Overall, programs that serve individual borrowers attract (or limit eligibility to) more experienced micro-entrepreneurs whose businesses, at the time of first loans, have larger gross receipts and numbers of employees than the businesses served by group lending programs.

What Has Been Learned: International Outcomes and Evidence of Success

In Latin America and in Hispanic communities in the United States, programs that provide relatively small loans in gradually increasing amounts to individual borrowers succeed consistently in using such loans to stimulate the growth of micro-enterprises. The success of these small loans is linked to the provision of opportunities for micro-entrepreneurs to acquire appropriate business skills, and to give each other mutual support. In Bolivia, for example, in 1989, external evaluators of PRODEM, ACCION's local affiliate, reported that after one year of program participation, borrowers' quarterly income increased on average from $2,372 to $5,553 (134 percent); labor expenses increased from $294 to $817; and profits increased from $581 to $831.[20]

Between April 1986 and July 1989, AVANCE (ACCION's affiliate in Costa Rica) made loans to 3,028 micro-enterprises. As a result of the loans, 536 new jobs were created and 1,555 jobs were strengthened. A detailed examination of 12 percent of the borrowers' businesses concluded that 29 percent increased employment (7 percent of them by more than 100 percent), 50 percent increased sales (22 percent by more than 100 percent), 50 percent increased assets (19 percent by more than 100 percent), and 37 percent increased net income (21 percent by more than 100 percent).[21]

In the southwestern United States, from 1987 to 1991, MICRO made 627 loans to more than 300 micro-enterprises. Between October 1, 1990 and June 30, 1991, MICRO clients stabilized 156 full-time and 10 part-time jobs. As for new employment, thirty-two full-time and forty-five part-time jobs were created. Average wages for new and stabilized jobs were $5.33 for full-time positions (more than 20 hours per week) and $4.50 for part-time.[22] The average cost per job (calculated by adding the number of jobs stabilized to the number of jobs created, and dividing that number into the total costs of program operation for the period) was $1,078.07.

Micro-enterprise development programs in Latin America that use the Grameen Bank or solidarity group model also report significant impacts on their clients' businesses. In Colombia, the Association of Solidarity Groups (an ACCION affiliate) found in 1990 that borrower income rose, on average, 58 percent for micro-producers and thirty-six percent for micro-vendors in a year. Some 30 percent of these borrowers increased their incomes by at least 100 percent during that period. From 1983 through 1990, 18,712 micro-entrepreneurs received loans from the Association. During that time, 14,000 jobs were created or strengthened (from part-time to full-time, or from temporary/seasonal to year-round).[23]

Genesis, an ACCION affiliate in Guatemala, offers loans to both individuals and groups. An independent evaluation of the program, prepared in October 1989, allows for some comparison of the two methods:

> About 91% of sampled individual borrowers and 90% of solidarity group members increased their gross sales after participating in the Genesis project. For individual borrowers, sales increased by an average of $906 over an 8-month period, or three loans. Growth rates per borrower range from 26% to 300%, with an average growth rate of 50%. While 63% of individual micro-businesses had gross sales of less than $1,481 prior to participating in Genesis, only 36% did so after receiving their third loan. . . .
>
> For solidarity groups, sales increased an average of $285 over a 7-month period, or 6 loans. Whereas 80% of the sampled group borrowers had gross sales of less than $1,481 prior to their participation in Genesis, this figure dropped to 60% after their sixth loan. . . .
>
> Net profits show substantial increases for 91% of the sampled individual borrowers and 70% of solidarity group members. Prior to their participation in the program, the net profits of individuals averaged $244 a month in comparison to $470 after the third loan. This represents a 92% increase in 8 months. For solidarity group members, average net profits grew from $224 to $314 over 7 months. . . .
>
> Interviews with sampled borrowers revealed that 80% of them presently keep records (bookkeeping), as opposed to only 30% of them before joining Genesis.[24]

Loan programs which use group lending techniques regularly report higher repayment rates than do programs which make loans to individuals. ADEMI, an ACCION affiliate in the Dominican Republic, offers loans both to individual borrowers and to solidarity groups. From May, 1987, to May, 1988, ADEMI financed 3,430 micro-enterprises, creating 10,829 jobs. The organization has found that the informal sector was capable of creating a new job for every $822 invested.[25] The rate of late repayments for solidarity group members was 6 percent; the rate for individual borrowers was 17 percent.[26]

What Has Been Learned: Outcomes and Evidence of Success in U.S. Tribal Communities

Several micro-enterprise development programs in Asia and Latin America can draw on ten to fifteen years of data to demonstrate the effectiveness of their methods. To tribal communities in the United States, however, micro-enterprise development programs are relative newcomers, and their track records are comparatively short. The Lakota Fund, in mid-1992, had eleven circles with five borrowers apiece after two years of operation; the Sicangu Enterprise Center, after eighteen months, had five circles. By June, 1992, the most senior members of the Lakota Fund's borrowers circles had taken, at most, two loans, and the first clients of the Sicangu Enterprise Center were completing repayment of their first loans. Nonetheless, these programs report that early measures (both quantitative and qualitative) of effectiveness are consistent with results of similar programs elsewhere, with one notable difference—the center at Rosebud, despite geographic isolation and low population density, grew more rapidly than comparable centers in urban areas (see table 12.1).

An informal survey of clients of the Lakota Fund in May 1992 indicated that approximately one-fifth of the borrowers founded entirely new enterprises with their loans. Preexisting businesses reported increases in sales ranging from 30 percent to 100 percent. Several Lakota Fund clients, particularly artists and craftspeople, found that the general impoverishment of their communities limited their volume of sales and held down the prices that they could receive on the local market; several of these artists have used their new business skills and access to credit to establish markets beyond the borders of the Pine Ridge Reservation.

A formal survey of participants in the Sicangu Enterprise Center in August 1992 indicated that 85 percent of respondents had increased their monthly income since joining a peer group. Half of the fourteen participants surveyed indicated that the monthly income from their enterprise exceeded $200. Participants reported that they found the center's training on record-keeping, management, and pricing to be helpful; nearly all respondents requested additional training in management and bookkeeping, and also wanted additional collective activities to help market micro-enterprise products.

Table 12.1: Summary of Data from Neighborhood Enterprise Center Pilot Projects

Program Characteristics	Rosebud	Jackson	Pasadena	West Philadelphia
Date started	6/90	3/90	4/90	9/90
Date of first loan	11/90	8/90	10/90	6/91
Number of groups	6	4	8	5
Number of peer group members	30	17	42	26
Number of borrowers	30	13	20	20
Number of minority borrowers (%)	29 (97%)	13 (100%)	18 (90%)	20 (100%)
Number of women borrowers (%)	16 (53%)	8 (62%)	14 (70%)	6 (30%)
Number of loans to date	49	15	31	22
Number of loans repaid	24	3	9	15
Number of loans outstanding	25	6	20	7
Number of defaults	0	6	2	0
Dollar value loans to date	$41,000	$25,500	$19,500	$36,400
Dollar value loans repaid	$23,113	$4,500	$5,500	$23,007
Dollar value loans outstanding	$17,887	$9,070	$13,200	$13,393
Dollar value defaults	$0	$11,930	$800	$0
Lifetime Default rate	0%	47%	4%	0%
Minimum loan size	$100	$100	$100	$100
Maximum initial loan size	$500	$1,500	$500	$1,500
Average loan size	$837	$1,700	$629	$1,654
Interest rate charged	12.5%	8.5–12%	10–10.5%	8.5–10.5%
Line of credit dollar amount	$65,000	$20,000	$40,000	$50,000
Do clients contribute to reserve?	yes: 5% of loan (PG savings also)	yes: 5% of loan	yes: 5% of loan	1st yr. yes: 5% of loan

Source: The Commercial and Economic Development Department, Neighborhood Reinvestment Corporation. 1993. Nelson, Candace.

Half of the respondents mentioned that they derived benefit from getting to know other micro-entrepreneurs better during the orientation process; participants identified the opportunities to share business plans and success stories, and to build trust and confidence, as particularly helpful.

More than 90 percent of the Rosebud respondents used their early loans to purchase supplies; one-third of the group used loan funds to buy or repair equipment. (This is consistent with the experiences of Lakota Fund and MICRO borrowers; the creation of additional jobs among MICRO clients does not ordinarily take place until after the third loan.) [27] Two-thirds of the group planned to use future loans to increase or improve the working space for their enterprise so that the business facilities could be more separate from family living areas. A majority (57 percent) of entrepreneurs planned to expand their businesses to provide full-time employment for themselves; a similar proportion planned to expand their enterprises to provide more employment for family members or non-related individuals.

Members of the Sicangu Enterprise Center indicated that they had learned to set their prices to provide themselves with a reasonable wage according to local standards:[28]

Less than $3.99 per hour	21%
$4.00 to $4.99 per hour	14%
$5.00 to $10.00 per hour	50%
More than $10.00 per hour	14%

One-third of the respondents volunteered that they used different pricing structures depending on whether the purchaser was poor, Indian, or from a reservation community on one hand, or employed, non-Indian, or from off the reservation on the other.

Another indicator of success for the Grameen Bank techniques is provided by repayment rates. The circle banking technique has better records for repayment in Pine Ridge and Rosebud than any alternative approach to micro-enterprise or small business development. The Bureau of Indian Affairs, for the area that includes both reservations, reported repayment rates of less than 10 percent in the mid-1980s on its small business loan program; the program was eventually terminated. The Lakota Fund, when it began, made small loans only to individual entrepreneurs; when the default rate headed past 30 percent during the first year, the managers of the fund closed their doors and rethought their organization's strategy. After the

Lakota Fund adopted the Grameen Bank methodology, defaults and delinquency rates fell virtually to zero.

Differences in repayment rates may be attributable at least in part to the differences in types of borrowers between the two kinds of lending programs. Small business loan programs have, on reservations, generally targeted new businesses and startups, which have high likelihoods of failure; the circle lending programs have, for the most part, served clients who have already been in business for a number of years, and who use their loans to expand existing enterprises. Differences in target groups may not, however, account for all differences in repayment and default rates. Staff of all North American Indian programs argue strongly that the social nature of the Grameen Bank model—the peer pressure, mutual support, and sharing of information that the peer groups supply—is critically important in nurturing successful businesses and maintaining high repayment rates.

Program staff in both the U.S. and Canadian programs report that both attitudes and behaviors of participants change markedly during their involvement with their peer groups. Savings rates increase, because of both the mandatory savings that result from the surcharge and group members' voluntary savings plans. More notably, the entrepreneurs begin to view their activities as businesses, not just as informal money-raising activities. As the entrepreneurs begin to take their own activities more seriously, they begin to view their relationships with suppliers and customers as business relationships to be handled using business techniques and methods.

Peer group members increase their understanding of business terms and techniques and over time become more confident of their own abilities. Likewise, participants become more clearly aware of the value of their products and services. At the same time, they become more comfortable in addressing directly their own developmental needs. Circles in Rosebud have requested, after their certification, that program staff provide them with additional training and information on marketing. Groups in both Pine Ridge and Rosebud have spent time addressing issues of family dysfunction and substance abuse, topics crucially important to household-based enterprises in communities hit hard by these problems.[29]

Peer group members readily share information within their circles, and regularly make suggestions about business techniques that other members might find useful. Some collaborative projects have emerged among peer group members; in one case, the proprietor of a computer software enterprise has begun to use his graphics capabilities to design stencils for a tee-shirt/sweatshirt business. Additionally, borrowers have begun to request meetings of all participants reservation-wide to exchange information and discuss shared experiences. Such sharing, over time, becomes a primary source of technical assistance for borrowers, who thus acquire information in terms they can understand, from sources they respect, at times when they can use it.

Staff of circle banking projects in Indian country are unanimous in considering the sharing of information among borrowers as the single most important part of the program for the development of the enterprises. Borrowers report relatively profound effects on their businesses even when the amounts of credit involved are small. Joining a borrower's circle appears to assist the participants to mobilize their own—and each others's—energies and skills in ways that amplify the effects of the monetary investments.

Initial community responses to the peer group methodology on both the Pine Ridge and Rosebud Reservations have been highly favorable. Experienced entrepreneurs—and some elected tribal officials—appreciate the lack of government involvement in the projects, which are relatively insulated from both the vagaries of policy changes and the pressures of political favoritism.[30] The projects serve other reservation needs as well. Childcare and transportation are scarce in most reservation communities; residents recognize that this technique of supporting micro-enterprise development allows business persons to continue to work out their own solutions to these problems.

Additionally, tribal members, whether they participate or not, frequently observe that the methods fit comfortably with traditional Lakota cultural values, which emphasize both a strong commitment to collaborative action within families, and an equally strong recognition of the importance of personal and individual achievements. Similar reactions of cultural appropriateness have come from the Canadian Ojibwa and Cree communities that participated in the Calmeadow Foundation pilot projects.

Despite general community approval of the concept of group lending, individual micro-entrepreneurs on each of these reservations have accepted these loan programs with caution born of experience. Individuals who have very gradually built their own businesses in the adverse and inhospitable economic conditions of reservations tend to be skeptical of outside intervention. As managers, they are moderately risk-averse, and are unwilling to bite off more than they know that they can chew. They understand clearly the limitations on supplies of labor and materials imposed by their local environment, and see no point in expanding too rapidly. As a result, in both Rosebud and Pine

Ridge, significant increases in participation rates have occurred only in the second years of the programs. Most micro-entrepreneurs in these communities prefer to watch the experiences of others in the program for months or years.[31] Only after the techniques have clearly demonstrated their usefulness under local conditions do participation rates begin to build.[32]

The development of a circle banking project in a reservation community requires considerable staff time and effort. Start-up activities for each of the U.S. programs took at least a year prior to making the first loan. The directors of the Lakota Fund and the Sicangu Enterprise Center felt that their initial staffing plans had significantly underestimated the needs of their programs for development and initial organizing.[33] In each case, the local organization also received considerable support and training from an off-reservation institution with access to national resources.) Given the relatively small populations within reservations, and the consequent limits on the volume of loans that any program can generate, it is unlikely that any program on a single reservation can become totally self-supporting on the basis of revenue from loan surcharges.

Are these programs—slow, incremental, small-scale—worth the social investment necessary to develop and sustain them in American Indian communities? The evidence from Bangladesh, from MICRO, from ACCION affiliates in Latin America, and from the Canadian programs, is strongly positive.[34] The evidence from Pine Ridge and Rosebud is consistent with the patterns seen elsewhere: participants have already reported increased sales and household income; participation rates in the programs are increasing; borrowers both report and demonstrate increased knowledge of useful business methods; and the tribal communities respond favorably to development that is seen to proceed at an appropriate pace under local control.

Slow, incremental, and small-scale are virtues in many tribal communities, which have found that control of rapid, large-scale, high-cost projects frequently eludes them. Tribal cultures and Indian individuals have long experience in successful economic adaptation and evolution, as long as the tempo is right and the resources are adequate. The circle banking technique allows entrepreneurs to convert their skills, their character, and their knowledge of local markets and individuals into economic assets. For those lenders and policymakers who know the strengths of many tribal communities, reliance on the knowledge and skills of Indian entrepreneurs makes this approach to development and investment both prudent and promising.

While the Grameen Bank methodology works well in tribal communities, it is also demonstrating its effectiveness in other rural areas, with non-Indian populations. The Good Faith Fund in Pine Bluff, Arkansas, serves rural, African-American communities in the Mississippi River delta, and has made $200,000 worth of loans to peer groups since 1988—again resulting in steady, incremental improvements in the businesses and the lives of the borrowers. Most of the Fund's clients, unlike entrepreneurs at Rosebud and Pine Ridge, use their loans to start new businesses.

What are indicators of potential success for a peer-group lending program in a rural area? High population density does not seem to be essential. The presence of an active group of existing micro-enterprises appears to be helpful, but not absolutely necessary. Likewise, the presence of Lakota or other tribal values of community and relationship appear to be very useful, but not critical. Very important, however, is the existence of a significant population that does not have access to sources of small amounts of credit or useful preparation or training for business development. Also essential is the presence within the community of information networks that transmit news efficiently about the character and trustworthiness of local residents. Finally, the community itself must be stable enough to permit the development of a borrowers' organization without undue interference from political or other external sources. If these conditions are met, peer-group lending techniques appear to be robust enough to serve the needs of rural micro-entrepreneurs in a wide variety of locations and cultures.

Acknowledgments

The author gratefully acknowledges the generous assistance of the staff and members of micro-enterprise loan programs, and in particular: Eileen Emery Lunderman of the Sicangu Enterprise Center, Mission, South Dakota; Elsie Meek of The Lakota Fund, Kyle, South Dakota; Gord Cunningham of The Calmeadow Foundation and Patti MacGregor of The First Peoples Fund, Toronto, Ontario; Frank Ballesteros of the Micro Industry Credit Rural Organization, Tucson, Arizona; Laura Junglas of the Commercial and Economic Development Division, Neighborhood Reinvestment Corporation, Boston, Massachusetts; and the staff of the Good Faith Fund, Pine Bluff, Arkansas. David Selvage, of the Sisseton-Wahpeton Tribal Housing Authority, provided information about his community. The families of Wadi and Amjad Wadi explained peer-group lending practices in their home Palestinian community. Kathleen Pickering conducted the interviews and tabulated the data for the survey of the Sicangu Enterprise Center participants. Gabriela Romanow of ACCION International, Cambridge, Massachusetts, was especially helpful in providing data, not otherwise available, on Latin American programs.

NOTES

1. U.S. Census, 1990.

2. Nancy Adler, *International Dimensions of Organizational Behavior*, second edition (Boston: PWS-Kent Publishing Company, 1991), pp. 80–81, 96–98.

3. This theme in federal policy is explored extensively in Brian W. Dieppe, *The Vanishing American: White Attitudes and U.S. Indian Policy* (Middletown, CN: Wesleyan University Press, 1982).

4. Douglas Johnson, "A Study of The Twenty-five Poorest Counties in the Continental U.S.A. in 1986" (New York: National Program Division, General Board of Global Ministries, The United Methodist Church, 1987), p. 10.

5. Johnson, p. 13.

6. Paul Szabo, "Job Survey of Todd County" (Rosebud, SD: Sinte Gleska University, 1985), p. 1.

7. Evidence from those tribes (particularly the Sisseton-Wahpeton Sioux Tribe of South Dakota) that have organized their own land leasing operations, indicates that returns on BIA leasing are significantly below market rates (personal communications, David Selvage, August 1991).

8. Stephen Cornell and Joseph Kalt, *Public Choice, Culture, and American Indian Economic Development* (Cambridge, MA: The Harvard Project on American Indian Economic Development, The John F. Kennedy School of Government Energy and Environmental Policy Center, Harvard University, June 1988), pp. 32–33.

9. Cornell and Kalt, pp. 31–38, present a basic analytic framework for the consideration of constraints and stimuli to economic development on reservations.

10. Johnson, p. 13.

11. Richard T. Sherman, "A Study of Traditional and Informal Sector Micro-Enterprise Activity and Its Impact on the Pine Ridge Reservation Economy," submitted to the Aspen Institute for Humanistic Studies, Washington, DC, September, 1988, p. 42.

12. Eileen Lunderman, "Feasibility Study for The Rosebud Reservation Enterprise Center," submitted to the Commercial and Economic Development Division of Neighborhood Reinvestment Corporation, Boston, MA, 1989. The study was performed as an initial effort to identify, locate, and describe existing micro-enterprises on the Rosebud Reservation, and not as a comprehensive assessment of informal sector activity.

13. Laura Junglas, personal communication, 18 December 1991.

14. Gord Cunningham, in *The Local Economy and Micro-Enterprise Sector of A Native Community: A Case Study of Wikwemikong (Unceded) Indian Reserve #26.* (Guelf: The University School of Rural Planning and Development, University of Guelph, 1990) reported unemployment rates fluctuating sea-

sonally between 45 and 63 percent. Public sector employment provided 75 percent of all jobs, pp. 58–61.

15. The author is grateful to the family of Wadji and Amjad Wadi, of Minneapolis, MN, for their explanations of the *jamiyla,* a Palestinian version of the borrowers' circle technique (personal communication, December 28, 1990).

16. "The Grameen Bank," an interview with Dr. Muhammed Yunus, conducted by David Cayley, broadcast on *Ideas,* 5 March 1991, the Canadian Broadcasting Corporation, Toronto, Ontario. Transcript ID 9099, pp. 2–7.

17. In 1990, the Commercial and Economic Development Division of Neighborhood Reinvestment Corporation, as pilot projects, supported the founding of four micro-enterprise development loan programs; each program uses the Grameen Bank techniques. Of these, the Sicangu Enterprise Center was both the only project in a rural area, and the only project with a Native American client base. The others are located in Pasadena, CA, Jackson, MS, and Philadelphia, PA. Significantly, the pace of development of the Rosebud center, measured by numbers of circles and numbers of participants, has equalled or exceeded that of the other three centers, despite the larger potential service populations for the urban programs. Neighborhood Reinvestment staff have suggested that Rosebud residents have been more readily able to form peer groups because tribal members know more about each other when they enter the program. Reservation populations are, overall, less transient than urban populations, and family and social connections provide ample access to information about potential peer group members (Laura Junglas, personal communication, Sept. 24, 1991). Rosebud residents also have little access to other sources of credit for small loans (pawnshops, informal or non-legal lenders) and few other sources of information about business development; for both of these goods, the reservation enterprise center on the reservation has virtually no local competition.

18. The Lakota Fund uses a total of six sessions; the material covered is essentially the same as in the three sessions at Rosebud.

19. Personal communication, Frank Ballesteros, May 1992.

20. The evaluation was conducted by the United States Agency for International Development; figures were cited by PRODEM, La Paz, Bolivia, in an application to the Inter-American Foundation, August 1989 (personal communication from Gabriela Romanow).

21. Informational/promotional pamphlet by and about AVANCE, San Jose, Costa Rica, 1990.

22. Micro Industry Credit Rural Organization (MICRO); A Division of PPEP Housing Development Corp. (PHDC), *Annual Report: Program Year 1990–91.* MICRO's staff does not expect micro-enterprises to expand significantly until the second or third round of loans is completed; until that point, entrepreneurs may simply be keeping their businesses alive while they learn new management skills, revise their approaches to pricing and marketing,

and change their own expectations of their enterprises. In its annual report, MICRO defines job stabilization as being in business "anytime from October 1990 to June 30, 1991, and the enterprise is still in business at the end of this reporting period, June 30, 1991."

23. *Consolidacion Y Expansion de Programas de Grupos Solidarios,* proposal for CODESPA Foundation, presented by the Association of Solidarity Groups of Columbia, February, 1990.

24. John Hatch and Arelis Gomez, *An Evaluation of Guatemala's Micro-business Promotion Project* (Draft), October 1989.

25. A.C. Lewin, *Al Borde de la Cumbre,* October, 1991.

26. Margaret Bowman, "ADEMI: Scaling Up and Decentralizing a Loan Program," in Charles S. Mann, Merilee S. Grindle, and Parker Shipton (eds.), *Seeking Solutions: Framework and Cases for Small Enterprise Development Programs,* p. 119, footnote 2.

27. Personal communication, Frank Ballesteros, May 1992.

28. Indian people who reside on the Rosebud Reservation are entitled to medical care from the federal Indian Health Service, and may qualify for other federal assistance by virtue of income level. The importance of these supports in providing an encouraging environment for micro-enterprise on reservations has not yet been evaluated, but appears to be quite significant; entrepreneurs who are currently employed, should they move into self-employment, do not face the barrier of significant increases in health-care costs when they lose employer-subsidized health coverage.

29. The Grameen Bank pays considerable attention to questions of social values and personal self-development among borrowers. Neighborhood Reinvestment Corporation staff did not emphasize this component as explicitly in the pilot programs, but the concern with values and their implications for personal development has emerged spontaneously from the peer groups themselves.

30. Personal communication, Alex Lunderman, President, Rosebud Sioux Tribe, June 1988.

31. In Rosebud, the initial participants in the project have not been the poorest of the poor; the first borrowers have mainly been individuals who are employed outside the home, but who seek to develop their micro-enterprise into a full-time source of income. Individuals without formal employment have tended to join only after the program is well-established.

32. This caution of Native American micro-entrepreneurs parallels the attitudes and behavior of Bangladeshi participants in the Grameen Bank, according to Muhammed Yunus. *Ideas* interview, p. 3.

33. The Calmeadow Foundation reports similar staffing patterns for its projects, with a minimum of one full-time person, plus support services, on each reserve.

34. The Calmeadow Foundation is conducting an extensive evaluation of the pilot programs it sponsored; final data were unavailable in time for this article.

REFERENCES

Adler, Nancy J., *International Dimensions of Organizational Behavior*, second edition (Boston, MA: PWS-Kent Publishing Company, 1991).

Ashe, Jeffery, *PISCES Phase One: Assisting the Smallest Scale Economic Activities of the Urban Poor: Summary and Recommendations for Practitioners* (Cambridge, MA: ACCION International/AITEC, 1981).

Cornell, Stephen, and Kalt, Joseph. P., *Public Choice, Culture, and American Indian Economic Development* (Cambridge, MA: The Harvard Project on American Indian Economic Development, John F. Kennedy School of Government, Harvard University, 1988).

Cunningham, Gord, *The Local Economy and Micro-Enterprise Sector of a Native Community: A Case Study of Wikwemikong (Unceded) Indian Reserve #26* (Guelf, Ont.: The University School of Rural Planning and Development, University of Guelph, 1990).

Dieppe, Brian W., *The Vanishing American: White Attitudes and U.S. Indian Policy*, (Middletown, CT: Wesleyan University Press, 1982).

The Grameen Bank, interview conducted by David Cayley, broadcast on *Idea*. Transcript ID 9099 (Toronto, Ont.: The Canadian Broadcasting Corporation, 1991).

Hargreaves, Margaret Barnwell, and Chang, Hedy Nai-Lin, "The Impact of Federal Welfare Reform in Indian Country: A Case Study of the Rosebud Reservation," in *What Can Tribes Do? Strategies and Institutions in American Indian Economic Development*, edited by Stephen Cornell and Joseph P. Kalt, (Los Angeles: The American Indian Studies Center, The University of California, Los Angeles, 1992).

Johnson, Douglas, *A Study of The Twenty-Five Poorest Counties in the Continental U.S.A. in 1986* (New York: National Program Division, General Board of Global Ministries, The United Methodist Church, 1987).

Lunderman, Eileen Emery, *Feasibility Study for The Rosebud Reservation Enterprise Center*, (Rosebud, SD: Rosebud Reservation Enterprise Center, Sinte Gleska University, 1989).

Mann, Charles S., Grindle, Merilee S., Shipton, Parker (eds.), *Seeking Solutions: Framework and Cases for Small Enterprise Development Programs* (West Hartford, CT: Kumarian Press, 1989).

Nelson, Candace, *Evaluation of the Neighborhood Enterprise Center Program as of September 30, 1992: A Pilot Program of Neighborhood Reinvestment Corporation* (Boston: Neighborhood Reinvestment Corporation, 1993).

Otero, Maria, *A Handful of Rice: Savings Mobilization by Micro-Enterprise Programs and Perspectives for the Future*, (Washington, DC: ACCION International, 1989).

Ross, David P., and Usher, Peter J., *From The Roots Up: Economic Development as if Community Mattered* (Ottawa, Ont.: Canadian Council on Social Development, 1986).

Sherman, Richard T., *A Study of Traditional and Informal Sector Micro-Enterprise Activity and its Impact on the Pine Ridge Reservation Economy* (Washington, DC: The Aspen Institute for Humanistic Studies, 1988).

Smith, Timothy, "Strategies for Financing Economic and Business Development on Indian Reservations," (St. Paul, MN: Northwest Area Foundation, 1989).

Szabo, Paul, "Job Survey of Todd County," (Rosebud, SD: Sinte Gleska University, 1985).

CHAPTER 13

Helping the Unemployed Start Businesses: A Potential Rural Development Strategy

JULES H. LICHTENSTEIN[1]

Introduction

Developing effective strategies for rural development has been an ongoing concern of policymakers, public officials, and rural constituencies.[2] One approach has been to stimulate small business development and job creation in rural America. Emphasis has been placed on targeting federal credit programs to rural areas.[3] An example of this approach is the Small Business Administration's (SBA) Microloan Demonstration Program.[4] Until recently, little attention has been given to a potential development strategy—the use of self-employment/reemployment as a potential tool for assisting the return of the unemployed to productive work. Even less discussion has been devoted to the applicability of the self-employment strategy to rural versus urban areas. This would involve examining the significance of an urban versus rural setting for the success of this strategy. Specifically, do the characteristics of rural areas—i.e., their remoteness, lack of access to information and specialized services, the small and undiversified nature of their labor markets, and the characteristics of their labor force—significantly affect the potential use of a self-employment/reemployment strategy?

The focus of this chapter is to briefly outline the self-employment strategy and to examine the applicability of self-employment/

reemployment strategies to the unemployed living in rural versus urban areas in the United States. Can these opportunities be extended to help in the reemployment of unemployed workers? What are the differences in the success of these strategies in rural versus urban areas?[5]

The Self-Employment/Reemployment Strategy

The self-employment/reemployment strategy involves providing unemployed workers in an area with either a lump sum payment or periodic payments in lieu of unemployment benefits to help them set up and run a business. Various forms of technical assistance are also provided to individuals under this strategy.

The current interest in self-employment as a reemployment option for unemployed workers and as a potential development strategy is the result of a variety of factors. Underlying this interest are basic American values that entrepreneurship and the ability to start a business should be opportunities available to everyone. Other considerations include the widely acknowledged contribution of small business to job creation, the relatively modest financial requirements for starting many types of new businesses,[6] and the experience of many European countries with self-employment initiatives including the French Chomeurs Createurs "Unemployed Entrepreneurs" program and the British self-employment allowance program. Several federally-assisted demonstration programs have been initiated and designed to examine self-employment as a reemployment option.[7] Interest in using this approach in rural areas is based on efforts to revitalize rural areas and stem the decline in growth and development in these areas.

Examining the viability of the self-employment approach in a rural versus an urban setting entails looking at self-employment employment trends and business growth in rural (nonmetropolitan) versus urban (metropolitan) areas. It is also important to examine relevant research that attempts to explain the transition to self-employment of unemployed versus employed workers, and the effect of rural/urban residence on the transition. In addition, early evaluation results of self-employment/reemployment demonstration projects will be examined.

Small Business versus Micro-Business

Self-employment/reemployment strategies need to be placed in perspective. This includes a look at self-employment or the micro-business—how it is defined and related to small business, what the general trends look like, and what we know about self-employment in rural versus urban areas.

Micro-Business in the United States

The dominant form of organization in American business is the small business. When we think of businesses in the United States, we imagine businesses with employees. In reality, the typical business in the United States is a micro-business; i.e., a business with one individual working less than full time—a part-time business with few receipts. The next most common business is an individual working full time without employees. Of the 20 million businesses in the United States, 6 million (about 30 percent) are full-time businesses with employees, 9 million (45 percent) are full-time businesses without employees, and the rest (5 million, or 25 percent) are part-time businesses without employees.[8]

Definitions

There is no universally accepted definition of a micro-enterprise, i.e., the smallest small businesses.[9] Probably the most common term used to describe a micro-enterprise is self-employment. "Self-employment," simply defined, is working for yourself. The official definition used by the Census Bureau includes both sole proprietors and partners with no distinction, and leaves out owners of incorporated business who are considered wage-and-salary workers. Also left out are individuals who work for wages and salaries and have side businesses, i.e., so-called "moonlighters."[10] A broader definition of self-employment and business ownership might provide a better measure of total entrepreneurial activity (table 13.1).

Self-Employment Data and Trends

The definition of self-employed used will have dramatic effects on the counts of the self-employed or micro-businesses and any analysis of self-employment or business trends and behavior. In addition, the data sources available will have a significant effect on the kinds of analysis that can be undertaken. Possible data sources include Census surveys, IRS data, and listings of businesses from yellow and white page directories.

Based on the official Census definition of self-employment and data from the Current Population Survey, the number of self-employed employed increased 81 percent between 1968 and 1993—from 5.1 million to 9.2 million (table 13.2).[11] Another dramatic self-employ-

Table 13.1: Distribution of Employment in Nonagricultural Industries by Class of Workers

Class of Worker	Number (Thousands)	Percent of Total Employment
Total Nonagricultural Employment	95,918	100.0%
Unincorporated Self-Employed,	7,482	7.8
Self-Employed Only	(7,190)	(7.6)
Self-Employed with Wage-and-Salary Employment	(192)	(0.2)
Wage-and-Salary Workers	88,053	91.8
Incorporated Self-Employed	(2,590)	(2.7)
Wage-and-Salary Workers Only	(82,585)	(86.1)
Wage-and-Salary Workers with Self-Employment	(2,878)	(3.0)
Unpaid Family Workers	384	0.4
Total Self-Employed,	12,950	13.5
Unincorporated Self-Employed	(7,482)	(7.8)
Incorporated Self-Employed	(2,590)	(2.7)
Wage-and-Salary Workers with Self-Employment	(2,878)	(3.0)

Note: Numbers in parentheses are subtotals.

Source: U.S. Department of Commerce, Bureau of the Census, Current Population Survey, May 1983, unpublished data. *The State of Small Business: A Report of the President* (Washington, DC: U.S. Government Printing Office, 1986), Table 4.3.

ment phenomenon evident from the Census data is the growth of women entrepreneurs. Men are more likely to be self-employed than women, but the number of unincorporated self-employed women has been increasing over *four* times faster than the number of self-employed men and more than *three* times as fast as women wage-and-salary workers (table 13.2). This increase has occurred most strongly in the last decade.

Micro-Businesses in the Rural United States

In addition, analysis of unpublished data from the Current Population Survey shows where the self-employed live. Almost 70 percent of all self-employed workers live in metropolitan areas (table 13.3).[12] Except for the incorporated self-employed, self-employed workers are more geographically concentrated in nonmetropolitan areas than workers employed in wage-and-salary jobs only. The incorporated self-employed are significantly more likely to live in metropolitan areas than are the unincorporated self-employed—77 percent compared with 68 percent. Incorporated self-employed individuals have usually been in business longer and typically earn more than the unincorporated self-employed.[13] There is relatively little difference in the location of full-time versus part-time unincorporated self-employed. When compared with total U.S. population residing in

Table 13.2: Nonfarm Self-Employed Individuals, 1963–1993 (Thousands)

Year	Total	Male	Female
1993	9,218	6,140	3,078
1988	8,519	5,564	2,955
1983	7,575	5,136	2,439
1978	6,429	4,614	1,814
1973	5,474	4,055	1,419
1968	5,102	3,870	1,232
1963	6,114	4,743	1,371
Annual Percent Change, 1963–1993	1.7%	1.0%	4.2%

Source: U.S. Department of Labor, Bureau of Labor Statistics, *Employment and Earnings*, (Washington, DC: U.S. Government Printing Office, various issues).

Table 13.3: Percentage Distribution of Employed Nonagricultural Workers by Selected Characteristics

	Total Population[j]	OB[a] FT[f]	SE[b] FT	SE[b] PT[g]	ISE[c] FT	WSSE[d] FT	WSO[e] FT	WSO[e] PT
Number[h]	NA	2,719	3,393	1,551	1,470	650	16,748	5,788
Metropolitan area[i]	75.8	69.5	67.7	65.5	77.3	63.7	74.2	72.2
Nonmetropolitan area	24.2	30.5	32.3	34.5	22.7	36.3	25.8	27.8

a. Owners of businesses, including the self-employed (unincorporated), incorporated self-employed, and wage and salary workers with self-employment.
b. Self-employed (unincorporated).
c. Incorporated self-employed.
d. Wage and salary workers with self-employment.
e. Wage and salary workers only.
f. Full-time workers.
g. Part-time workers.
h. Number of records in sample. All other figures in percent.
i. Standard Metropolitan Statistical Area. On all jobs held during the survey week.
j. Data are estimated from published Census data. Statistical Abstract, 1985.

Source: Simon and Company, Inc. *A New Perspective on Business Ownership: Phase II Final Report* (Washington, DC: U.S. Small Business Administration, Office of Advocacy, report prepared under contract no. SBA-8559-AER-84, July 15, 1985), Table 4. Tabulations by Simon and Company of unpublished data from March-May 1983 CPS.

Table 13.4: Percentage Distribution of Full-time Employed Nonagricultural Workers by Selected Characteristics: Males and Females, May 1983

	Males			Females		
	OB[a]	SE[b]	WSO[c]	OB	SE	WSO
Number[d]	2,135	2,518	9,684	584	875	7,064
Metropolitan area[e]	69.7	68.3	74.5	68.7	65.7	73.7
Nonmetropolitan area	30.3	31.7	25.5	31.3	34.3	26.3

a. Owners of businesses, including the self-employed (unincorporated), incorporated self-employed, and wage and salary workers with self-employment.
b. Self-employed (unincorporated).
c. Wage and salary workers only.
d. Number of records in sample. All other figures in percent.
e. Standard Metropolitan Statistical Area.

Source: Simon and Company, Inc. *A New Perspective on Business Ownership: Phase II Final Report* (Washington, DC: U.S. Small Business Administration, Office of Advocacy, report prepared under contract no. SBA-8559-AER-84, July 15, 1985), Table 6. Tabulations by Simon and Company of unpublished data from March-May 1983 CPS.

metropolitan areas, all self-employed workers except for the incorporated self-employed are more concentrated in nonmetropolitan areas than metropolitan areas. In addition, there is very little difference in the proportion of men and women who are self-employed in metropolitan and non-metropolitan areas (table 13.4).

Looking at selected major occupations, the unincorporated self-employed in metropolitan areas are more likely to be in executive, administrative, and managerial occupations than their counterparts in nonmetropolitan areas and significantly more likely to be in professional specialties (table 13.5). The proportion of self-employed workers in the professional occupations residing in nonmetropolitan areas is less than that of wage-and-salary workers. The self-employed in metropolitan areas are also more likely to earn more than their counterparts in nonmetropolitan areas (table 13.6).

Another source of Census data on the self-employed is the Survey of Income and Program Participation (SIPP). This data source provides information on the size of businesses operated by self-employed individuals. It also provides information on the legal form of business.[14]

Clearly, sole proprietorships are much more likely to have only one individual in the business (the owner) compared with corporations and partnerships—78 percent versus 12 percent for corporations and partnerships combined (tables 13.7 and 13.8). SIPP business ownership data for rural versus urban areas is available but can only be tabulated from unpublished sources. Further information about the self-employed is available from the Characteristics of Business Owners Survey (CBO) undertaken by the Census Bureau in both 1982 and 1987. The CBO is one of the most comprehensive surveys of the

Table 13.5: Percentage Distribution of Full-time Employed Nonagricultural Workers by Selected Characteristics: Selected Major Occupations, May 1983

	Executive, Administrative, and Managerial		Professional Specialty		Sales		Service[a]		Precision Production Craft, and Repair	
	SE[b]	WSO[c]	SE	WSO	SE	WSO	SE	WSO	SE	WSO
Number[d]	640	1,999	515	2,387	798	1,566	394	1,349	639	2,235
Metropolitan area[e]	71.4	81.9	77.2	75.8	64.6	78.0	64.7	72.0	63.5	71.3
Nonmetropolitan area	28.6	18.1	22.8	24.2	35.4	22.0	35.3	28.0	36.5	28.7

a. Excludes workers in protective and private household occupations.

b. Self-employed (unincorporated).

c. Wage and salary workers only.

d. Number of records in sample. All other figures in percent.

e. Standard Metropolitan Statistical Area.

Source: Simon and Company, Inc. *A New Perspective on Business Ownership: Phase II Final Report* (Washington, DC: U.S. Small Business Administration, Office of Advocacy, report prepared under contract no. SBA-8559-AER-84, July 15, 1985), Table 7. Tabulations by Simon and Company of unpublished data from March-May 1983 CPS.

demographic and financial characteristics of businesses and their owners. It is essentially a dataset of young and small businesses, with emphasis on businesses owned by minorities and women. The sample represents about 11 million businesses and 14 million owners. About three quarters of these businesses lack workers (table 13.9).[15]

Table 13.6: Percentage Distribution of Employed Nonagricultural Workers[a] by Selected Characteristics: Earnings in 1982

	1982 Earnings: Less than $10,000			1982 Earnings: $10,000 or more		
	OB	SE	WSO	OB[b]	SE[c]	WSO[d]
Number[e]	1,025	759	6,720	1,110	735	11,786
Metropolitan area[f]	62.4	59.5	69.0	75.4	74.0	77.0
Nonmetropolitan area	37.6	40.5	31.0	24.6	26.0	23.0

a. Employment and class of worker status as of May 1983.
b. Owners of business, including the self-employed (unincorporated), incorporated self-employed and wage and salary workers with self-employment.
c. Self-employed (unincorporated).
d. Wage and salary workers only.
e. Number of records in sample. All other figures in percent.
f. Standard Metropolitan Statistical Area.

Source: Simon and Company, Inc. *A New Perspective on Business Ownership: Phase II Final Report* (Washington, DC: Office of Advocacy, report prepared under contract no. SBA-8559-AER-84, July 15, 1985), Table 9. Tabulations by Simon and Company of unpublished data from March-May 1983 CPS.

Table 13.7: Distribution of Business by Legal Form of Business and Number of Employees, 1983[a] (Percent)

	Number of Employees[b]				
Category	1	2	3 to 5	6 or more	Total
Total	100.0	100.0	100.0	100.0	100.0
Sole proprietorship[c]	93.8	51.1	47.7	16.0	70.7
Casual sole proprietorship[c]	3.8	0	0	0	22.3
Noncasual sole proprietorships	90.0	51.1	47.7	16.0	48.4
Partnerships and incorporated businesses	6.2	48.9	52.3	94.0	29.3

a. SIPP reference periods June to September 1983 through September to December 1983.
b. Employment in primary business. Owner or owners and unpaid family workers included in count of employees.
c. Includes sole businesses with expected gross receipts of less than $1,000 in next 12 months. Some of these sole businesses may be partnerships or incorporated businesses.

Source: For an analysis of SIPP data on the self-employed see, Sheldon E. Haber, Enrique J. Lamas, and Jules H. Lichtenstein, "On Their Own: The Self-Employed and others in Private Business," *Monthly Labor Review* (May 1987), Table 5.

Results from Research and Demonstration Projects

There are numerous ways in which the potential for self-employment as a reemployment strategy can be approached. First, it is possible to analyze secondary data to determine how successful the unemployed are compared with the employed in entering self-employ-

Table 13.8: Distribution of Business by Number of Employees and Legal Form of Business, 1983[a] (Percent)

Category	Number of Employees[b]				
	1	2	3 to 5	6 or more	Total
Total	56.9	12.3	14.5	14.3	100.0
Sole proprietorships[c]	78.2	8.9	9.7	3.2	100.0
Casual sole proprietorships[c]	100.0	0	0	0	100.0
Noncasual sole proprietorships	66.1	13.0	14.2	4.7	100.0
Partnerships and incorporated businesses	12.5	20.6	25.8	41.1	100.0

a. SIPP reference periods June to September 1983 through September to December 1983.

b. Employment in primary business. Owner or owners and unpaid family workers included in count of employees.

c. Includes sole businesses with expected gross receipts of less than $1,000 in next 12 months. Some of these sole businesses may be partnerships or incorporated businesses.

Source: For an analysis of SIPP data on the self-employed see, Sheldon E. Haber, Enrique J. Lamas, and Jules H. Lichtenstein, "On Their Own: The Self-Employed and others in Private Business," *Monthly Labor Review* (May 1987), Table 5.

Table 13.9: Number of Sole Proprietorships in 1987 by Type of Owners[a]

	Nonminority Male-Owned Business	Women-Owned Business	Minority-Owned Business
	(1,000s)	(1,000s)	(1,000s)
Total[b]	8,755 (100.0)	4,114 (100.0)	1,223 (100.0)
With No Paid Employees	6,075 (69.4)	3,496 (85.0)	973 (80.0)
With Paid Employees	2,680 (30.6)	618 (15.0)	250 (20.0)

a. Figures in parentheses are for percentage of total.

b. Data for each of these ownership groups cannot be summed to a total for all firms because firms can be included in multiple groups (e.g., a firm could be both Black and women-owned.)

Source: U.S. Department of Commerce, Bureau of the Census, *1987 Characteristics of Business Owners* (Washington, DC: U.S. Government Printing Office, April 1992), p. 18.

ment. A second approach is to directly examine the results of ongoing experiments and demonstration projects.

Research into Self-Employment Entry by Unemployed versus Employed Workers

It is possible that those who enter self-employment from employment differ significantly from those who enter from unemployment. The differences in backgrounds and motivations of the employed and unemployed suggest differences in their ability to enter self-employment, start a business, and succeed in business. For example, those who enter self-employment from wage-and-salary work may be better prepared to handle the tasks involved in starting a business than those who enter from unemployment. Previously employed business owners are more likely than the unemployed to have assets available to facilitate a business startup and are therefore more likely to succeed in self-employment.[16]

The fact that many unemployed are likely to be less able to enter and succeed at self-employment than employed individuals is probably due to some extent to the fact that unemployment is often unexpected. In addition, unemployment frequently brings about a reduction in savings, and therefore assets, available for starting a business. Unemployed workers may look at self-employment as a temporary condition that provides temporary income while trying to find a suitable wage-and-salary job. On the other hand, the likelihood of expiring unemployment insurance benefits may motivate some unemployed individuals to enter self-employment—this may represent employment of last resort.

The Office of Advocacy recently funded research to address many of these questions.[17] Using Census' Current Population Survey data for 1968 through 1987, an effort was made to analyze several relevant factors, including metropolitan/nonmetropolitan differences. Findings indicate that living in an urban (versus a rural) area appears to have an effect on self-employment entry. Employed individuals living in urban areas are less likely than their counterparts in rural areas to become self-employed—all other factors held constant. On the other hand, the urban/rural factor does not have an impact on whether an unemployed individual enters self-employment.[18]

The study also probed (1) the frequency of small business formation by employed and unemployed workers; (2) the frequency of small business dissolution by workers who were employed or unemployed prior to the business start; and (3) the earnings of unemployed workers who started a business relative to unemployed workers who returned to wage work and employed workers who started small businesses.

Overall, the analysis found that self-employment does provide an outlet for unemployed workers. However, unemployed workers do not do very well at self-employment. They leave self-employment more often and earn less in the first year than self-employed workers who were employed prior to starting their businesses.[19]

But the fact that many unemployed workers who entered self-employment remain self-employed rather than returning to wage work may suggest that they would do even more poorly at wage work or it may indicate they are more satisfied being self-employed. The survival of a business over time is also a function of the ability of a business to grow and add jobs. Recent research has shown that 23.7 percent of all firms fail within the first two years of their startup date. However, the failure rate for those young firms adding at least one job is only 8 percent during this period compared with 29.5 percent for non-growing firms.[20]

The Western European and Canadian Experience with Self-Employment Initiatives

As indicated earlier, interest within the United States in the self-employment/reemployment strategy has been stimulated by the European experience with self-employment initiatives. These programs have focused on assisting dislocated workers (those workers who are permanently laid off from their jobs due to structural economic conditions) return to employment. The focus of the programs has been to promote self-employment and microbusiness creation for individuals eligible for unemployment benefits through the national insurance program. The two largest European self-employment programs are those of Britain and France.[21] In France, the Chomeurs Createurs is estimated to generate between 20 and 25 percent of all new businesses. In England, the Enterprise Allowance Scheme is estimated to account for 20 percent of new self-employment.[22]

The programs in France and England provide two different ways in which self-employment programs might be structured. The French Chomeurs Createurs ("Unemployed Entrepreneurs") program provides a lump-sum payment that varies according to the length of previous employment and current unemployment. The British program provides a weekly self-employment allowance in place of regular unemployment benefits, which continues for a year while participants develop and operate their businesses.[23] However, neither the French nor the British program appears to use different approaches in assisting the unemployed in rural versus urban areas.

The financial assistance provided in other European countries is also based on these two basic types—lump-sum payments for capitalization of a business based on unemployment benefits; or periodic payments in lieu of regular unemployment benefits that provide individuals with income during business formation and early stages of operation.

In addition to financial support, most of the European programs provide some sort of package of business services including business counseling, entrepreneurial training, technical assistance, exemptions from certain business taxes and legal requirements (e.g., exemption from social security contributions in France), and preferential access to business loans and grants from sources outside the program. It is unclear whether other European countries have programs that differentiate between urban versus rural areas.

In Canada, on the other hand, the Self-Employment Incentive Option is part of the Community Futures Program, an umbrella initiative to assist rural communities experiencing or anticipating high unemployment. Self-employment is part of a comprehensive regional economic development strategy.[24]

The U.S. Experience with Self-Employment Demonstration Projects

The European experience has attracted considerable U.S. interest over the last few years and has acted as a catalyst to stimulate interest in self-employment as an option for reemployment of unemployed workers in the United States.

These experiences have led the U.S. Department of Labor to explore the possibility of promoting self-employment as a reemployment option for unemployed workers. In 1987, the Labor Department initiated a research demonstration project in the State of Washington to test the cost effectiveness of using a one-time, lump-sum unemployment benefit payment to assist self-employment. This approach was similar to the French program.[25]

Later in 1987, the Congress enacted legislation titled the "Demonstration Program to Provide Self-Employment Allowances to Eligible Individuals" that authorized the Department of Labor to proceed with self-employment demonstration projects in other states. This resulted in a second demonstration, in Massachusetts, which was designed to test a program that provides unemployed workers

with periodic payments during the early stages of business development similar to the British Enterprise Allowance Scheme program.[26]

Potential Target Populations

A wide range of groups have been identified as possible target
populations for a self-employment program. Certain groups have
been identified by demonstration program staff as the most likely
candidates for a self-employment assistance program: Unemployment Insurance recipients, dislocated workers, older workers, AFDC
recipients, and "at-risk" youth.

Within each group there are likely to be some individuals who
have better potential for success in self-employment than others.
Some groups emerge as more likely candidates to succeed. Demonstration program staff have found that older workers, unemployment insurance recipients, and dislocated workers are more likely to
have work experience and personal maturity to assist them in
starting a new business. They may also have access to state- and
federally-supported training programs and entitlements.

An important question is the extent to which these groups are
located in rural versus urban areas. Attempting to judge the potential
for self-employment among such a varied group requires attention to
sub-groups within it. It seems likely that one sub-group, although
small in relation to the total U.S. dislocated worker population,
which has significant potential for self-employment would be unemployed farmers and ranchers. They tend to have an array of marketable skills, usually know the community, and are likely to understand the fundamentals of business management. Though they
would need to translate their experience into a new context in a
depressed local economy, a study of the Council of State Policy and
Planning Agencies shows a high number of successful businesses
were started by former farmers in Iowa.[27]

Demonstration Project Evaluations

Interim evaluations of the Washington State experiment—the
Washington Self-Employment and Enterprise Development (SEED)
Demonstration—and the Massachusetts Unemployment Insurance
Self-Employment Demonstration have been conducted by the Labor
Department.[28] The primary purpose of these demonstrations was to
determine the viability of self-employment as a reemployment option
for unemployed workers.

The evaluation of the demonstrations consists of three parts: (1) an implementation and process analysis; (2) an impact analysis; and (3) a benefit-cost analysis.

The interim results of the Labor Department's evaluations of the Washington and Massachusetts demonstrations indicate that self-employment programs increase the likelihood of entry into self-employment and accelerate its timing for UI claimants who were interested in self-employment. In addition, the results indicate that self-employment programs increase the likelihood of total employment as well as the duration of this employment.

Preliminary analysis of the SEED Demonstration indicates that the interest in self-employment was greater in urban areas with lower unemployment rates and vibrant local economies than in rural areas with weaker economies and relatively high unemployment rates. Analysts indicate that it is not possible at this time to determine whether the difference in interest was primarily due to the employment conditions or to the urban/rural nature of the area.[29] The SEED Demonstration was initiated at a time when Washington State's economy was very strong and the condition of the state's economy could have significant implications for the success of demonstrations in local areas.

Characteristics of the participants in the programs varied significantly from rural to urban areas. Participants in urban areas were more likely (1) to have higher levels of education; (2) to be employed in professional, technical, or managerial occupations; (3) to have been employed in manufacturing or services sectors; (4) to have higher UI payments; (5) to be unmarried; (6) to have a higher expectation of being called back by their previous employer; and (7) to have more assets than participants in rural areas.[30]

These encouraging findings from the Washington and Massachusetts UI Self-Employment Demonstrations have been used by supporters of self-employment programs to assist unemployed workers in becoming self-employed. In November 1993, Congress passed the North American Free Trade Agreement (NAFTA, P.L. 103–182), which allows states to establish self-employment assistance programs as part of the state unemployment compensation system. UI claimants will now be able to obtain self-employment training and financial assistance from state employment security systems. To date, four New England states (Connecticut, Rhode Island, Maine, and Vermont) have enacted enabling legislation to implement self-employment assistance programs for the unemployed. A number of other states, including New York and California, have recently introduced bills to enact similar legislation.

The provisions of the act give states the ability to add self-employment programs to the current mix of reemployment policy tools available to help dislocated workers. To qualify for these self-employment allowance payments, program participants must attend entrepreneurial training courses and receive other technical assistance services in support of their self-employment effort. The cost of administering the program will be paid from UI administrative grants.

Summary and Conclusions

The applicability of self-employment/reemployment as a potential rural development strategy in the United States cannot be clearly determined at this time. Analysis of Census data indicates that the population density is not significantly related to whether an unemployed individual enters self-employment. However, a more direct assessment is needed to fully explore the self-employment/reemployment strategy as it relates to rural areas. Analyses of self-employment/reemployment demonstration projects in the states of Washington and Massachusetts have not yet been completed. These evaluations are designed to explore the differences across demonstration sites and examine how impacts may differ by urban/rural areas or employment conditions.[31]

NOTES

1. Jules H. Lichtenstein, Ph.D., is Chief of the Applied Policy Branch in the U.S. Small Business Administration's Office of Advocacy. Points of view or opinions stated in this chapter are those of the author and do not necessarily represent the position or policies of the U.S. Small Business Administration.

2. Various strategies have been proposed and focus on improving the infrastructure of rural areas through regional or rural development efforts and improving the human capital of rural areas. For an analysis of the latter see, Economic Research Service, *Education and Rural Economic Development: Strategies for the 1990's* (Washington, DC: U.S. Department of Agriculture, September 1991). Also see, Economic Research Service, *Infrastructure Investment and Economic Development: Rural Strategies for the 1990's*, Staff Report No. AGES 9069 (Washington, DC: U.S. Department of Agriculture, November 1990).

3. "Impact of Credit Reform on Lending Programs and Rural Development," Hearing before the Subcommittee on Procurement, Tourism, and Rural Development of the House Committee on Small Business, Washington, DC (April 30, 1991). See also Economic Research Service, *Financial*

Market Intervention as Rural Development Strategy, ERS Staff Report No. AGES90-70 (Washington, DC: U.S. Department of Agriculture, November 1990).

4. The purpose of this program, which was authorized in 1991, is to provide assistance to new or existing small business concerns in need of small-scale financing and technical assistance. As a result, SBA makes direct loans and grants to selected intermediary lenders and technical assistance providers that contribute matching funds and, in turn, make microloans and provide technical assistance to eligible small businesses. The program's target population is women, low income, and minority entrepreneurs and business owners as well as small businesses in areas suffering from a lack of credit due to economic downturn. At least 50 percent of the lenders who participate in the program are required to serve rural areas. As of June 1994, 43.2 percent of the loans have been made in rural areas.

5. For the purposes of this chapter an urban area will be defined as a metropolitan area (i.e., a metropolitan statistical area (MSA)) and a rural area will be defined as a nonmetropolitan area (i.e., a non MSA). However, data are presented for Standard Metropolitan Statistical Areas—the concept is similar to but preceded the MSA concept.

6. Analysis of the Characteristics of Business Ownership (CBO) data indicates that about half of all proprietors started or acquired their businesses with less than $5,000. See Faith Ando & Associates, Inc. *Minorities, Women, Veterans and the 1982 Characteristics of Business Ownership Survey: A Preliminary Analysis*, Report No. PB 89-115091/AS (Springfield, VA: National Technical Information Service, 1989; prepared under award no. SBA-3026-OA-88).

7. In 1987, the Labor Department initiated demonstration projects in the states of Washington and Massachusetts.

8. Statistics published by the Internal Revenue Service provide the broadest measure of non-farm businesses in the United States. An estimated 21.3 million tax returns were filed in 1992. See *The State of Small Business: A Report of the President* (Washington, DC: Government Printing Office, 1993), p. 37.

9. The terms "micro-enterprise," and "micro-business," and "self-employment" are used interchangeably in this paper.

10. For an extended discussion of self-employment as a small business phenomenon, see Jules H. Lichtenstein, "Self-Employment as Small Business," *The State of Small Business: A Report of the President* (Washington, DC: U.S. Government Printing Office, 1986), 105–49. If we expand the definition to include the incorporated self-employed and "moonlighters," the Office of Advocacy has estimated that about 13 million Americans are self-employed entrepreneurs (see table 13.1). The Office of Advocacy is currently updating this research.

11. This trend does not include the even more dramatic trend in other components of the self-employed not included in the official definition. For example, the Office of Advocacy estimated that moonlighters increased 468

percent from 1979 to 1983 (to almost 2.9 million) according to the latest analysis available.

12. For the most recent analysis completed by the Small Business Administration's (SBA) Office of Advocacy of unpublished CPS data that provides information on the self-employed by metropolitan/non-metropolitan area, see Simon & Company, Inc. *A New Perspective on Business Ownership: Phase II Final Report* (Washington, DC: U.S. Small Business Administration, Office of Advocacy, report prepared under contract no. SBA-8559-AER-84, July 15, 1985). The definition of the self-employed used in this report includes owners of businesses, including the self-employed (unincorporated), incorporated self-employed and wage-and-salary workers with self-employment.

13. *The State of Small Business, 1986, op. cit.,* p. 130.

14. As indicated earlier, published Census data from the CPS on the self-employed cover only unincorporated self-employed, which includes but does not distinguish between sole proprietorships and partnerships. It is possible to obtain information on incorporated self-employed from unpublished CPS data. Unpublished SIPP data permits a breakout of all legal forms—sole proprietorships, partnerships and corporations—for the self-employed. For an analysis of SIPP data on the self-employed, see Sheldon E. Haber, Enrique J. Lamas, and Jules H. Lichtenstein, "On Their Own: The Self-Employed and Others in Private Business," *Monthly Labor Review* (May 1987), pp. 17–23. SIPP business ownership data for rural versus urban areas are available but can only be tabulated from unpublished sources.

15. While it is possible to examine metropolitan/nonmetropolitan differences in business ownership using both the 1982 and 1987 CBO database, as yet, this has not been undertaken by researchers.

16. Jacob M. Benus and Terry Johnson, "Entry Into Self-Employment," draft paper presented at the Association for Public Policy Analysis and Management's Thirteenth Annual Research Conference, October 24–26, 1991, Bethesda, Maryland, pp. 7–8.

17. David S. Evans and Linda S. Leighton, *Small-Business Formation by Unemployed Workers* (Washington, DC: U.S. Small Business Administration, Office of Advocacy, prepared under contract award no. SBA-2102-AER-87, January 1989), pp. i–iv.

18. *Ibid.,* pp. 10–11.

19. According to the analysis of CPS data, of the white men who started a small business after being unemployed, 51.5 percent returned to wage employment after a year. Of white men who were employed before starting a business, only 37.0 percent returned to wage employment after a year. The results are roughly the same for minorities—54 percent for the unemployed versus 38.0 percent for the employed. On the other hand, there is relatively little difference for white women—42.3 percent for the unemployed versus 41.2 percent for the employed. The samples, however, are much smaller and the results less reliable for white women and minorities. *Ibid.* p.ii.

20. *The State of Small Business: A Report of the President* (Washington, DC: Government Printing Office, 1989), pp. 24–25.

21. Self-employment programs focused on the unemployed have also been tried in Belgium, Denmark, Finland, Germany, Greece, Ireland, Italy, Luxembourg, the Netherlands, Norway, Portugal, Spain, and Sweden. Australia and Canada have also implemented programs. See Stephen A. Wandner and Jon C. Messenger, "From Unemployed to Self-Employed: Self-Employment As a Reemployment Option in the United States," paper prepared for the Association of Public Policy Analysis and Management's Thirteenth Annual Research Conference, October 24–26, 1991, Bethesda, Maryland, p. 3.

22. Jacob M. Benus and Terry Johnson, *op. cit.*, p. 3.

23. *Ibid.*, p. 4.

24. *FIRMSTART: A Study of the Viability of Self-employment for Unemployed and Low-Income People* (Washington, D.C.: U.S. Department of Labor, Employment and Training Administration, 1989) , p. 5.

25. Stephen A. Wandner and Jon C. Messenger, *op. cit.*, p. 13.

26. In addition to the Labor Department-sponsored projects, the Corporation for Enterprise Development is coordinating a third demonstration project called the Self-Employment Investment Demonstration. This project has a different target population—recipients of social welfare benefits in the Aid to Families with Dependent Children (AFDC) program.

27. *FIRMSTART, op. cit.*, p. 32.

28. Jacob Benus, Michelle Wood, and Neelima Grover. "A Comparative Analysis of the Washington and Massachusetts UI Self-Employment Demonstrations," in *Self-Employment as a Reemployment Option: Demonstration Results and National Legislation,* January, 1994 (Unemployment Insurance Occasional Paper 94-3, U.S. Department of Labor, 1994).

29. Interest is measured by the proportion of all targeted claimants who receiving an invitation letter who submitted at SEED application.

30. Jacob M. Benus and Terry Johnson, *op. cit.*, p.16.

31. The final impact report for both demonstrations is scheduled to be released in January 1995.

CHAPTER 14

Targeting Market Failures in Natural Resource Industries as a Rural Development Strategy: The Case of the Maine Potato Market Improvement Fund

STEWART N. SMITH

Background

Business firms make investment decisions based on the best information available. In rural areas, small firms are heavily dependent on a
local infrastructure[1] of private and public goods and services providers for much of their information. When that infrastructure fails to
provide adequate information, or the information is not acted upon,
firms and industries become noncompetitive and rural economies
suffer. Government can correct the market failure by directly providing the necessary services if it wants to stay involved indefinitely, or
by encouraging the development of an adequate infrastructure if it
wants to be able to withdraw. Regardless of which track is chosen,
distinguishing between correcting a market failure and providing a
subsidy can be a tricky exercise, especially when performed in the
public arena, but it becomes critical to effectively allocating scarce
public resources to improve rural economies over the longer term.
The Maine Potato Market Improvement Fund offers a case study of
how government resources, targeted to a specific market failure, can
improve the competitiveness of a natural resource industry and the
economy of a rural area by correcting a market failure.

In response to concerns in Aroostook County, Maine, arising
from the potential closing of a major military facility, its citizens
engaged in a regional economic development process. The Maine
Potato Market Improvement Fund (PMIF), created by the Maine

legislature in 1981, was a direct result of that process, which represented a cooperative federal, state, and local effort.

Aroostook, the northernmost county in the state, bordered on three sides by Canada,[2] is the largest geographic county in Maine. It has a population density of only thirteen persons per square mile, one-third the average density of the state and one-fifth that of the nation. Agriculture, forestry, and the military account for three-quarters of the export[3] economy, in about equal proportions. Potato production comprises 85 percent of total farm income, representing 95 percent of the state and 6 percent of the national potato supply. Frozen french fry potato processors use about 30 percent of the crop, and seed production for sale represents 20 percent. The balance is shipped in the fresh form, primarily as table stock, with a substantial proportion of that packed on the farm.

In the late 1970s, Loring Air Force base in Aroostook was proposed for reduction or closure, prompting the citizenry to initiate a planning process, including identifying economic activities to mitigate the impact of such a decision.[4] The planning process was supported by federal and state funds, with the governor providing a full-time staff person to work closely with the executive director of the planning committee.

The highest priority recommendation of the agriculture task force was to improve the marketing of potatoes by (1) shifting more potato packing from on-farm facilities to larger central facilities, where tighter quality standards could be consistently enforced, and (2) improving the storage of potatoes by adopting more state-of-the-art environmental (air pressure and humidity) control technology, which was generally utilized in other major potato production areas but not in Aroostook.

PMIF Program

Theoretical Basis

A dual component program, authorized as the Potato Market Improvement Fund (PMIF), was designed on the premise that public loan programs, targeted to specific outcomes, could affect individual economic behavior by (1) creating a network of suppliers and information providers to make appropriate goods and information more readily available to the private sector, and (2) offering low-cost targeted credit. PMIF was funded by a $5 million general obligation bond issued by the state.

Rather than simply providing low-cost loans, the program was designed to correct a market failure by creating an infrastructure network of suppliers and information providers necessary to support specific private economic activity. Private businesses make investment decisions based upon anticipated costs and revenues, which are estimated from available information. Small businesses, especially those in rural areas with less access to global information, are particularly dependent on a local network of suppliers for information, including primary information suppliers such as the Cooperative Extension Service, and providers of private goods and services such as equipment suppliers and lenders for whom information transfer is a secondary activity. Since competition is often less acute and opportunity for growth less likely in regions of decline or no growth, suppliers often do not invest actively in those areas, resulting in stale information provided by local networks.

PMIF was developed on the premise that a relatively large infusion of assured capital allocated to a specific use could expand infrastructure support that, when combined with low-cost credit, would result in farmers making better decisions regarding investments in storage and marketing facilities for their crops. That premise should be valid for other situations, and would be especially appropriate in natural resource industries where support networks fail to keep abreast of new demands and technologies and therefore fail to offer necessary information to their users because of relative isolation. These are cases of market failure where a particular group of market participants do not have adequate information to make appropriate investment decisions. In the case of the Aroostook potato industry, loss of market share and farm profits due to quality degradation of product was generally recognized. There was less agreement on the need for improved storages and central packing, despite considerable evidence that central packing facilities and more closely controlled storage environments were providing improved quality in some other potato producing regions. PMIF was aimed at overcoming this market failure and may serve as an instructive model for other regions with similar market defects.

Administrative Parameters

PMIF legislation provided substantial operational guidance, including a relatively high credit standard for borrowers. Since PMIF credit was designed to encourage adoption of certain technologies and not as a credit source of last resort, the program was limited to borrowers with strong credit capabilities. The notion of using state loan programs to influence the adoption of technologies, rather than providing credit to farmers who could not qualify elsewhere, was a new concept to some legislators and potential borrowers.

A second legislative provision encouraged participation by other lenders.[5] In an effort to build a stronger lender infrastructure, PMIF limited state funds to 45 percent of a project and required only 10 percent equity contribution by the borrower. By subordinating its interest to those of participating lenders, the state assumed most of the risk and opened a window of opportunity for other lenders.

Administering the program by an agency with responsibility beyond agriculture was also considered critical by some. In an effort to maximize general support beyond the agricultural constituency, the Commissioner of the Department of Agriculture, Food and Rural Resources (DAFRR), who is statutorily responsible for the program, contracted administration to the Finance Authority of Maine (FAME), which operates most other state business finance programs.[6]

PMIF Results

This chapter evaluates the effectiveness of PMIF in meeting its objectives. It considers both program outcomes and economic impact. To successfully achieve its program objectives, PMIF would have led to the creation of an infrastructure that could support the development of central packing facilities and environmentally controlled storage units beyond the extent of PMIF funding. To meet the economic intent of the original planners, the program would have resulted in increases in economic activity in Aroostook County, specifically increases in construction activity and in Aroostook's share of the national potato market.

Program Outputs

Through 1990, 137 projects had been financed in Aroostook with PMIF funds, including ten packing sheds, sixteen packing equipment projects, sixty-eight new storage facilities, and forty-three retrofitted storage units. Total project activity was $17.4 million, including PMIF funds of $7.7 million,[7] participating lender funds of $5.9 million, and equity capital from borrowers of $3.6 million. The typical project involved over $100,000. Overall storage capacity improved by new construction and retrofitting totalled 4.0 million hundredweight (cwt), about 20 percent of industry capacity. Central packing facilities built or improved had the capacity to load out 4,485 truckloads annually, or about 23 percent of the average annual industry loadout. Since the program was initiated in 1983, there have

Table 14.1: PMIF Direct Activities

Program Year	# of Projects	Total $ ($ 000)	PMIF $ ($ 000)	Other Lender $ ($ 000)	Table Potato Price ($/cwt)
1983[a]	4	882	331	304	5.83
1984	9	682	316	207	3.29
1985	9	740	330	409	0.82
1986	16	1,291	521	486	5.08
1987	18	2,540	1,109	816	3.32
1988[b]	12	1,835	772	625	6.99
1989	33	4,063	1,877	1,148	7.41
1990	36	5,368	2,478	1,699	4.68
TOTALS	137	17,401	7,735	5,694	4.04

a. Does not include an early project, subsequently liquidated, to which PMIF contributed 9 percent financing.

b. PMIF direct activity projects were reduced because FAME directed $1.1 million of a one-time energy conservation fund to projects that otherwise would have used PMIF funding. These are treated as indirect activities rather than PMIF projects. If these projects were included, 1988 would have shown a steady growth with over $3 million in projects.

been no defaults on PMIF loans and no loans were non-performing at the end of 1990.[8]

Although the fund was fully committed by the end of the 1990 lending year, it grew rather slowly at first, as seen in table 14.1. Both the program and the premise of improved marketing were somewhat suspect during the initial years. Potential participating lenders were wary of public credit programs. Some creditors associated PMIF with government credit programs of last resort and were concerned about political intervention. Many farmers were not convinced that the Maine natural environment, which is more humid than that in western states where the technology was prominent, required similar investment.

However, the first years of the program provided confidence to both participating lenders and farmers. Participating lenders found the loans were sound and saw their clients financially improved as a result of the projects. The program was also enticing since PMIF assumed a subordinate interest in the collateral, protecting the participating lender from most of the risk.

Farmers also became converts. Considerable information-sharing between program users and farmers evaluating new or improved storage facilities proved to be effective. Much of the sharing was done directly and often by group visits organized by the Cooperative Extension Service. Since the storage projects were strengthening the balance sheet of participating farmers, farm suppliers encouraged use of the program after the initial years. In an industry like Aroostook potatoes, where substantial production credit is advanced by suppliers, this can be an important incentive.

The program undoubtedly benefitted from unusually strong potato prices in 1989 and 1990. While the program grew at a steady rate, the heaviest use coincided with those years of high potato prices. If price trends of the earlier years had continued, the program would likely have grown to full utilization, but more slowly.

Infrastructure Creation

While measuring the impact on infrastructure is less precise than measuring program outputs, interviews with infrastructure providers proved consistent: goods and services providers evolved because of PMIF. The employment by PMIF of a storage engineer located in Aroostook County and dedicated full time to providing technical assistance on potato storage and packing facilities to the private sector is considered extremely helpful by industry members. Prior to PMIF, public service potato storage engineering was provided by the Cooperative Extension Service through partial assignment of an agricultural engineer located at the land grant campus, some 150 miles from the center of Aroostook.

Private firms supplying storage equipment represent a second element of infrastructure development. Six firms representing five manufacturers, three of which are located in Aroostook and formed since the inception of PMIF, now actively provide environmentally-controlled storage equipment and services. Before PMIF, only two supply firms served the industry in Aroostook County, one directing only part of its business to Aroostook facilities and the other representing part-time work for its owner.

Increased creditor capacity, both in the number and capabilities of lenders, represents a third infrastructure element. Prior to PMIF, private creditors made very few loans for storage and packing sheds. Most lender activity was provided by FmHA and the Aroostook Farm Credit System; neither required state-of-the art building or equipment standards and neither financed off-farm central packing facilities.

Six private banks and the Aroostook Farm Credit System are currently qualified as participating lenders, although the volume of credit provided by the banks is relatively small. In all cases, however, participating lenders have adopted project requirements established by PMIF, which include minimum insulation and equipment standards and professional oversight during the construction or installation phase. In addition, six individuals from five credit institutions participate in one or more of the three PMIF administrative committees—Program Evaluation, Project Review, or Credit Review.

Interviews with various participants in the region suggest that the increased infrastructure has had a synergistic effect. There is a general perception that attitudes concerning the storage and shipping of potatoes have changed noticeably since PMIF was initiated. While these new attitudes are not always explicitly attributed to the program, they are often attributed to the infrastructure enhancement cited above which was created by PMIF.

Economic Impacts

PMIF generates two types of economic activity: construction activity lasting only through the project development phase, and increased potato marketing activity that can extend over the life of the facilities. The program creates direct activities from projects financed by PMIF, and indirect activities from projects not funded by PMIF but developed because of the new environment created by PMIF.

The clearest measurable impact is the construction activity of projects directly financed by PMIF.[9] Increased potato marketing results from increased volume and higher prices. Volumes can be increased through reduced weight loss from dehydration (air shrink), tuber decomposition (rot), and culling. Higher prices can result from generally improved product quality and extended seasonality, i.e., the ability to market during a greater part of the year.[10]

PMIF adds a further increase in marketing of processed potato products, primarily frozen french fries. In addition to increasing the volume of potatoes available for local processors, controlled environment storage also provides an improved raw product that has allowed the processors to expand their share of markets over what it would have been without that improvement. A portion of potatoes received by Maine processors result in Grade B finished products, which can be sold only at a price lower than Grade A. Storage units built to PMIF standards result in a higher proportion of Grade A finished product. This shift in grades results in an increased value of processed potato products due to PMIF and produces a greater local multiplier than if those potatoes were exported in raw form.

The values of increased potato marketings[11] have substantially exceeded the public investment in PMIF, as seen in table 14.2, which shows the value of increased marketing at both the farm and processor level due to PMIF activity.[12] Increased farm value for the program through 1990 totaled about $12 million, somewhat less than

Table 14.2: PMIF: Estimated Impacts on Potato Marketings

Program Year	PMIF (cum.) ($ 000)	Proj. (cum.) ($ 000)	Potato Price (composite) ($/cwt)	Marketing Impacts		
				Farm ($ 000)	Proc. ($ 000)	Total ($ 000)
1983	331	882	5.96	225	18	243
1984	647	1,564	4.06	315	33	348
1985	978	2,304	2.03	198	110	308
1986	1,499	3,595	5.57	1,212	322	1,534
1987	2,607	6,135	3.95	1,083	434	1,517
1988	3,380	9,068[a]	7.75	2,433	537	2,970
1989	5,257	13,131	7.82	3,304	790	4,094
1990	7,735	18,499	5.33	3,212	1,019	4,231
Total	7,735	18,499	5.31	11,982	3,263	15,245
1991–2001[b]	4,884	16,014[c]	5.33	35,369	10,018	45,387
TOTAL	12,619	34,513	5.32	47,351	13,281	60,632

a. Includes $1.098 million indirect activity contributed by energy conservation fund.
b. Projected and not cumulative.
c. Includes indirect activity at estimated 1990 level.

the $18.5 million total investment in facilities but exceeding the $7.7 million of PMIF funding to date. If the program continues to reinvest its loan repayments and the projects have a useful life of twelve years,[13] the program will result in a total increase of farm marketings of about $47.4 million over its useful life.[14]

Although not shown in table 14.2, the various marketing segments are also influenced differently because of price differentials. The seed producing sector has benefitted more than the other sectors considering it comprises only 20 percent of the industry, due to the generally high prices that prevail in that sector and the disproportionately higher use made of the program by seed producers.

Return to processors from increased quality has totalled about $3.3 million to date, some of which is passed onto the farm level. Assuming the projects continue to perform adequately over their expected lifespan, the return to processors should be about $13.3 million. Aroostook's share of the national potato market will have increased by $60 million by the year 2001 over what it would have been otherwise due to the PMIF program, representing an annual increase of 5 percent when the fund is fully utilized.

The above returns represent an increase in the value of marketings to potato farmers and processors, not an equivalent increase in net income. A substantial portion of those increased funds are spent in the local county for labor, supplies, and services, creating the multiplier effect desired by the program planners. Likewise, the construction expenditures have a multiplier effect although they are one-time activities.

The impacts of these multiplier effects on the regional economy were estimated using the IMPLAN regional economic modelling system.[15] To date, the PMIF program direct activities have increased the gross county product (the total economic activity in Aroostook County) by $50 million, $24 million resulting from increased potato marketing and $26 from construction activity. This has resulted in increases in Aroostook incomes of $22 million, nearly 60 percent in wages and the balance in property income, primarily returns to equity and other property of farmers and businesses (see table 14.3).

Construction activity from direct PMIF funds will be slowed in the future as those funds are fully committed. New construction from direct projects will be limited by the amount of annual repayments by borrowers.[16] However, similar projects will likely be undertaken with alternative capital sources. Increased potato marketing should continue to generate multiplier activity over the life of the current projects regardless of future construction activity. Based on performance to date, PMIF will contribute through year 2001 an increase of $144 million to total economic activity in Aroostook, including increased incomes of $66 million. As seen in table 14.3, however, the proportion of income from wages will decline from 60 percent to 48 percent since the construction industry is more labor intensive than farming and food processing.

Table 14.3: PMIF: Estimated Impacts on Aroostook Economy ($000)

	1983–1990	1991–2001	Total
Potato Marketing			
Gross County Product	23,883	71,110	94,933
Total Income	11,606	34,613	46,218
Wages	4,461	13,338	17,798
Property income	7,145	21,275	28,420
Construction			
Gross County Product	26,341	22,802	49,143
Total Income	10,626	9,198	19,824
Wages	8,709	7,539	16,248
Property income	1,917	1,660	3,577
Total Impacts			
Gross County Product	50,224	93,912	144,136
Total Income	22,232	43,811	66,043
Wages	13,169	20,877	34,046
Property income	9,063	22,935	31,997

Discussion

Relative to the state investment, the PMIF program has provided substantial returns to both the agricultural industry and the local economy. The reported returns to individual borrowers indicate they should have made such investments even without PMIF, suggesting a market failure in which the infrastructure supporting farmer investment decisions had nearly broken down and a program such as PMIF was necessary to refocus attitudes and resources. A review of critical program factors suggests key provisions determined the success of the program and the conditions under which they might be generalized to other situations.

Program Development

While there is little recognition in the industry of the genesis of the program, two factors stand out as crucial to obtaining state funding. The first was the role of the governor. By assigning a staff person from his office to the program planning process, he effectively committed support for the results. That support proved crucial, especially in voter approval of the bond issue. The second critical factor was the involvement of the DAFRR in the planning process. While the planning effort was locally initiated and controlled, DAFRR participated at the outset and was active in developing the agricultural recommendations. When the local recommendations came to the governor, DAFRR was ready to translate the agricultural component into a legislative proposal.

Program Implementation

There is some question raised concerning the efficacy of administering the program outside DAFRR. While the program is given high marks for administration, some suggest that it could have started faster, with earlier benefits, if DAFRR had initially assumed the administration. On the other hand, much of the broad support the program currently enjoys can be traced to its being well administered by an agency perceived to be competent with responsibilities across the economic spectrum.

The program undoubtedly benefitted from not being a lender of last resort. The fund has been preserved and the strong credit of borrowers has allayed fears of participating lenders that PMIF loans would be uneconomical. On the other hand, there is concern among some farmers and legislators that the program supports well-financed borrowers while turning down those less able to get financing elsewhere. Despite that difference of value judgments, the clarity of purpose has likely protected PMIF administrators from detrimental political involvement.

The PMIF experience also demonstrates the value of targeting program outcomes. Without targeting a specific technology to a specific area and industry, the modest PMIF funds would likely have been dissipated without building the infrastructure necessary to continue beyond the amount of government funding. With the targeting, the program benefits were adequate to attract an infrastructure to service the demand for this rather narrow component of Maine agriculture. It is unlikely the infrastructure would have developed without the targeting. Likewise, without the targeting, it is doubtful that there would have been as much interest from farmers. By having several different industry segments promoting advantages of particular technologies, farmers became aware of the benefits before they would have without the focus. On the other hand, some complain that the program should address a more broad spectrum of farm problems. While it is not possible to do so under current legislation, this complaint does serve notice that even effective targeted programs will have critics. It seems clear from the PMIF experience, however, that the effectiveness of the program would have been severely curtailed without the targeting.

Program Limitations

While achieving both program and economic objectives, the program has certain limitations. It is not clear at this time that program administrators and users want PMIF displaced by private sector activity. The original intent was to develop an infrastructure adequate enough to continue funding new projects with the presumption that PMIF funds would be used elsewhere; for example, to address other market failures. That strategy is not promoted now. While it is recognized that more individuals and firms are now involved in developing PMIF-type facilities, it is not viewed that this infrastructure could or should displace PMIF funds.

FAME is currently searching for ways to replenish the fund rather than for ways to withdraw state funding without reducing the level of project development. Industry representatives are generally in favor of this replenishment strategy. If withdrawing PMIF funds as the market failure was corrected was an important strategy, the legislation should have contained a mechanism that assured the withdrawal of the program as alternative, preferably private, resources developed.

There is a more specific infrastructure concern regarding partici- pating creditors. While seven lenders have participated in PMIF in Aroostook County, the Farm Credit System has provided over 80 percent of that activity. The other six, all private banks, have limited involvement primarily due to what one describes as noncompetitive conditions; i.e., the Farm Credit System, because of its access to national capital markets and federal government relationship, offers loans at lower interest rates than the banks. While it may not be the responsibility of PMIF or any state loan program to level the playing field for all lenders, the unevenness should be recognized as inhib- iting broad participation by lenders.

The most intensely stated complaint about the program is advanced by others as a strength. Some charge that the program is unduly cumbersome, requiring more paperwork than is necessary. FAME requires forms similar to its other lending programs with some lessening of burden due to the nature of farm records. While some farmers charge it is still overly cumbersome, others claim the information requested is essential to making good project decisions for borrowers as well as lenders. The latter view also maintains that the requirements are helpful in forcing farmers to be more specific in their planning and projections generally. Since there is evidence that a lack of good records has been detrimental to many farmers in that particular industry, on balance, the information required by PMIF is probably positive for the industry.

Generalizing PMIF Successes

Critical elements of the program suggest that the PMIF can be generalized under certain conditions. First, program development is critical. PMIF might have failed if the same level of funds had been dispersed in a less targeted way. Targeting specific technologies was a key to the PMIF success. It focused enough funds on a single use to encourage the formation of an adequate suppliers' network. While the total amount of public funds was relatively small—less than 5 percent of the annual sales of the industry at the farm level—because it was very focused it was adequate to encourage new business firms to provide the necessary products and services.

A corollary critical programmatic element was the determina- tion not to use the program as a lender of last resort. If the borrowers had been weak credits, private creditors probably would have been much more cautious. As it was, the private sector embraced the program rather slowly and overcame their reluctance only as they saw the strength of the borrowers. The clarity of purpose in the legislation also gave program administrators political cover. While local legislators occasionally advocated for their constituents, because the statute was clear, the program was never politically threatened because of its perceived insensitivity to farmers who were poor credit risks. Other programs with limited funds might do well to emulate these two aspects of PMIF.

PMIF worked because it was directed at overcoming a specific market failure. A lack of sound information about storage and packing technologies and an inadequate network of lenders and suppliers to support projects resulted in the private sector failing to make profitable investments in storage and packing facilities. In the case of PMIF, that market failure resulted in reduced market share and profits and was highlighted by the successful use of technology in other regions of the United States. The test for a successful program in other regions or industries might not be that obvious. More subtle market failures resulting in less dramatic outcomes than those in the Aroostook potato industry at the inception of PMIF might still be improved with this type of program. For example, a similarly targeted program could be successful even when the industry is actually expanding market share, if the program led to faster expansion. In addition, the technology would not necessarily have to be in place elsewhere; it could be coming out of an experiment station. However, the test should be that the technology would not have been adopted fast enough to maximize social returns without the program.

The program need not be limited to technology development. It could apply to any situation where lack of available knowledge and information is inhibiting market efficiency. For example, if a market segment for a product that can be profitably produced locally is not being met because the private sector is not adequately aware of the opportunity or reluctant to assume the market development risk, the state might provide financial support during a transition period for farmers or processors to shift their production to meet the unmet demand. Technical and financial assistance to local fish processors, small scale food processors in rural areas, or wood products manufacturers could be beneficial.

To meet the PMIF standard, however, a market failure would have to be clearly defined, although not necessarily agreed upon or generally recognized. Government funding, even for transitions, would not be appropriate in cases where markets are functioning properly, unless that funding led to reduced costs due to scale or scope economies. In rural areas, market deficiencies involving new technologies or new products are probably quite common. Without the existence of market deficiencies, those intervention would be market distorting, and the government program could not be withdrawn without loss of economic activity. PMIF succeeded because it was built on a limited government role and addressed a defined market failure. Market failures in other regions and industries can probably be overcome with public investment programs similar to PMIF.

Summary

PMIF was developed from an integrated state and local planning effort that enjoyed federal financial support. The combination of all three was probably crucial to the success of the program.

The PMIF program has demonstrated that a state government credit program, targeted to specific outcomes and providing low-cost loans, can influence investments made in the private sector and contribute to its competitiveness by improving market efficiency. Much of the success of PMIF can be attributed to its design to encourage the development of an infrastructure network to support those investments.

PMIF targeted specific technologies that were established in other areas and had a fast payoff to individual borrowers. Technologies that were not as well proven or that had slower payoffs might not attract a similar response. The payback to individual borrowers is sufficiently high that, if private markets are adequately efficient, government credit should become unnecessary in the longer run.

For political reasons, it is not clear that PMIF will be displaced. It is clear, however, that without the focus and capital base created by PMIF, the infrastructure and attitudes necessary to overcome the existing market failure by supporting appropriate private investment decisions would not have emerged.

NOTES

1. Infrastructure as used here represents the comprehensive supply of goods and services, public and private, utilized by business firms. This is a broader concept than that representing only certain components of public provisions like highways and bridges, as often used in economic development literature.

2. The province of New Brunswick borders on the east and north, Quebec on the west.

3. "Export" refers to sales of goods or services to buyers located outside Aroostook County.

4. Loring is now closed under more recent military base closing legislation.

5. Private banks had effectively abandoned Aroostook potato farm lending to the Farmers Home Administration, the Farm Credit System, and private suppliers.

6. Prior to the creation of FAME the program was administered by the Maine Development Foundation, a quasi-state development group, under contractual arrangements with DAFRR.

7. Loan totals exceed the original $5 million of bond proceeds since the program is authorized to utilize repaid principal, earned interest and fee income for program objectives.

8. One project, which represented a unique case since PMIF provided only 9 percent of the financing, was voluntarily liquidated with no PMIF loss.

9. Since there was practically no similar activity prior to PMIF, it is assumed that these projects would not have been undertaken without PMIF. Indirect activity of PMIF, estimated to be about 20 percent of direct activity, is included in impact measures only where noted.

10. Extended seasonality provides farmers and packers with the ability to service accounts year round rather than only during the winter season. While it was generally reported that this provides substantial benefit to the shipper and the region beyond direct price enhancement, this chapter does not attempt to quantity that benefit.

11. Since results were not estimated from a controlled survey, the values are conservatively estimated. The increased volumes and price premiums attributed to improved facilities are calculated from values representing judgments of industry participants and anecdotal information from program users; it was deemed prudent to use the lower values of those judgments. Price differentials and season average prices were calculated from data reported in "Marketing Maine Potatoes" annual summaries published by the Federal-State Market News Service and in the Maine Potato Market Advisory weekly reports. Market share shifts of processed potato products are based on informal information from one of the industry's two processors. In estimating the marketing value of PMIF projects, it is assumed that all improved storage units are filled to capacity annually, since improved storage units represent only 20 percent of industry capacity and it is reported that improved storage units are utilized before unimproved ones.

12. As seen by the relatively low values in 1985, for example, farm marketing values created by PMIF are substantially influenced by season average market prices. Given the volatility of potato prices, program impacts will vary substantially from year to year, even after the program is fully implemented. During the PMIF program through 1990, four of the eight years have shown relatively high potato prices, reflecting higher prices than normally found in similar eight-year periods over the past thirty years. Consequently, program returns are higher than they would have been if potato prices had been more normal over that time period.

13. This is a conservative estimate that assumes new technologies will erode the competitive advantages of the current systems twelve years after installation.

14. Projections of future impacts assume market prices similar to 1990 and are comparative; they estimate the impact of the program but are not a forecast of the industry. Other events will influence industry earnings in the future. For example, shifts in consumer preference may result in the Aroostook potato economy losing a substantial share of its market; or other changes may result in a substantial gain. The projections in this chapter represent the differences in values only as a result of the PMIF program.

15. The IMPLAN model was specified for regions in Maine by Dr. Steven Deller at the University of Maine. See Deller, Steven, "A Collection of Regional Economic Models for the State of Maine: An Application of the IMPLAN System," Agricultural Experiment Station Miscellaneous Report #351, University of Maine; Orono, 1990.

16. FAME is currently seeking ways to replenish the PMIF fund.

PART V

Strategic Thinking for Rural Development

Some Communities Are Successful, Others Are Not: Toward an Institutional Framework for Understanding the Reasons Why

GEORGE R. McDOWELL[1]

Introduction

Some communities are successful and others are not. That is, some communities are able to set reasonable goals for themselves and achieve them. Usually those goals include measures of economic well-being such as jobs and income. The explanations for success, or lack thereof, among communities are exceedingly elusive. They are for the most part beyond the scope of the economic rationale employed in assessing community resources and community development potentials. Some very useful sociological research suggests community attributes that are empirical correlates of successful communities. However, there is little conceptual development in either economics or sociology that does much to explain why some communities are successful and others are not.

This chapter explores the elements in a conceptual framework for understanding the community processes that give rise to, or defeat, local development. This conceptual framework is based in analytical institutional economics.

Local Economic Development Processes and Their Explanation

In the literature on economic development, the importance of community leadership, community and local business attitudes, and a variety of other relatively "soft" variables are consistently identified as the bottom line explanations of successful local economic development. The work of John et al. (1986), *A Brighter Future for Rural America*, is classic in this regard. The authors developed an econometric model involving twelve "hard" variables that included population; the percentage employed in manufacturing, mining, and farming; the percentage with high school educations; and the percentage of commuters. After the model involving the hard variables explained only twenty percent of the variation in economic development success in a sample of rural communities, the authors concluded from community interviews that there were eight keys to the success of communities in economic development.

The eight keys were: (1) recruitment and entrepreneurship; (2) manufacturing and services; (3) progressive firms; (4) sustained local economic development activities; (5) a pro-growth attitude; (6) finance, sites, buildings, and infrastructure; (7) leadership: partnerships and sparkplugs; and (8) support from outside. Clearly, "progressive firms," "a pro-growth attitude," "leadership," and even several dimensions of the other keys to economic success are, by any stretch of the imagination, "soft" variables.

A number of researchers have tried to clarify some of the specific community attributes that are either themselves among the soft variables or are unexpected correlates with community economic success. Flora and Flora (1990; 1992) and others have examined the characteristics of "entrepreneurial" communities and of communities that have generated successful self-development projects. According to Flora and Flora's research, entrepreneurial communities have the following attributes:

1. They accept controversy as normal (indicated by a newspaper willing to print controversy).
2. There is a long-term emphasis on academics (as compared to sports) in the schools.
3. There are enough personal financial resources to allow for some collective risk-taking.
4. There is a willingness to invest that surplus in local private initiatives.
5. They are willing to tax themselves to invest in a rural infrastructure.
6. They are able to define community broadly (so that consolidation has meant larger boundaries for communities rather than a win-lose battle between jurisdictions).

7. They have the ability to network vertically and horizontally to direct resources, particularly information, to the community.
8. They have a flexible and dispersed community leadership.

These characteristics of entrepreneurial communities clearly move our attention beyond economic variables into the functioning of the community itself. In the process of giving meaning to the results of their research, Flora and Flora employ the notion of "social infrastructure" and specifically identify the importance of internal community linkages (networks) as well as external linkages.

In another conceptual effort to more clearly describe the elements and outcomes of community processes that contribute to the long-term success of a community, Shaffer and Summers (1988) set forth the notion of "Community Vitality."

Community Vitality is "the capacity of a local social system to generate income and employment in order to maintain, if not improve, its relative economic position" (Shaffer and Summers 1988). Some of the important characteristics of vital communities include the explicit recognition of the need to adapt to changing conditions, the need to use and maintain the resource base of the community, and the need to measure success in relation to other comparable communities.

Community economic development is thus seen as a dynamic process that creates or loses opportunities depending on the community's preparedness, willingness, and capacity to respond. The concept of resource maintenance recognizes that development is a long-term effort and cannot be achieved through short-term exploitation of human and physical resources. The notion of relative position means that the community is interested in how well it is doing in comparison to similar communities; such comparisons indicate the degree to which the community and its citizens have access to externally generated opportunities. They also indicate the degree to which members of the community are able to attain a particular standard of living that is defined by the culture of the larger society.

McDowell and Shaffer (1989) have used the concept of community vitality as a means to integrating the various economic methodologies and paradigms that relate to the analysis of community economic issues. To this end, they identify the following as the fundamental resources that a community must manage as it seeks to become vital:

1. *Land, water, and other natural resources (public or private)*. These are the resources over which the community has the greatest amount of control within our form of democracy.
2. *Labor or human capital*. Some decisions, both private and public, will cause some people to leave and others to come to the community.
3. *Capital*. Although there are few direct tools that local communities have that control the flow of capital, both public and private stocks of capital within the community and public investments to be made can influence private investments. There are also some institutional arrangements such as community development corporations that can directly facilitate the flow of capital into a community.
4. *Institutions*. These are the rights and obligations, or social, political and legal rules, governing what has to be taken into account in the use of the other resources of the community.

There is likely to be a constant conflict within most communities over issues relating to continuity versus change (maintenance or protection versus use of resources). That conflict will also occur over the use and change of the institutions of the community. The positions people take will be influenced by their time preference or personal discount rate, with the conservationists having a lower discount rate than the developers.

It is through the wise use and maintenance of resources and the willingness and ability to adapt to a constantly changing environment that a community becomes, or continues to be, a vital community. The conceptual frameworks in economics that are commonly used to figure out the wise use of these resources generally come out of regional economics and production economics.

The regional economic theories emphasizing demand, such as export base theory and central place theory, build on the idea that the focus of policy is to respond to some market, whether local or nonlocal. It is assumed that the enterprises within the community can supply the market in a competitive fashion, but the critical effort is to determine what and where that market is and what its characteristics are. This form of analysis generates local strategies that build on the idea of expanding the local export sector or having local businesses provide previously imported items for local consumers.

Regional economic theories emphasizing supply aspects and production theory build on the idea that the focus of policy is to use capital, labor, and technology to supply a market. The community increases its development by shifting resources from lower- to higher-valued uses, using unemployed or underemployed resources, importing resources, and/or adopting new technology. Community strategies that are suggested by these approaches are characterized by labor training/retraining, technology transfer, upgrading management skills, increasing the availability of capital, and the production and management of publicly provided services.

The importance of resource maintenance to continuing the existing level of resource use, and thus community vitality, is clearly seen in examples where a natural resource is exhausted or rendered unusable. Reduction of aquifers through overuse and loss of agricultural land through imprudent zoning are just a couple of examples of problems in resource maintenance. The theories and conceptualizations of natural resource economics contribute significantly to calculating the value to communities of maintaining such resources.

The analysis of the problems of communities in maintaining their private and public stock of physical capital or their stock of human capital generally falls to the theories of public finance and welfare economics. However, few areas of community decision making are as difficult to assess or are as contentious as the issue of public capital investment. Recent concerns with infrastructure problems and theory would seem to support this contention.

Community vitality is a long-run concept that requires more than just the efficient use of resources in the short run to generate profits, jobs, and income for current community residents. Markets for products and services come and go, along with changing preferences and changing definitions of acceptable living standards. Changing technology has a profound influence on production and consumption patterns, on the use of resources, and on the comparative advantage of specific uses and users.

These dynamic conditions in the economy and society make it necessary for a community and its people to be flexible, adaptable, and capable of making decisions on resource uses—decisions that adjust to change. Indeed the major message of both Drucker (1985) and Birch (1987) in their discussions of the changing national economy is that individuals, and presumably communities, must be adaptable and prepared for change. Macro economic and development economic theories are useful in describing, predicting, or estimating the magnitude of the changes that communities face, and what some of their adjustments should be.

Community Institutional Resources: The Key to Vitality

The resource maintenance issue and the adaptability of a community to change are discussed together here because both have a major institutional dimension. The mechanisms for both maintenance and change are the community's institutional resources. However, in addition to the set of institutional arrangements that are under the control of the community itself, there are a host of institutional empowerments and constraints that are available from, or imposed by, other levels of government.

The institutional aspects of local economic development can be divided into two components. The first emphasizes the rules of the game—the current rules regarding resource use and maintenance. A substantial amount of community development activity involves explaining to local people in both the public and private sectors what the rules are that constrain and empower them with respect to directions they wish to take.

Extension workers and other development specialists advise communities and citizens on issues of development rights related to the retention of agricultural land; zoning; planning; the rights, duties, and responsibilities of various local officials; whether industrial revenue bonds can be used to refinance a manufacturing firm or to fund commercial development; and the kinds of federal or state grant programs that are available and who is eligible.

The second institutional dimension of communities has to do with the institutional forms of decision making in the community; these institutions can expand or circumscribe the capacity of the community to decide where it wishes to go. The structure and functioning of the many organizations, boards, committees, and departments in both the public and private sector in a locale cause it to function as a community.

While the theoretical constructs of micro and macro economics, regional economics, public finance economics, and resource economics appear to explain the consequences of resource maintenance or the need for change in the use of resources, everyone, and no one, is an expert on the design of institutions. Most of what we know about institutions and their functioning at the local level is descriptive— not analytical—and falls into the first category—the rules of the game. Considerably less is known about how the design of new institutions and institutional arrangements impacts on local society, values, and culture. For example, we know little about the impact of institutions on such things as the mutual trust in a community that makes controversy an acceptable and normal state of affairs. We know little about what generates a diverse and broadly based leadership structure.

Institutions, Culture, and Community

Institutions—in the most conceptual sense property rights or simply rights—have their origin in some minimal sense of community. "It's mine," not because I assert it is, or even because I have a gun to defend it, but because you agree that it is. Taylor (1966) calls this minimum sense of relationship a "covenant." The covenant creates the self-restraint or forbearance—the acknowledgment that "it's yours"—that creates the rights. Some of these agreements between people are then codified and become law.

Most economists acknowledge that the market is not an exchange of goods but an exchange of rights (see Schmid 1987; Taylor 1966; and Bromley 1989) and that the rights have their origin in some kind of public choice. There is general recognition of this collective or community basis of the market and the economy, of the rights exchanged therein, and of the institutions that guide exchange in that market.

After this acknowledgement by economists, much of the economics dealing with property rights or institutions speaks in terms of the conflicts over those specific rights that are codified in formal law and that are adjudicated through legal institutions. Much less attention is paid to informal or nonformal institutions, and seemingly completely forgotten is the covenant or sense of community that creates rights in the first place. This predisposition to deal with codified rights or formal institutions limits the treatment of institutions or rights to a subset of all institutions—only those that are formally codified. Many of the "soft variables" relevant in local economic development are likely the result of institutions, or arrangements between people, that are not codified but are simply the way of doing business in one community and not in another.

Fallows (1989) describes the set of institutions that are more subtle than those that are codified in his discussion of economically relevant dimensions of culture and why culture matters in explaining the economic performance of a society. "In the long run, a society's strength depends on the way that ordinary people voluntarily behave. Ordinary people matter because there are so many of them. Voluntary behavior matters because it's too hard to supervise them all of the time. . . . This voluntary behavior is what I mean by 'culture' "(Fallows 1989: 13). In Taylor's (1966) discussion of the origin of rights, these notions of culture are aspects of the covenant or the set of rights within which economic activity takes place.[2]

In an effort to identify the elements of life, particularly economic life, over which culture has a major influence, Fallows goes first to Myrdal's *Asian Drama* (1968). As Myrdal attempted to explain the roots of poverty throughout Asia, he identified the cultural traits that productive cultures have in common and that are useful for development. Myrdal, reports Fallows, identified the following thirteen traits: (1) efficiency; (2) diligence; (3) orderliness; (4) punctuality; (5) frugality; (6) scrupulous honesty (pays off in the long run); (7) rationality in decisions on actions (approaching the rationally calculating "economic man" of Western liberal ideology); (8) preparedness for change; (9) alertness to opportunities as they arise in a changing world; (10) energetic enterprise; (11) integrity and self-reliance; (12) cooperativeness; and (13) willingness to take the long view (and forego short-term profiteering).

Myrdal argues throughout *Asian Drama* that Indian culture, rather than encouraging these traits, encourages unproductive behavior by ordinary people.

As Fallows further refines the cultural norms that are economically productive, he reports on some work by Lawrence Harrison, a long-time United States Agency for International Development (US-AID) official with extensive experience in Latin America. Harrison's list of the elements of culture useful for development are the following: (1) the expectations of fair play; (2) the availability of educational opportunities; (3) the availability of health services; (4) the encouragement of experimentation and criticism; (5) the capacity to match skills and jobs; (6) rewards for merit and achievement; and (7) stability and continuity.

The elements of culture that empower people such that their voluntary actions contribute to development can be reduced even further to two crucial items, argues Fallows: whether the radius of trust is large enough and whether people feel they can control their destiny. Different societies, he argues, establish the radius of trust and the sense of controlled destiny in very different ways. These differences, and the unique way that the United States establishes those elements in its culture, are the subject of his book.

In Fallows' terms, a vital community will create a culture, a sense of itself, that lets people know the rules of the local economic game, encourages them to play as hard as they can within those rules, and reminds them of their obligations to the rest of the community—the elements of "control of destiny" and "radius of trust."

In a rather similar vein, Edward Banfield's *Moral Basis of a Backward Society* (1965) describes a culture in southern Italy in the 1950s that is unable to act together for the common good because there is virtually no trust or sense of obligation to anyone outside of the extended family. This "amoral familism" says Banfield, is responsible for the impoverishment of the region, rather than the lack of resources or economic opportunity.

Whether these dimensions of culture defined by Fallows— sense of control over destiny and radius of trust—are an adequate basis to describe the cultural differences between successful and unsuccessful communities is not now known. Alternatively, whether they provide a set of categories in which to place the soft variable correlates of successful and unsuccessful development is also not clear. They do, however, suggest a direction for further exploration.

Areas for Further Exploration

The Domain in Which Leadership Operates

In *Community and the Politics of Place* (1990), Kemmis explores the role or domain of leadership, one of the clearest yet most elusive of the soft variables often identified as keys to economic development. Kemmis takes the reader back to the debate between Madison and Jefferson about the character of the U.S. Constitution. Jefferson sought, in the Constitution, to create a document that would challenge citizens to the noblest of ". . . 'civic virtues' upon which real citizenship depended." (Kemmis 1990: 21). Madison, argues Kemmis, believed that a constitution must protect citizens from their meanest instincts. Because Madison prevailed, we have a set of governance institutions that are essentially aimed at preventing tyranny, not at encouraging development.

Kemmis illustrates his point by describing the hearing process, a normal and familiar procedure in local, state, and national decision making in the United States. Because the hearing procedure is essentially adversarial and adjudicative, parties with different points of view on a matter come to the hearing and take the most extreme position possible—not one they would necessarily accept in a negotiated outcome. But they seldom really do negotiate with each other, because the rules—institutions—either do not permit it or certainly do not facilitate it. Because our constitutional ethic and the institutions that flow from it control our meanest instincts rather than appeal to our noblest virtues we are stuck with zero-sum choices to a certain degree.

Is it possible that this is the domain of leadership? If development is more than zero-sum, and the economy is a system of claims (rights) rather than of commodities, then local development must be able to create new rights. But a set of governance procedures that are by their nature adversarial and not arbitrable, adjudicative and not negotiative, will not likely generate the new understanding between people—the new covenants—that will lead to the new rights and to development.

Is this the role of leadership, whether in official cum political roles or in civic cum volunteer roles? Do leaders move people, parties, and interests from zero-sum to positive-sum positions, from seeking adjudication or choice between conflicting rights to entering negotiations that can create new rights?

The Community as a Commons or a Common Property Resource

It is even more difficult to initiate a strategy that will result in successful development in a community than to detect the major influences that distinguish successful from unsuccessful communities. This is true whether the action is initiated from within the local governance structure or outside that structure, within the civil/voluntary realm of the community. From both the within-government and the outside-government perspectives, individuals and groups seeking to take actions come up against the community institutions, must deal with them, and frequently must change them.

In addition to the adjudicative norms of those institutions described above, there is another set of considerations that makes change in those institutions difficult and affects the behavior of people. Just like many of the land, water, and air resources of the community, the communities' institutional resources have common property characteristics.

These institutions are supposed to be accessible to all citizens, and the rules on changing them—the institutions for changing institutions—frequently require more than a simple majority to change them. Simple indifference, rather than opposition, on the part of many citizens may defeat the change being attempted. This is a free-rider problem.

Therefore, those who seek to change or use institutions extensively will encounter many of the difficulties more often associated with natural, common property resources. Such difficulties include the free-riders and unwilling-riders[3] that follow from the high exclusion costs and joint impact attributes associated with common property resources (see Schmid 1987: 44). Elinor Ostrom, in *Governing the Commons* (1990), suggests that neither government nor the market is uniformly successful in solving common property resource management problems.

The importance of recognizing this dimension of community and community economic culture is that it may explain some of the great difficulty in both the analysis of community economic development issues and in the practical work of carrying out successful local economic development strategies. Such efforts are frequently defeated, not because free-riders are evil, but because they are busy doing other things.

Conclusions

Local people are desperate to know what actions will develop their communities. The elements that give rise to local success in local development are unpredictable from one locale to another. Successful development is phenomenological if not purely serendipitous, that is, it is an unusual and unpredictable occurrence.

Some of the things that can lead to this conclusion include: (1) the great differences between communities with respect to community resources and location attributes; (2) the degree to which regional, national, and international economic forces influence what happens locally and the limited span of control any locale has over those forces; (3) our lack of understanding of the major elements that give rise to local economic success; (4) our lack of much theoretical insight into the same issues; and (5) the rather consistent evidence that when successful development in rural communities does occur, it frequently depends on the special initiatives, local attitudes, or leadership and actions of some individual(s) who prove all the experts wrong.

This is the beginning of an attempt to untangle what is serendipity for some communities, and random, uncontrolled disaster for others; hopefully thereby to increase the chances for any community to be successful.

NOTES

1. Work on this subject is partially supported by a grant from the Ford Foundation.

2. The notion of culture used here does not deal with issues such as the unique anthropological attributes of northern Europeans in communities of the upper midwest, or the Scotch-Irish of Appalachia. Nor is it intended to include the unique cultural circumstances generated by the work and

industry of mining, or lumbering, or some other industry, though some authors such as Hibbard attach this meaning to the term "economic culture." The focus here, and in Fallows, is on the cultural dimensions of communities that cause some upper midwest communities to succeed and others to fail, some Appalachian communities to be successful and others not to be, and some mining or lumbering or farming communities to be successful and others not.

3. Free-riders, like private residents adjacent to public lands, obtain extra benefits without contributing. Unwilling-riders, like homeowners adjacent to landfills, have extra costs imposed on them against their wills.

REFERENCES

Banfield, Edward. 1965. *The Moral Basis of a Backward Society*. New York: The Free Press.

Birch, David. 1987. *Job Creation in America*. New York: The Free Press.

Bromley, Daniel W. 1989. *Economic Interests and Institutions*. New York: Basil Blackwell.

DeWitt, John, Sandra S. Batie, and Kim Norris. 1988. *A Brighter Future for Rural America? Strategies for Communities and States*. Washington, DC: National Governors' Association.

Drucker, Peter F. 1985. *Innovation and Entrepreneurship: Practices and Principles*. New York: Harper & Row.

Fallows, James M. 1989. *More Like Us: Making America Great Again*. Boston, MA: Houghton Mifflin.

Flora, Cornelia B., and Jan L. Flora. 1990. "Developing Entrepreneurial Rural Communities." *Sociological Practice* 8.

Flora, Jan, and Cornelia Flora. 1992. "Local Economic Development Projects: Key Factors." Unpublished manuscript.

Green, Gary P., Jan L. Flora, Cornelia B. Flora, and Frederick E. Schmidt. 1990. "Local Self-Development Strategies: National Survey Results." *Journal of the Community Development Society*, 21 (2):55–73.

Harrison, Lawrence E. 1985. *Underdevelopment Is A State of Mind: The Latin American Case*. Co-Published by: Maryland: Center for International Affairs, Harvard University. London: University Press of America.

Kemmis, Daniel. 1990. *Community and the Politics of Place*. Norman, OK: University of Oklahoma Press.

McDowell, George R. 1990. "Local Development Strategies: Do We Do What We Know, Do We Know What We Are Doing?" Unpublished paper presented at International Symposium on Economic Change, Policies, Strategies and Research Issues, July 4–7, Aspen, Colorado.

McDowell, George R., and Ron Shaffer. 1989. "Toward An Integrating Framework For Rural and Community Economics." Unpublished Paper, Department of Agricultural and Applied Economics, VPI&SU. Department of Agricultural Economics, University of Wisconsin, Madison.

Mydral, Gunnar. 1968. *Asian Drama: An Inquiry Into The Poverty of Nations*. (3 Vols) New York: 20th Century Fund.

Osborne, David. 1988. *Laboratories of Democracy*. Boston, MA: Harvard Business School Press.

Ostrom, Elinor. 1990. *Governing the Commons: The Evolution of Institutions for Collective Action*. Cambridge and New York, Cambridge University Press.

Schmid, A. Allen. 1987. *Property, Power, and Public Choice*, 2d ed. New York: Praeger.

Shaffer, Ron, and Gene F. Summers. 1988. "Community Economic Vitality." Chapter 1 in *Community Economic Vitality: Major Trends and Selected Issues*. Ames, IA: The North Central Regional Center for Rural Development, Iowa State University.

Taylor, John F. A. 1966. *The Masks of Society*. New York: Meredith Publishing Company.

Western Governors' Association. 1992. *Small Towns: Culture, Change, and Cooperation*. Western Governors' Association, January.

CHAPTER 16

Successfully Matching Development Strategies and Tactics with Rural Communities: Two Approaches

DAVID W. SEARS AND J. NORMAN REID

Introduction

We have used the term *rural development strategy* repeatedly throughout this book. When we refer to such a strategy, we are speaking of a carefully crafted and orchestrated set of tactics that are intended, as a package, to move a rural community or region in the direction of a specific development goal. This package of tactics is likely to include some that are implemented simultaneously and some that are implemented sequentially.

Thus, the construction of a rural development strategy requires a set of tactics. As we use the term, a *rural development tactic*[1] is an action (or set of actions) that is (are) focused on a relatively narrow portion of the total array of activities that might be undertaken to enhance the economy of a specific rural community or region. Thus, airport improvement would be one rural development tactic; technical assistance to small businesses is a second; upgrading the quality of the local K-12 school system is a third.

The Interaction of Strategy and Community

Strategy choices interact with community characteristics, leading to rural development results that are more successful in some situa-

tions, and less successful in others. Pertinent community characteristics include population and demography, geography, physical
characteristics, the economy, social structure, institutional climate,
and governmental climate. An additional key community characteristic is the context (physical, economic, social, political, and administrative) in which the community is located.

Thus, rural development success depends upon a good match
of strategy and community.[2] But since communities vary along many
dimensions, and a very large number of potential strategies exist as
well, getting the "right" fit—or, more realistically, a "good" fit—is
not an easy task.[3]

Matching Strategies and Communities

In an attempt to choose highly compatible pairs of strategies and
communities, one route is to start with a strategy and look for
appropriate communities, while a second route is to start with a
community and search for appropriate strategies. We refer to these
two different routes as the *Program-Centered approach* and the
Community-Centered approach.

The starting point for the Program-Centered approach is the
expectation that strategy X will be more successful in the community
of Oakdale than in the somewhat different community of Smithville.
In brief, the Program-Centered route (1) focuses on a particular
strategy, and then (2) searches among communities, asking "where
would this strategy work best?" or, at least, "where would this
strategy *work well*?"

In contrast, the starting point for the Community-Centered
approach is the expectation that using strategy X in Oakdale will be
more successful than using strategy Y. Thus, the Community-
Centered route (1) focuses on a particular community (or a particular
type of community), and then (2) searches among strategies asking
"what strategy would work best in this (type of) community?" or, at
least, "what strategy would *work well* in this (type of) community?"

Two Approaches to Matching Tactics and Communities

In terms of analysis, it is often the tactic rather than the strategy that
is examined. This is especially true for the Program-Centered approach. The reality is that the rural development field has no set of
"standard" strategies sitting on the shelf ready to be applied in
specific communities. And there is no central supplier capable of
providing even one such strategy to willing communities.[4] What

Figure 16.1. Matching Development Strategies and Tactics with Rural Communities: Two Approaches

Approach	Study Focus	Central Question
Program-Centered	A specific development strategy or tactic	In what community, or type of community, will this strategy or tactic work well?
Community-Centered	A specific community or type of community	What development strategy or tactic will work well in this community, or this type of community?

does exist, though, is a range of "standard" tactics that are available through a variety of regional, state, and federal programs. Thus, the Program-Centered approach often turns out to be the following: (1) to focus on a particular tactic, and then (2) to search among communities asking "where would this tactic work best?" or, at least, "where would this tactic *work well?*"

The Community-Centered approach, in contrast, is actually frequently used for strategy selection; that is, often a community will think about choosing or designing a strategy that will enable the community to move toward achieving a rural development goal. The Community-Centered approach is, however, also used for selecting tactics. When looking for appropriate tactics, the Community-Centered route (1) focuses on a particular community (or a particular *type* of community), and then (2) searches among tactics asking "what tactic would work best in this (type of) community?" or, at least, "what tactic would *work well* in this (type of) community?"

Program Managers and Local Development Specialists: Which Approach to Use?

Across the variety of persons operating in the rural development arena, the perceived utility of these two approaches will vary. In particular, program managers and local development specialists are likely to view the utility of these two approaches differently.

Program managers may use neither of these approaches, but when they do, it will almost always be the Program-Centered approach. The manager of a state highway department, for instance, will have only one rural development tactic to work with—building or upgrading highways; but he or she can search the state looking for local areas where the economic development payoffs from highway investments will be the greatest. The state highway department is simply not in a position to use the Community-Centered approach.

Local development specialists and community planners also may use neither of these approaches, but when they do, it will nearly always be the Community-Centered approach. The local development specialist for Oakdale, for instance, will have only one community to work with—Oakdale; but he or she can search among a variety of specific tactics looking for those that will produce the greatest economic development payoffs. Even better, if Oakdale has a well-articulated economic development strategy, he or she can search for tactics that will, collectively, make a strong contribution toward implementing that strategy. In practice, however, local development specialists often have not chosen tactics that would contribute to a carefully conceived development strategy, nor have they even considered a very wide range of tactics.

How Is the Choice of Approach Related to the Governance Model?

In chapter 1 of this book we described some of the new thinking that has emerged over the past several years on the ways that government might be organized. One of the most thought-provoking ideas is that defining government in terms of programs has some negative features; one of the deficiencies of program-defined government is the inertia that is built into the system, as a program that made sense under one set of circumstances continues to survive long past its useful lifespan. Another weakness of program-driven government is that each program is typically incapable of responding flexibly to needs and opportunities that will vary from place to place.

Program-defined government, with its several weaknesses, is often consistent with choosing the Program-Centered approach. At the extreme, the Program-Centered approach is constrained to moving within the confines of a very narrow box; this is a box in which the set of tactics to be considered is limited to the set of individual programs that are in place. In this situation, for instance, if the state has a program to provide technical assistance to unemployed farmers attempting to start businesses, then the provision of such assistance is a rural development tactic; and, on the other hand, if the state does *not* have such a technical assistance program, then the provision of such assistance is *not* a rural development tactic.

Not surprisingly, each program manager is prone to look at his or her own program as a useful tactic. And, of course, almost all programs will have some usefulness, at least under some circumstances. Thus, program managers are likely to feel very comfortable with the Program-Centered approach.

Local development specialists and community planners, on the other hand, do not have to buy into this model of development—and, in fact, most do not. They are better able to see the world from the "reinventing government" perspective, searching for useful rural tactics beyond those defined by current programs.

We want to be careful, however, not to imply that those choosing the Program-Centered approach are always from the "old governance" school, while those choosing the Community-Centered approach are necessarily from the "reinventing government" school. It is easy, of course, to use the Program-Centered approach to focus on existing programs as the only tactics worthy of consideration, but using the Program-Centered approach is not inconsistent with looking at a whole new array of tactics not defined by current programs.

Likewise, while the Community-Centered approach lends itself to thinking about new and different rural development tactics, using the Community-Centered approach is also compatible with looking only at existing programs as possibilities. We suspect that many small communities, often pressured by the constraints of volunteer labor to get most public business done, and falling into familiar habits, do not look beyond the array of existing programs when thinking about economic development.

What Happens When Neither of These Approaches Is Used?

A program manager might use neither of these approaches—not even the "obvious" Program-Centered approach—because he or she has not chosen to focus program resources on places where the economic development payoffs will be the highest. The manager may choose to allocate program resources on some other basis.[5] For instance, the state highway department might choose to allocate highway spending to state legislative districts based on (1) the relative power of the districts' legislators; or (2) the number of local highway fatalities in the past thirty-six months; or (3) the number of miles of substandard state highways.[6]

In short, each program will not necessarily be viewed by its managers as a rural development program; thus, program allocations will not always be aimed at having strong impacts on economic development. It is nevertheless possible that allocations based on other criteria (e.g., safety or highway conditions) may have good economic development results—i.e., stimulating economic development is not necessarily incompatible with achieving safety objectives or improved highway conditions.

A local economic development specialist might use neither of these approaches—not even the "obvious" Community-Centered approach—because he or she is not thinking in terms of choosing strategies and related tactics with the best economic development payoffs. Rather, the local specialist may be simply on the lookout for good opportunities to expand the level of resources coming into the community. For instance, if the state department of environmental protection notifies all local governments that twenty-five communities in the state will be given grants to upgrade local sewer systems, Oakdale's economic development specialist might view this as an opportunity and thus might apply for the grant program, without worrying about whether other tactics might produce substantially better development payoffs for the community. Of course, this opportunistic approach is not necessarily incompatible with achieving good economic development results.

Local communities that are locked into a "crisis reaction" mode of operation will be especially unlikely to select tactics because they fit into a carefully conceived development strategy; in the "crisis" mode the tendency is to grab anything that's available.

Analysts: Which Approach to Use?

The role of analysts and researchers is to provide information that will be useful to decision makers (both program managers and local economic development specialists) when they are trying to find matches of strategies and tactics with rural communities that will produce good economic development results. In the attempt to uncover this useful information, analysts might profitably use either framework.

Research to date, however, has concentrated almost exclusively upon the Program-Centered approach. Clearly all the work in this volume is based on the Program-Centered approach. That is, each chapter in this book takes a particular tactic and examines a number of aspects of that tactic, including—for several of the chapters—looking at where the tactic would work well. This emphasis—conducting research on the Program-Centered approach—is a useful one. Obviously, the information produced can be used directly by the program managers working with the tactics studied; for instance, the manager of a state aviation facilities capital improvement program will be able to directly use the information presented in chapter 10 on the importance of local airports to rural businesses.

Research studies on the Program-Centered approach can also provide useful information for those decision makers (e.g., many local economic development specialists) using the Community-Centered approach. For instance, one Program-Centered study may show that investment in fiber optic telecommunications systems has a higher payoff in communities with a highly skilled work force than in communities with low skills. A second Program-Centered study may show that marketing assistance has a higher payoff in communities with many small businesses than in communities where employment is concentrated in a few large firms. A third Program-Centered study may show that investments in upgrading airports has a higher payoff in communities located more than 50 miles from a major airport than in communities closer to an existing large airport. Together, these three studies would not tell the economic development specialist from Oakdale whether to choose investment in fiber optics, marketing assistance to local businesses, or upgrading the local airport as the most appropriate rural development tactic in that locality. But, the studies do give him/her more information to work with than he/she would have had without the three studies—perhaps helping to focus on the strengths and weaknesses of each of these three tactics. In general, such studies would help guide local leaders and economic development specialists to ask more probing questions and to seek more thoughtful answers.

The rural strategy research community has barely begun to scratch the surface in conducting Program-Centered studies. Many tactics have not yet been studied at all. And, as we pointed out in an earlier review of rural strategy studies,[7] most of the existing studies have a number of serious limitations. We therefore see a continuing need for strong Program-Centered studies.

The situation is very different for Community-Centered studies. In a Community-Centered study, the analyst would look at a particular community—or, preferably, a *type* of community—and try to determine what strategy or tactics would work well in this (type of) community. A Community-Centered study will clearly be more directly useful than a Program-Centered study to the decision maker who is attempting to use a Community-Centered approach to the matching of tactics with communities.[8]

Few such Community-Centered studies currently exist, and—reflecting the overall field—there are none in this volume. One reason that Community-Centered studies are not often found is that they are more difficult than Program-Centered studies to carry out.

A useful, if not mandatory, step that will precede the conduct of Community-Centered studies is the establishment of a comprehensive list of rural development tactics. This list might be highly aggregated; for instance, individual tactics might be identified as

(1) infrastructure investment, (2) education and training, (3) business assistance, and so on. Or, the list might be highly disaggregated; for instance, business assistance might be broken down into numerous individual actions: (1) marketing assistance, (2) accounting assistance, (3) site location assistance, (4) provision of capital for high-risk ventures, (5) provision of key economic information, (6) enterprise zones, (7) business incubators, and so on. No generally accepted classification of tactics has been developed. In fact, obtaining basic information on individual tactics is often the primary concern of community-level developers.

What might be called a "partial" Community-Centered study could, however, be carried out without first establishing a comprehensive list of rural development tactics. Under the "partial" Community-Centered study, the analyst would not look through the entire comprehensive list of tactics, but would only examine a selected subset of tactics, such as those related to business assistance, searching for those that would work well in a particular (type of) community.

One also can envision a Community-Centered strategic study—one that is looking for useful strategies, not just useful tactics, for a community. Community-Centered strategic studies open the range of inquiry to include the interactions and complementarities among the specific tactics that together constitute a strategy. It is likely that many such studies would find that the joint effects of using several tactics simultaneously and/or sequentially are much greater than (or much less than) the sum of the effects that would occur had each tactic been used only in isolation.

Such Community-Centered strategic studies have advantages— they should be more useful than Community-Centered studies of tactics. But they have disadvantages as well—they will prove to be more difficult to conduct than Community-Centered studies of tactics.

Prior to conducting a Community-Centered study focused on strategies, a comprehensive list of strategies might be established. We think the field is currently a long way from establishing such a list. The field currently contains, however, a rough cut at a list of general strategies: (1) encourage growth, (2) manage growth, (3) control growth, (4) cope gracefully with decline, (5) upgrade substandard services and facilities to minimum standards, and (6) ease transitions from one economic base to another. These six represent some of the most prominent general strategies available to rural communities. To be very useful in guiding development in any specific community, however, a much more specific strategy would have to be designed. For instance, if Oakdale chose to encourage growth as its general strategy, the local planners would want to spell out that strategy in some detail, specifying what economic sectors would be encouraged to grow and how that encouragement might be orchestrated through the use of specific tactics.

Another difficulty of Community-Centered research studies is that a single Community-Centered study will necessarily be much larger in scope than a single Program-Centered study. Simply put, a solid Community-Centered study is likely to involve several times more resources than a solid Program-Centered study. For instance, an accurate and thorough description of a community's characteristics—required for a Community-Centered study—is a laborious task, and that is only the beginning of an effort that must also track the interactions of a number of tactics with these characteristics.

Community-Centered studies can be useful in a variety of ways. First, and most importantly, a Community-Centered study will be useful to decision makers using a Community-Centered approach; for instance, the development specialist in Oakdale will find a study of the relative merits of several strategies or tactics in Oakdale-type communities (e.g., manufacturing-dependent places with few natural amenities located far from metro areas) to be exceedingly useful.

Second, a Community-Centered study can be useful to program managers using the Program-Centered approach. For example, the director of the state highway program would be interested to know that, based on a Community-Centered study, one of the best ways to promote development in places like Oakdale is investment in upgrading highways; this information could be used by the manager to supplement the information available from a Program-Centered study of highway investment as a rural development strategy. Thus, Community-Centered studies can provide some basis for thinking about the ways in which programs might best be targeted to communities with particular characteristics.

Third, for the research community, the addition of Community-Centered studies to the body of rural strategy research will enhance the entire effort. Specifically, Community-Centered studies will provide useful input into Program-Centered studies; for instance, several Community-Centered studies that concluded jointly that telecommunications investments in growing communities produced better development results than such investments in declining communities could be used as input for a Program-Centered study of telecommunications investment as a rural strategy. In addition, a careful periodic examination of the results from both Program-Centered and Community-Centered studies will help researchers prepare a stronger and more policy-relevant rural strategy research agenda than would be possible with only one type of study.

Fourth, and finally, well-executed Community-Centered studies will force the field of rural development to more clearly begin to come to terms with interactions among tactics. The field needs to focus more squarely on identifying groups of tactics that are complementary, other groups that are internally inconsistent and incompatible, and still other groups where some tactics may be good substitutes for others.

Policymakers will thus find it useful for rural researchers to conduct a range of studies, including those that flow from each of the two approaches. They must acknowledge the greater difficulty and cost of the Community-Centered studies, and should stand ready to support these studies as well as the more traditional studies.

How Should Analysts Respond to Ideas about the Governance Model?

As indicated in an earlier section of this chapter, the Program-Centered approach should not be equated with "old governance" nor should the Community-Centered approach be equated with "reinventing government."

Even with the prodding of a "reinventing government" president and "reinventing government" governors in some states, it is reasonable to believe that the world will not change overnight from the "old governance" program-defined system to the "reinventing government" results-oriented system. Thus, it seems to us that researchers who are interested in producing findings useful to real-world decision makers should conduct studies that look at existing programs as possible tactics and should also conduct studies that look at non-program-defined tactics. We think that into the foreseeable future both "old governance" strategies and tactics and "reinventing government" strategies and tactics can be useful subjects of rural research studies.

The utility of "old governance" strategy studies is quite obvious: as long as existing programs are viewed by program managers and local development specialists as candidate tactics, then research indicating the best matches between particular tactics and communities will be very useful. We believe that "reinventing government" strategy studies will also be useful, however, for somewhat different reasons. "Reinventing government" strategy studies will help push the field of rural development forward by focusing attention on new ways of trying to promote and sustain rural development.

Weaknesses in Current Rural Strategy Research

In chapter 1, we described in some detail recent trends in the perceived proper and useful role of government, especially as reflected in the notion that we need to "reinvent" government. These changing perceptions have major implications for future rural strategy research. First is the fact that the development process has multiple goals and is served by multiple programs. For example, while infrastructure construction is clearly part of development, it represents only one among many developmental objectives. Others include the creation of business activity, the development of community institutions, and the development of a work force able to participate in increasingly complex and lucrative workplaces. Numerous individual government programs are available to support the achievement of these many goals.

Typically, rural strategy research has focused on a narrow range of programs and policy objectives. Yet in a world that is increasingly complex and interconnected, partial understanding provides an unsatisfactory basis for meaningful advice about policy options. To be effective, rural strategy research must be capable of accommodating the simultaneous effects of multiple programs, as well as the trade-offs among multiple developmental goals.

Second, and related, are the interactions that occur among programs. Program effects do not occur in isolation. Often, they depend on each other for their success. The classic case is the relationship between job creation and job training. Training programs cannot place workers in jobs if none are available. Likewise, most businesses are unlikely to succeed without properly trained workers. Few rural strategy studies to date have taken program interactions into account. It is increasingly clear, however, that such approaches are called for.

Third, rural strategy research typically examines program impacts within a narrow range of time. Studies that track progress over a period of a year or two are common. Development, however, is a process that may unfold only over the course of decades, if not generations. It may be helpful to think of development as occurring in stages.[9] Rural policy impacts can be fully understood only in the context of these longer time periods. What is required of rural strategy research is the capacity to accommodate a long-term perspective that includes, wherever possible, longitudinal methods.

The failure of most rural strategy research to meet these needs characterizes a discipline that is unable to accurately reflect the world of reality. The conduct of research is largely based on targets of opportunity, choosing means that are readily at hand; it is, in effect, a supply-driven system of research. What is now required is a rural strategy research field that is driven instead by real needs for information about specific strategies and tactics and their likelihood of success under existing conditions in rural communities. In short, rural strategy research must be driven not by supply, but by demand.

For the most part, however, this is a response the rural research community has been unprepared to make. In the 1992 Special Symposium on Rural Development,[10] we reviewed a selection of rural strategy research, concluding that while there has been a large quantity of policy-oriented research on rural development issues, serious concerns remain about the quality and usefulness of that work. To quote ourselves:

> Our disappointments are centered on the shallowness of existing research, its lack of sensitivity to both differences of context and diversity of developmental outcomes, and to shortcomings of method and data quality. Much rural development policy research . . . can only be described as rudimentary. While encouraging exceptions to this generalization occur in the literature, our overwhelming impression is that a need exists for major improvements in the quantity and quality of rural policy research.[11]

In the time since that earlier volume appeared, we have seen no reason to modify our overall judgment about the need for major improvements in the rural strategy research field.

Recommendations

It is our view that there are an enormous number of exciting and useful studies that need to be conducted in the rural strategy research field. We cannot, however, point to just one subset of these studies that should be emphasized, to the exclusion of all others. We see clear value in conducting each of three different types of studies:

- *Program-Centered "old governance" studies of tactics.* Because the world generally changes slowly, many "old governance" approaches are still prominent in the rural development toolbox, and are likely to remain so for a number of years. Thus, Program-Centered "old governance" studies are needed so that program managers can more clearly see the likely consequences of some of their primary development options. These studies are not intended to move the field rapidly in a new direction, but will help managers make better choices within a limited set of traditional tactics. The quality of these studies can, and should, be improved (see the 1992 *Policy Studies Journal* symposium (vol. 20, no. 2) for how such improvements might be made).

- *Program-Centered "reinventing government" studies of tactics.* Many promising new rural development tactics have emerged in recent years, and there is every reason to believe that still others will be developed over the next several years. Solid research on these newer tactics is important to provide well-grounded non-anecdotal information on these tactics (for instance, is the latest approach just a fad, or does it really work?). In addition, good research can help draw attention to new tactics that should be included in the set of mainstream development tools.
- *Community-Centered studies.* As difficult to conduct as Community-Centered studies are likely to be, their importance cannot be denied. Narrower studies will generally lead to narrower thinking about government activities; narrower thinking, in turn, will mean fewer options will be considered. We cannot reinvent government unless we think expansively. Community-Centered studies, much more so than Program-Centered studies, are likely to push policymakers to think expansively. Thus, Community-Centered studies are *high risk* studies—the costs are likely to be high (because they are complex, and no good models for these studies exist) and the probability of inconclusive results is high. Nonetheless, the potential payoff in terms of more effective rural development strategies and tactics from such studies is extremely high.

If we headed up a large national effort on rural strategy research, we would be inclined to split our budget among these three categories of studies on a 50:25:25 basis over the next three to five years. This reflects a need to provide information immediately useful to decision makers while simultaneously attempting to move the field forward.

Whatever research agenda is chosen, it is important to step back quite frequently and evaluate progress and failures, so that the agenda can be modified to respond to what we learn about both (1) the interaction of rural strategies and tactics with community characteristics, and (2) the success of various research methodologies.

What we are calling for is a revolution in rural research—in the subjects addressed as well as in our methods—that is suitable to the complexity of today's rural development problems. What we are asking for will not be easy, but with diligence and creativity, it will enable the rural strategy research field to make a substantial contribution to helping front-line program managers and economic development specialists more wisely choose from among the array of rural strategy and tactical possibilities. The greatest contribution can be made in enabling policymakers to better match strategies and specific tactics with community characteristics. We are confident that strong research will ultimately lead to solid answers to the questions of how best to match development strategies and tactics with the needs and opportunities of rural communities.[12]

NOTES

1. Ray Vlasin of Michigan State University suggested that we use the term *tactic*.

2. Clearly, the success of results—in terms of achieving development objectives—also depends upon the ways in which the strategies and tools are chosen and implemented. We acknowledge the importance of these details in assuring success, but for this chapter we are largely ignoring this key factor.

3. Malecki—in *Technology and Economic Development* (Harlow, England: Longman Scientific and Technical, 1991)—discusses the relationship between community characteristics and economic development on pp. 22–30.

4. In fact, we would argue strongly that such "standard" strategies should not be provided. It makes much more sense for each community to customize its own unique strategy, using the combination of tactics that seems to fit best.

5. This chapter, of course, focuses on economic development. But we do not want to be narrow-minded about the objectives of public programs. We acknowledge that (1) some very useful public programs will have objectives not aimed at economic development, and (2) some other very useful public programs will have multiple objectives, in which economic development is just one objective among several.

6. Many other allocation approaches could be used. Equal distribution per jurisdiction or equal distribution per capita are, for instance, other possibilities.

7. See David W. Sears and J. Norman Reid. 1992. "Rural Strategies and Rural Development Research: An Assessment." *Policy Studies Journal*, 20(2): 301–309.

8. Community-Centered studies must be based on a good understanding of how various community characteristics interact with development tactics to produce good (or poor) rural development outcomes.

9. See, for example, W.W. Rostow. *The Stages of Economic Growth: A Non-Communist Manifesto.* 3rd ed. (Cambridge: Cambridge University Press, 1990).

10. Special Symposium on Rural Development, *Policy Studies Journal*, 20(2).

11. David W. Sears and J. Norman Reid. 1992. "Rural Strategies and Rural Development Research: An Assessment" *Policy Studies Journal* 20(2): 308.

12. Thanks to Ray Vlasin, George McDowell, and Pat Sullivan for their helpful comments on an early draft of this chapter.

Index

Summers, Gene, 271
Survey of Income and Program
     Participation (SIPP), 237

Tactic, 282–84, 288–89, 291
"Target 2000," 50
Technical assistance, 154–55.
  disadvantaged groups and,
     158–59
  effectiveness of, 157–58
  entrepreneurship and, 153–55
  evaluation of, 157
  importance of, 152–53
  lack of usage, 156–57
  most popular, 156
  users of, 155–56
Technology adoption, 252–53
Technology development, 262
Tribal communities and micro-
     enterprise development,
     220–26
Tribal governments, 206–207

Unemployment Insurance Act
     (Canadian), 66
United Methodist Church study,
     205–206
United States Constitution, 277
United States Department of
     Labor, 243–44
University of Nebraska at Omaha,
     34
University of Wisconsin
     Cooperative Extension, 13
Unwilling-riders, 278–79, 280
Urban area, defined, 247

Visual Flight Rules, 174
Volunteer Visitor Business
     Retention and Expansion
     (VVR&E) program, 138–49
  characteristics of, 140
  coordinators, 141–43, 149

employment impacts, 141–43
goal and objectives, 138–39, 143
program structure, 141–43
state sponsors, 139, 140–41
successful programs,
     characteristics of, 144, 148
survey results, 142–43
  coordinator responses, 144–47
  firm responses, 147
volunteers, 139, 142
Volunteers, 10, 139

Wisconsin Community Economic
     Analysis Program. *See*
     Community Economic
     Analysis Program
Wisconsin, economic
     development, 13–27
  airports and, 174–79
Worker cooperatives, 84–100
  advantages of, 85–86
  agri-industrial, 90–91
  barriers to, 96–97
  criticisms of, 87
  failure, 86–88
  forestry, 88–90
  goals of, 97
  industrial, 91–94
  job quality and, 96
  principles of, 85
  productivity, 86
  rural versus urban, 88
  success, conditions for, 84–88
Worker's Owned Network
     (WON), 94
Would You Like to Swing on a Star?,
     102, 115
Wyoming Aeronautics
     Commission's "User's
     Guide," 172

Yunus, Mohammed, 211–12
  confidentiality and, 215